D0838005

The best of
Mrs BEETON'S
Cakes
& Baking

The best of Mrs BEETON'S Cakes & Baking

WEIDENFELD & NICOLSON

First published in 2005 by the Orion Publishing Group Ltd
5 Upper St Martin's Lane
London
WC2H 9EA

Text selection © Orion Publishing Group Ltd 2005

Orion Publishing Group Limited hereby exclude all liability to the extent
permitted by law for any errors or omissions in this book and for any loss,
damage or expense (whether direct or indirect) suffered by a third party
relying on any information contained in this book.

All rights reserved. No part of this publication may be reproduced,
stored in a retrieval system, or transmitted, in any form or by any means,
electronic, mechanical, photocopying, recording or otherwise, without
the prior written permission of both the copyright holder and the above
publisher of this book.

Designed by seagulls
Index prepared by Indexing Specialists (UK) Ltd
Produced by Omnipress Ltd, Eastbourne
Printed and bound in the UK by
CPI Mackays, Chatham ME5 8TD

Contents

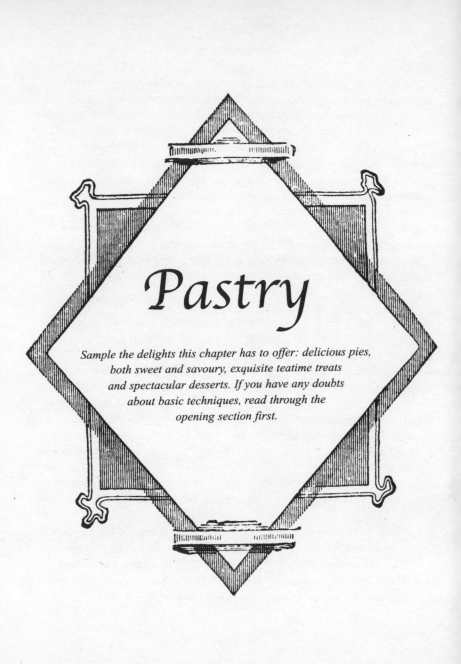

Pastry

Sample the delights this chapter has to offer: delicious pies, both sweet and savoury, exquisite teatime treats and spectacular desserts. If you have any doubts about basic techniques, read through the opening section first.

RUBBING IN

The first stage in making several types of pastry is to rub the fat into the flour. This basic technique is used for other purposes in cookery so it is worth getting right. Ensure that your hands and work surface are cool (marble is the traditional pastry-working surface), or the fat will melt and your pastry will be leaden. Cut the fat into small pieces and mix it with the flour. Using just the tips of your fingers, lift a little of the mixture and rub the fat with the flour once or twice. Let the mixture fall back into the bowl before lifting another small portion and rubbing again. Continue in this way until the mixture has the texture of fine breadcrumbs.

It is important that you lift the mixture and rub it lightly to incorporate air into it. If you pick up too much mixture and push it back into the palms of your hands, air will not mix with it and the pastry will be heavy. Once you have mastered the technique you will find it quick and easy to perform; in fact, the quicker the process is completed, the lighter the pastry.

ADDING LIQUID TO SHORT PASTRIES

The term 'short' is used to describe pastry that is not made heavy by the addition of too much liquid. The melt-in-your-mouth texture that is characteristic of good short pastry is the result of using the right proportion of fat to flour and just enough liquid to hold the pastry together as it is rolled. When making sweet pastry dishes, various types of short pastry may be used and the difference may be in the liquid added to bind the ingredients. Plain short crust pastry is bound with a little water. The water should be very cold (preferably iced) and just enough should be added to bind the rubbed in mixture into lumps. The lumps are gently pressed together so that the pastry just holds its shape. It should not be sticky.

Sweet short crust or richer pastry for making flans may be bound with egg yolk instead of, or as well as, a little water. Egg yolk contains a high proportion of fat so the resulting pastry will be very short. Adding sugar to pastry also tends to give a short and crumbly texture. Some rich pastry is made very short by adding extra fat, usually butter, to give a good flavour as well as a short texture.

ADDING LIQUID TO PUFF PASTRY OR FLAKY PASTRY

The dough for this type of pastry has only a small proportion of the fat rubbed in, with the majority of the fat incorporated by rolling it with the pastry. A little extra liquid is added to make a dough that is just slightly sticky. This type of dough holds the fat which is added in lumps or a block during rolling. The resulting pastry is not short; it is crisp and it forms distinct layers. Puff pastry is lighter and has more layers than flaky pastry.

The layers in puff and flaky pastry trap air to make the pastry rise during cooking. A strengthening substance called 'gluten' is naturally present in flour; this is developed by rolling the pastry. The process of rolling and folding actually serves to toughen the basic dough. Adding the fat each time the pastry is rolled means that the dough does not form into a solid mass but retains very fine layers. The air trapped between these layers expands as the dough is heated and so the pastry rises. Because the dough itself is toughened by the gluten, the layers set and give the finished pastry its characteristic crisp texture.

ROLLING OUT

Whatever type of pastry you are handling, you should always roll it out very lightly. Use a very light dusting of flour on the work surface. There should be just enough to prevent the pastry from sticking; short pastries usually require less than puff or flaky pastries. Too much flour at this stage may spoil the balance of ingredients. Never turn pastry over during rolling. The pastry should be lifted occasionally and turned round to prevent it sticking to the surface. Push the rolling pin away from you in short, quick strokes. Keep the rolling pin lightly dusted with flour.

When rolling out pastry, try to establish the shape as soon as you begin. For example, if you are lining a round flan dish, start with a ball of pastry which is flattened into a roughly circular shape. If you want to end up with an oblong sheet of pastry, form the pastry into an oblong lump and flatten it slightly before rolling it.

LIFTING ROLLED-OUT PASTRY

To lift a sheet of pastry, dust the rolling-pin lightly with flour and place it in the middle of the pastry. Fold half the pastry over the rolling pin to lift the pastry into position.

LINING A FLAN TIN OR DISH

Roll the pastry out to a size that will cover the base and come up the sides of the dish with a little extra to spare. Lift the pastry on the rolling pin, then lower it loosely over the tin or dish.

Quickly work around the dish, lifting the edge of the pastry with one hand and pressing it down into the corner of the dish with the forefinger and knuckle of the other hand. When the pastry is pressed neatly all around the base of the dish, press the excess around the edge of the dish so that it falls backwards slightly.

Roll the rolling pin across the top of the dish to trim off excess pastry. If you are lining a tin its edge will cut off the pastry; if using a dish you will gently have to pull away the excess pastry edges, or run a knife around the rim.

BAKING BLIND

Pastry cases that are cooked and cooled before they are filled have a sheet of greaseproof paper and baking beans placed in them to prevent the base of the pastry from puffing up. This is known as baking blind. The paper and backing beans are usually removed once the pastry has been cooked enough to set, and the pastry case returned to the oven to allow it to brown slightly.

In some recipes, the pastry case is partially baked before it is filled, and the cooking is completed with the filling. The technique of baking blind would be used for this preliminary baking of the pastry case.

Clear instructions are given in individual recipes. Ceramic baking beans may be purchased for baking blind, or ordinary dried peas or beans may be used. These are sprinkled over the greaseproof paper to weight the pastry slightly. Dried peas or beans used for this purpose may be cooled and stored in an airtight container and used over and over again. However, they may not be cooked to be eaten in another recipe.

COMMON FAULTS WITH PASTRY AND HOW TO AVOID THEM

SHORT CRUST PASTRY (OR SIMILAR PASTRIES)

Hard, tough pastry
- Too little fat used
- Too much liquid added
- Pastry handled too much or too heavily
- Too much flour used for rolling out
- Grainy, flaky or blistered pastry
- Fat not rubbed in sufficiently
- Water not mixed in well
- Pastry rolled out twice
- Too much flour used for rolling

Pastry too short, very crumbly (collapses)
- Too much fat used
- Fat overworked into flour
- Too little liquid used

PUFF OR FLAKY PASTRY

Pastry hard and tough
- Warm fat used
- Too much water used
- Dough overkneaded
- Oven temperature too low during cooking

Unevenly risen
- Fat not mixed in evenly during rolling
- Unevenly folded and rolled
- Pastry not chilled before use

Pastry flat, not light
- Warm fat used
- Dough not folded and rolled sufficiently

Soggy pastry with a hard crust
- Oven too hot; pastry browned and hardened before it had time to rise

SUET CRUST PASTRY

Hard and tough
- Too much water added
- Cooked in a low oven for too long

Solid, lumpy pastry
- Plain flour used in a recipe that stipulated self-raising flour or plain flour plus a raising agent
- Pastry cooked too quickly (suet has not melted)
- Pastry has got wet during steaming
- Home-grated suet was lumpy

HOT WATER CRUST PASTRY

By comparison with other pastries, hot water crust is a heavy dough. Plain flour is bound to a dough with a mixture of water and lard, heated together until boiling.

Hot water crust pastry should be mixed, then lightly kneaded until smooth. If it is overworked it becomes greasy. Once mixed, the pastry should be kept warm in a bowl placed over hot (not simmering) water. To prevent the surface from drying, the dough should be closely covered with a polythene bag.

As the pastry cools it becomes more difficult to manage and tends to crack on the surface. When moulding pie cases around the outside of a container, the pastry has to be cooled before it may be filled and covered; during this time the pastry for the lid should be kept warm over hot water. The method which gives a better finish is to line a mould with pastry, then fill and cover it at once.

If the sides of a mould are removed so the pastry may brown, it is important to work quickly once the mould is not supporting the pie, otherwise the soft pastry may collapse. Before removing the sides of the mould, have beaten egg ready to brush the pastry. Brush the pastry quickly and put the pie back into the oven. The egg helps to strengthen and seal the pastry quickly.

If the sides of a moulded pie begin to bulge, quickly wrap a double-thick band of foil around the pie, placing it halfway up the depth. Return the pie to the oven until the pastry sets.

SHORT CRUST PASTRY

225 g / 8 oz plain flour
2.5 ml / ½ tsp salt
100 g / 4 oz margarine (or half butter, half lard)
flour for rolling out

Sift the flour and salt into a bowl, then rub on the margarine until the mixture resembles fine breadcrumbs. Add enough cold water to make a stiff dough.

Press the dough together with your fingertips. If time permits, wrap in grease-proof paper and rest in the refrigerator for 30 minutes. To use, roll out on a lightly-floured surface.

MAKES ABOUT 225 G / 8 OZ

VARIATION

• **Wholemeal Short Crust Pastry** Although wholemeal flour may be used on its own, this does tend to create a rather chewy pastry. Using 100 g / 4 oz each of plain and wholemeal flour gives a very satisfactory result.

COMMON SWEET SHORT CRUST

This old-fashioned sweet pastry is firm, not crumbly – a sweet equivalent of hot water crust. It may be used as a topping for fruit pies.

225 g / 8 oz plain flour
45 g / 1½ oz butter
25 g / 1 oz caster sugar
150 ml / ¼ pint milk

Put the flour into a bowl. Rub in the butter until the mixture resembles fine breadcrumbs, then stir in the sugar.

Bring the milk to the boil in a small saucepan. Add the boiling milk to the flour mixture and knead until smooth. Use at once by rolling out thinly on a lightly-floured surface.

MAKES ABOUT 350 G / 12 OZ

PATE SUCREE

200 g / 7 oz plain flour
1.25 ml / ¼ tsp salt
90 g / 3½ oz butter
50 g / 2 oz caster sugar
1 egg yolk
flour for rolling out

Sift the flour and salt into a bowl. Cut the butter into small pieces and rub into the flour until the mixture resembles fine breadcrumbs. Mix in the sugar, then the egg yolk, and add enough cold water to make a stiff dough. Roll out on a lightly-floured surface and use as required.

MAKES ABOUT 350 G / 12 OZ

BUTTER CRUST PASTRY

This excellent pastry forms crisp layers when cooked. It does not rise
as high as puff or flaky pastry but it has a pleasing, filo-like texture to the
separate flakes. It is ideal for topping savoury or sweet pies; for pasties
or small items like sausage rolls and for plaits and slices.

225 g / 8 oz plain flour, plus extra for rolling and dredging
75 g / 3 oz butter

Put the flour in a bowl. Add sufficient water (about 150 ml / ¼ pint) to make a smooth, soft dough.

Roll out the dough on a lightly-floured surface into an oblong measuring 30 x 15 cm / 12 x 6 inches. Mark roughly into thirds. Dot the middle third with the butter and dredge the fat lightly with flour.

Fold top and bottom thirds over the fat to enclose it completely then roll it out again. If time permits, wrap in polythene and rest in the refrigerator for 15 minutes. Repeat the rolling and folding three times, so that the butter is evenly distributed. To use, roll out on a lightly-floured surface.

MAKES ABOUT 350 G / 12 OZ

PUFF PASTRY

225 g / 8 oz plain flour
1.25 ml / ¼ tsp salt
225 g / 8 oz butter, chilled
5 ml / 1 tsp lemon juice
flour for rolling out

Sift the flour and salt into a bowl. Rub in 50 g / 2 oz of the butter. Add the lemon juice and enough cold water to mix the ingredients to a smooth, fairly soft dough. The mixture should take about 125 ml / 4 fl oz water but this must be added by the spoonful to avoid making the dough too wet. Wrap the dough in cling film and chill briefly.

Shape the remaining butter into a rectangle measuring about 10 x 7.5 cm / 4 x 3 inches, then chill again. On a lightly-floured surface, roll out the dough into an oblong measuring about 25 x 15 cm / 10 x 6 inches, or slightly smaller. Place the butter in the middle of the dough, then fold the bottom third over it and fold the top third down to enclose the butter completely.

Press the edges of the dough together with the rolling pin. Give the dough a quarter turn in a clockwise direction. Roll out the dough into an oblong as before, fold it again, the wrap in cling film. Chill for 30 minutes. Roll and fold the pastry 6 times in all, chilling well each time. To remember the number of rollings, mark dents in the dough with your fingertips.

After the process of rolling and folding is complete, chill the pastry again before using it as required.

MAKES ABOUT 450 G / 1 LB

ROUGH PUFF PASTRY

A slightly easier version of puff pastry; all the fat must be well chilled for success. For best results, chill the bowl of flour too; always make sure your hands are very cold by holding them under cold running water before handling the dough.

225 g / 8 oz plain flour
1.25 ml / ¼ tsp salt
175 g / 6 oz butter, cut in chunks and chilled
5 ml / 1 tsp lemon juice
flour for rolling out

Sift the flour and salt into a bowl. Add the butter and mix in lightly using a round-bladed knife. Mix in the lemon juice and enough ice-cold water to make a soft dough. The mixture should take about 125 ml / 4 fl oz (or very slightly more) but add the water a spoonful at a time to avoid making the dough too wet. The dough should be soft and very lumpy.

On a lightly-floured surface roll out the dough into an oblong, keeping the corners square. Mark the oblong of dough into thirds, then fold and roll it as for Flaky Pastry (page 11). Repeat the process four times in all, chilling the dough between each rolling or as necessary.

The rolled dough should be smooth. Wrap it in cling film and chill well before rolling it out to use as required.

MAKES ABOUT 450 G / 1 LB

FLAKY PASTRY

Flaky pastry does not have as many layers as puff pastry.
It contains less fat to flour and the dough is rolled and folded fewer times.

225 g / 8 oz plain flour
1.25 ml / ¼ tsp salt
175 g / 6 oz butter or 75 g / 3 oz each butter and lard, chilled
5 ml / 1 tsp lemon juice
flour for rolling out

Sift the flour and salt into a bowl. If using butter and lard, mix them together roughly. Rub in a quarter of the fat, keeping the remaining fat chilled. Stir in the lemon juice and enough cold water to mix the ingredients to a soft dough. The mixture should take about 125 ml / 4 fl oz water but this should be added by the spoonful to avoid making the dough too wet.

On a lightly-floured surface, roll out the dough into an oblong measuring about 25 x 15 cm / 10 x 6 inches. Mark the dough into thirds. Cut the fat into 3 equal portions. Dot one portion of fat over the top two-thirds of the dough, in neat lumps.

Fold the bottom thirds of the dough up over the middle portion, then fold the top third down so that the lumps of fat are enclosed completely. Press the edges of the dough together with the rolling pin. Give the dough a quarter turn in a clockwise direction, then roll out as before.

Repeat the process of dotting the dough with fat, folding and rolling it, twice more. Chill the dough briefly between each rolling. Finally, fold and roll the pastry once more, without any fat, then chill again before using it as required.

MAKES ABOUT 450 G / 1 LB

SUET CRUST PASTRY

200 g / 7 oz plain flour
5 ml / 1 tsp baking powder
pinch of salt
75 g / 3 oz shredded suet
flour for rolling out

Sift the flour, baking powder and salt into a mixing bowl. Stir in the suet, then add enough cold water (about 150–175 ml / 5–6 fl oz) to make a soft but not sticky dough. Use at once by rolling out on a lightly-floured surface.

MAKES 200 G / 7 OZ

CHOUX PASTRY

100 g / 4 oz plain flour
50 g / 2 oz butter or margarine
pinch of salt
2 whole eggs plus 1 yolk

Sift the flour on to a sheet of greaseproof paper. Put 250 ml / 8 fl oz water in a saucepan and add the butter or margarine with the salt. Heat gently until the fat melts.

When the fat has melted, bring the liquid rapidly to the boil, then add all the flour at once. Immediately remove the pan from the heat and stir the flour into the liquid to make a smooth paste which leaves the sides of the pan clean. Set aside to cool slightly.

Add the egg yolk and beat well. Add the whole eggs, one at a time, beating well after each addition. Continue beating until the paste is very glossy. Use at once.

MAKES ABOUT 175 G / 6 OZ

HOT WATER CRUST PASTRY

This pastry is used for pork, veal and ham, and raised game pies. It must be moulded while still warm.

200 g / 7 oz plain flour
2.5 ml / ½ tsp salt
75 g / 3 oz lard
100 ml / 3 ½ fl oz milk or water

Sift the flour and salt into a warm bowl and make a well in the centre. Keep the bowl in a warm place.

Meanwhile, heat the lard and milk or water until boiling. Add the hot mixture to the flour, mixing well with a wooden spoon until the pastry is cool enough to knead with the hands. Knead thoroughly and mould as required.

Bake at 220°C / 425°F / gas 7 until the pastry is set, then reduce the oven temperature to 180°C / 350°F / gas 4 until fully baked.

MAKES 350 G / 12 OZ

TO MOULD A RAISED PIE

Hot Water Crust Pastry (page 13)
fat for greasing
flour

Use a jar, round cake tin or similar container, as a mould: grease and flour the sides and base of the mould and invert it.

Reserve a quarter of the warm pastry for the lid and leave in the bowl in a warm place, covered with a greased polythene bag.

Roll out the remainder to about 5 mm / ¼ inch thick, in a round or oval shape. Lay the pastry over the mould, then ease the pastry around the sides. Take care not to pull the pastry and make sure that the sides and base are of an even thickness. Leave to cool.

When cold, remove the pastry case from the mould and put in the filling. Roll out the pastry reserved for the lid, dampen the rim of the case, put on the lid, pressing the edges firmly together. Tie 3 or 4 folds of greaseproof paper round the pie to hold it in shape during baking and to prevent it from becoming too brown.

MAKES ONE 13 CM / 5 INCH PIE

Using a Raised Pie Mould Decorative pie moulds may be purchased from cookshops. Usually oval in shape, they range in size from those which provide up to 6 servings, to others which make pies large enough to feed 40 people.

The two sides of the mould fit into a base and they are secured with clips. The sides should be secured and the inside of the mould should be well greased. The pastry should be rolled out to about two-thirds of the required size.

Lift the pastry into the mould and secure its edge just below the rim of the mould. Use your fingers to press the pastry into the mould, easing it upwards at the same time so that it comes above the rim of the mould when the lining is complete. The pie may be filled at once.

The sides of the mould should be removed about 15–30 minutes before the end of the cooking time. Brush the pastry with beaten egg immediately and return the pie to the oven promptly to prevent the sides from collasping.

RASIED VEAL PIE

If preferred, these ingredients can be made into 6 individual pies.
The eggs should be sliced and divided between the smaller pies.

Hot Water Crust Pastry (page 13), using 400 g / 14 oz flour
400 g / 14 oz pie veal
400 g / 14 oz lean pork
25 g / 1 oz plain flour
7.5 ml / 1½ tsp salt
1.25 ml / ¼ tsp ground pepper
3 hard-boiled eggs
beaten egg for glazing
about 125 ml / 4 fl oz well-flavoured, cooled
and jellied stock or canned consommé

Set the oven at 230ºC / 450ºF / gas 8. Line a 20 cm / 8 inch round pie mould with three-quarters of the pastry, or use a round cake tin to mould the pie as described opposite. Use the remaining quarter for the lid.

Cut the meat into small piece, removing any gristle or fat. Season the flour with the salt and pepper, then toss the pieces of meat in it. Put half the meat into the pastry case and put in the whole eggs. Add the remaining meat and 30 ml / 2 tbsp water. Put on the lid and brush with beaten egg. Make a hole in the centre to allow steam to escape. Bake for 15 minutes, then reduce the oven temperature to 140ºC / 275ºF / gas 1. Continue baking 2½ hours. Remove the greaseproof paper or mould for the last 30 minutes of the cooking time and brush the top and sides of the pastry with beaten egg.

Heat the stock or consommé until melted. When the pie is cooked, pour it through the hole in the lid using a funnel until the pie is full. Leave to cool.

SERVES SIX

RAISED PORK PIES

About 400 g / 14 oz pork bones
1 small onion, finely chopped
salt and pepper
300 ml / ½ pint stock or cold water
Hot Water Crust pastry (page 13), using 400 g / 14 oz flour
500 g / 18 oz lean pork, minced
1.25 ml / ¼ tsp dried sage
beaten egg for glazing

Simmer the pork bones, onion, salt, pepper and stock or water, covered, for 2 hours. Strain and cool. Make one 15 cm / 6 inch pie (as described page 15) or divide three-quarters of the pastry into 6 portions. Mould each piece using a jam jar, keeping the pastry about 5 mm / ¼ inch thick. Use the remainder for the lids. Set the oven at 220°C / 425°F / gas 7.

Season the pork with salt, pepper and sage. Divide between the prepared pie case or cases and add 10 ml / 2 tsp of the jellied stock to each. Put on the lids, brush with beaten egg, and make holes in the centres.

Bake for 15 minutes, then reduce the oven temperature to 180°C / 350°F / gas 4. Continue baking for 45 minutes (1 hour for a large pie). Remove the grease-proof paper for the last 30 minutes and brush the top and sides of the pastry with egg.

When cooked, remove from the oven and leave to cool. Warm the remainder of the jellied stock. Using a funnel, pour the stock through the hole in the pastry lids until the pies are full. Leave to cool.

SERVES SIX

VEGETABLE FLAN

200 g / 7 oz plain flour
100 g / 4 oz butter or margarine
salt and pepper
1 onion, chopped
50 g / 2 oz button mushrooms, thinly sliced
250 ml / 8 fl oz milk
100 g / 4 oz smoked Applewood cheese (or other hard cheese to taste)
2 eggs, separated
450 g / 1 lb cauliflower florets, lightly cooked
30 ml / 2 tbsp fine dried white breadcrumbs

Set the oven at 200°C / 400°F / gas 6. Place 175 g / 6 oz of the flour in a bowl and rub in 75 g / 3 oz of the butter or margarine. Add enough cold water to bind the mixture to a short dough – about 30 ml / 2 tbsp. Roll out the dough and use to line a 25 cm / 10 inch flan tin or dish.

Prick the pastry all over, line with greaseproof paper and sprinkle with dried peas or baking beans. Bake 'blind' for 15 minutes. Remove the beans and paper and continue to cook for a further 15 minutes, until the pastry is cooked.

Melt the remaining butter or margarine in a small saucepan. Add the onion and mushrooms and cook, stirring, over medium heat until the onion is soft and the mushrooms well cooked – about 15 minutes. Add the remaining flour and stir well. Gradually stir in the milk and bring to the boil, stirring all the time, to make a smooth, thick sauce. Stir in the cheese and salt and pepper to taste. Remove from the heat and beat in the egg yolks. Whisk the egg whites until stiff, then fold them into the sauce.

Arrange the cauliflower evenly over the base of the pastry case, then spoon the sauce over, teasing it down between the florets. Sprinkle with the breadcrumbs and bake for about 15 minutes, until set and golden brown on top. Serve at once.

SERVES SIX TO EIGHT

QUICHE LORRAINE

225 g / 8 oz rindless streaky bacon rashers
3 eggs
300 ml / ½ pint single cream
2.5 ml / ½ tsp salt
grinding of black pepper
pinch of grated nutmeg
25 g / 1 oz butter, diced

SHORT CRUST PASTRY
100 g / 4 oz plain flour
2.5 ml / ½ tsp salt
50 g / 2 oz margarine (or half butter, half lard)
flour for rolling out

Set the oven at 200ºC / 400ºF / gas 6. To make the pastry, sift the flour and salt into a bowl, then rub in the margarine until the mixture resembles fine bread-crumbs. Add enough cold water to make a stiff dough. Press the dough together.

Roll out the pastry on a lightly-floured surface and use it to line an 18 cm / 7 inch flan tin or ring placed on a baking sheet. Line the pastry with greaseproof paper and fill with baking beans. Bake 'blind' for 20 minutes until the rim of the pastry is slightly browned but the base still soft. Remove the paper and beans. Reduce the oven temperature to 190ºC / 375ºF / gas 5.

Cut the bacon in 2 cm x 5 mm / ¾ x ¼ inch strips. Dry fry for a few minutes. Drain and scatter strips over the pastry case. Press in lightly. Beat the eggs, cream, salt, pepper and nutmeg. Pour the mixture into the pastry case and dot with butter. Bake for 30 minutes. Serve at once.

SERVES FOUR TO SIX

CORNISH PASTIES

FILLING
1 large or 2 small potatoes
1 small turnip
1 onion, chopped
salt and pepper
300 g / 11 oz lean chuck steak, finely diced

PASTRY
500 g / 18 oz plain flour
5 ml / 1 tsp salt
150 g / 5 oz lard
60 ml / 4 tbsp shredded suet
flour for rolling out
beaten egg for glazing

Set the oven at 230°C / 450°F / gas 8. To make the pastry, sift the flour and salt into a bowl. Rub in the lard, then mix in the suet. Moisten with enough cold water to make a stiff dough. Roll out on a lightly-floured surface and cut into eight 16 cm / 6½ inch rounds.

To make the filling, dice the potatoes and turnip, then mix with the onion and add salt and pepper to taste. Add the meat and 30 ml / 2 tbsp water, and mix well. Divide between the pastry rounds, placing a line of mixture across the centre of each round.

Dampen the edges of each pastry round. Lift them to meet over the filling. Pinch together to seal, then flute the edges. Make small slits in both sides of each pasty near the top. Place the pasties on a baking sheet and brush with egg. Bake for 10 minutes, then lower the oven temperature to 180°C / 350°F / gas 4. Continue baking for a further 45 minutes, or until the meat is tender when pierced by a thin, heated skewer through the top of a pasty.

MAKES EIGHT

TRADITIONAL APPLE PIE

675 g / 1½ lb cooking apples
100 g / 4 oz sugar
6 cloves
caster sugar for dredging

SHORT CRUST PASTRY
350 g / 12 oz plain flour
4 ml / ¾ tsp salt
175 g / 6 oz margarine (or half butter, half lard)
flour for rolling out

Set the oven at 200°C / 400F / gas 6. To make the pastry, sift the flour and salt into a bowl, then rub in the margarine until the mixture resembles fine bread-crumbs. Add enough cold water to make a stiff dough. Press the dough together with your fingertips.

Roll out the pastry on a lightly-floured surface and use just over half to line a 750 ml / 1¼ pint pie dish. Peel, core and slice the apples. Place half in the pastry-lined dish, then add the sugar and cloves. Pile the remaining apples on top, cover with the remaining pastry and seal the edges. Brush the pastry with cold water and dredge with caster sugar.

Bake for 20 minutes, then lower the oven temperature to 180°C / 350°F / gas 4 and bake for 20 minutes more. The pastry should be golden brown. Dredge with more caster sugar and serve hot or cold.

SERVES SIX

VARIATIONS

- **Apricot Pie** Use two 375 g / 15 oz cans apricots, drained, instead of apples. Omit the sugar and cloves.
- **Blackberry and Apple Pie** Use half blackberries and half apples and replace the cloves with 2.5 ml / ½ tsp grated lemon rind.
- **Damson Pie** Use damsons instead of apples and increase the sugar to 150 g / 5 oz and omit the cloves.
- **Gooseberry Pie** Use cleaned, topped and tailed gooseberries instead of apples. Omit the cloves.

- **Redcurrant and Raspberry Pie** This is a winning combination. Use 450 / 1 lb redcurrants and 225 g / 8 oz raspberries instead of apples. Reduce the sugar to 30 ml / 2 tbsp and omit the cloves.
- **Rhubarb Pie** Use rhubarb cut into 2 cm / ¾ inch lengths instead of apples. Increase the sugar to 150 g / 5 oz.

MINCE PIES

Festive mince pies can also be made using flaky,
rough puff or puff pastry with mouthwatering results.
If using any of these pastries you will require 200 g / 7 oz flour.

350 g / 12 oz mincemeat
25 g / 1 oz icing or caster sugar for dredging

SHORT CRUST PASTRY
300 g / 10 oz plain flour
5 ml / 1 tsp salt
150 g / 5 oz margarine (or half butter, half lard)
flour for rolling out

Set the oven at 200°C / 400°F / gas 6. To make the pastry, sift the flour and salt into a bowl, then rub in the margarine until the mixture resembles fine bread-crumbs. Add enough cold water to make a stiff dough. Press the dough together with your fingertips.

Roll out the pastry on a lightly-floured surface and use just over half of it to line twelve 7.5 cm / 3 inch patty tins. Cut out 12 lids from the rest of the pastry. If liked, make holly leaf decorations from the pastry trimmings.

Place a spoonful of mincemeat in each pastry case. Dampen the edges of the cases and cover with the pastry lids. Seal the edges well. Brush the tops with water and add any pastry decorations. Dredge with the sugar. Make 2 small cuts in the top of each pie. Bake for 15–20 minutes or until golden brown.

MAKES TWELVE

LEMON TARTLETS

50 g / 2 oz butter
50 g / 2 oz sugar
1 egg, beaten
grated rind and juice of ½ lemon
10 ml / 2 tsp icing sugar

SHORT CRUST PASTRY
100 g / 4 oz plain flour
1.25 ml / ¼ tsp salt
50 g / 2 oz margarine (or half butter, half lard)
flour for rolling out

Set the oven at 200°C / 400°F / gas 6. To make the pastry, sift the flour and salt into a bowl, then rub in the margarine until the mixture resembles fine breadcrumbs. Add enough cold water to make a stiff dough. Press the dough together with your fingertips. Roll out and use to line twelve 7.5 cm / 3 inch patty tins.

Cream the butter and sugar in a bowl until pale and fluffy. Beat in the egg. Add the lemon rind and juice. Fill the pastry cases with the mixture.

Bake for 15–20 minutes until set. Leave to cool. Sift the icing sugar over the tartlets.

MAKES TWELVE

PUMPKIN PIE

1 (425 g / 15 oz) can pumpkin or 450 g / 1 lb cooked mashed pumpkin
150 g soft dark brown sugar
7.5 ml / 1½ tsp cinnamon
2.5 ml / ½ tsp salt
5 ml / 1 tsp ground ginger
2.5 ml / ½ tsp grated nutmeg
3 eggs
250 ml / 8 fl oz milk

SHORT CRUST PASTRY
225 g / 8 oz plain flour
2.5 ml / ½ tsp salt
100 g / 4 oz margarine (or half butter, half lard)
flour for rolling out

Set the oven at 200°C / 400°F / gas 6. To make the pastry, sift the flour and salt into a bowl, then rub in the margarine until the mixture resembles fine bread-crumbs. Add enough cold water to make a stiff dough. Press the dough together with your fingertips. Roll out on a lightly-floured surface and use to line a 25 cm / 10 inch pie plate. Chill in the refrigerator for 30 minutes.

In a large bowl, mix the pumpkin with the sugar, cinnamon, salt, ginger and nutmeg. Beat the eggs in a second bowl, add the milk and mix well. Stir the egg mixture into the pumpkin mixture. Pour into the pastry case.

Bake for 15 minutes. Lower the temperature to 180°C / 350°F / gas 4 and cook for a further 30–40 minutes, or until a knife inserted in the centre of the pie comes out clean. Cool the pie before serving.

SERVES SIX

SOUTHERN PECAN PIE

Pecan nuts are oval and red-shelled when whole; when shelled they resemble slim walnuts. Use unbroken halves of pecan nuts in the filling for this pie.

50 g / 2 oz butter
175 g / 6 oz soft light brown sugar
3 eggs
225 g / 8 oz shelled pecan nuts
150 g / 5 oz golden syrup
15 ml / 1 tbsp dark rum
2.5 ml / ½ tsp salt
double cream to serve

SHORT CRUST PASTRY
225 g / 8 oz plain flour
2.5 ml / ½ tsp salt
100 g / 4 oz margarine (or half butter, half lard)
flour for rolling out

Set the oven at 200°C / 400°F / gas 6. To make the pastry, sift the flour and salt into a bowl, then rub in the margarine until the mixture resembles fine bread-crumbs. Add enough cold water to make a stiff dough. Press the dough together with your fingertips. Roll out on a lightly-floured surface and use to line a 25 cm / 10 inch pie plate. Prick the base well.

Bake the pie case for 5 minutes, then cool. Lower the oven temperature to 180°C / 350°F / gas 4.

In a mixing bowl, cream the butter with the sugar until light. Beat in the eggs, one at a time. Stir in the rest of the ingredients. Fill the pastry case with the mixture and bake for about 40 minutes or until a knife inserted in the centre comes out clean. Serve warm or cold, with double cream.

SERVES SIX

LEMON MERINGUE PIE

300 g / 11 oz caster sugar
45 ml / 3 tbsp cornflour
45 ml / 3 tbsp plain flour
pinch of salt
30 ml / 2 tbsp butter
grated rind and juice of 2 lemons
3 eggs, separated

SHORT CRUST PASTRY
175 g / 6 oz plain flour
2.5 ml / ½ tsp salt
75 g / 3 oz margarine (or half butter, half lard)
flour for rolling out

Set the oven at 200°C / 400°F / gas 6. To make the pastry, sift the flour and salt into a bowl, then rub in the margarine until the mixture resembles fine breadcrumbs. Add enough cold water to make a stiff dough. Press the dough together lightly.

Roll out the pastry on a lightly-floured surface and use to line a 23 cm / 9 inch pie plate. Line the pastry with greaseproof paper and fill with baking beans. Bake 'blind' for 15 minutes; remove paper and beans. Return to the oven for 5 minutes.

Meanwhile, mix 50 g / 2 oz of the caster sugar, the cornflour, plain flour and salt in a saucepan. Stir in 300 ml / ½ pint water and bring to the boil, stirring.

Draw the pan off the heat and add the butter, lemon rind and juice. Put the egg yolks in a bowl, add a little of the cooked mixture, then add to the mixture in the pan. Beat well, replace over the heat and cook, stirring constantly for 2 minutes. Remove the pie from the oven and reduce the oven temperature to 180°C / 350°F / gas 4.

In a clean, grease-free bowl, whisk the egg whites until stiff. Fold in the remaining sugar. Pour the lemon custard into the baked pastry case and cover the top with the meringue, making sure that it covers the top completely. Bake for 12–15 minutes until the meringue is lightly browned. Cool before cutting.

SERVES SIX

MRS BEETON'S BAKEWELL PUDDING

strawberry or apricot jam
50 g / 2 oz butter
50 g / 2 oz caster sugar
1 egg
50 g / 2 oz ground almonds
50 g / 2 oz fine cake crumbs
few drops almond essence
icing sugar for dusting

SHORT CRUST PASTRY
100 g / 4 oz plain flour
1.25 ml / ¼ tsp salt
50 g / 2 oz margarine (or half butter, half lard)
flour for rolling out

Set the oven at 200ºC / 400ºF / gas 6. To make the pastry, sift the flour and salt into a bowl, then rub in the margarine until the mixture resembles fine breadcrumbs. Add enough cold water to make a stiff dough. Press the dough together lightly.

Roll out the pastry on a lightly-floured surface and use to line an 18 cm / 7 inch flan tin or ring placed on a baking sheet. Spread a good layer of jam over the pastry base.

In a mixing bowl, cream the butter with the sugar until pale and fluffy. Beat in the egg, then add the almonds, cake crumbs and essence. Beat until well mixed. Pour into the flan case, on top of the jam.

Bake for 30 minutes or until the centre of the pudding is firm. Sprinkle with icing sugar and serve hot or cold.

SERVES FOUR TO FIVE

VARIATIONS

- **Bakewell Tart** Make as above, but use raspberry jam and only 25 g / 1 oz bread or cake crumbs and 25 g / 1 oz ground almonds. Bake for 25 minutes.
- **Almond Tartlets** Line twelve 7.5 cm / 3 inch patty tins with the pastry. Replace the cake crumbs with an extra 50 g / 2 oz ground almonds and the almond essence with 2.5 ml / ½ tsp lemon juice. Bake for 12–18 minutes.
- **West Riding Pudding** Line a 500 ml / 17 oz dish with the pastry. Make as for Bakewell Pudding but substitute 75 g / 3 oz plain flour and 2.5 ml / ½ tsp baking powder for the cake crumbs and ground almonds. If the mixture seems stiff, add a little milk. Bake at 190°C / 375°F / gas 5 for 1 hour. Serve hot or cold.

PASTRY HORNS

Puff Pastry (page 9), using 100 g / 4 oz flour
flour for rolling out
beaten egg and milk for glazing

Roll out the pastry 5 mm / ¼ inch thick on a lightly-floured surface, then cut into strips 35 cm / 14 inches long and 2 cm / ¾ inch wide. Moisten the strips with cold water.

Wind each strip around a cornet mould, working from the point upward, keeping the moistened surface on the outside. Lay the horns on a dampened baking sheet, with the final overlap of the pastry strip underneath. Leave in a cool place for 1 hour.

Set the oven at 220°C / 425°F / gas 7. Brush the horns with beaten egg and milk. Bake for 10–15 minutes or until golden brown. Remove the moulds and return the horns to the oven for 5 minutes. Cool completely on a wire rack. When cold, fill the horns with a sweet or savoury filling.

MAKES EIGHT

TREACLE TART

An old favourite which is today as popular as ever.
Try it with cornflakes instead of breadcrumbs for a tasty change.

45 ml / 3 tbsp golden syrup
50 g / 2 oz soft white breadcrumbs
5 ml / 1 tsp lemon juice

SHORT CRUST PASTRY
150 g / 5 oz plain flour
2.5 ml / ½ tsp salt
65 g / 2½ oz margarine (or half butter, half lard)
flour for rolling out

Set the oven at 200°C / 400°F / gas 6. To make the pastry, sift the flour and salt into a bowl, then rub in the margarine until the mixture resembles fine bread-crumbs. Add enough cold water to make a stiff dough. Press the dough together with your fingertips.

Roll out the pastry on a lightly-floured surface and use just over three-quarters of it to line a 20 cm / 8 inch pie plate, reserving the rest for a lattice topping.

Melt the syrup in a saucepan. Stir in the breadcrumbs and lemon juice, then pour the mixture into the prepared pastry case.

Roll out the reserved pastry to a rectangle and cut into 1 cm / ½ inch strips. Arrange in a lattice on top of the tart. Bake for about 30 minutes.

SERVES SIX

VARIATION

- **Treacle Jelly Tart** Make as above, but omit the breadcrumbs and add 1 beaten egg to the syrup. Bake in a 180°C / 350°F / gas 4 oven until golden brown. When cold, the filling sets like jelly.

MRS BEETON'S APPLE FLAN

6 eating apples
4 cloves
45 ml / 3 tbsp medium-dry sherry
30 ml / 2 tbsp soft light brown sugar
3 egg whites
45 ml / 3 tbsp caster sugar

SHORT CRUST PASTRY
175 g / 6 oz plain flour
2.5 ml / ½ salt
75 g / 3 oz margarine (or half butter, half lard)

Peel and core the apples, cutting each into 8 sections. Place in a heatproof bowl, add the cloves and sherry and cover closely. Place the bowl in a deep saucepan. Add boiling water to come halfway up the sides of the bowl and cook for 20 minutes until the apple sections are tender but still intact.

Set the oven at 200°C / 400°F / gas 6. Sift the flour and salt into a bowl, then rub in margarine. Add enough cold water to make a stiff dough.

Roll out the pastry on a lightly-floured surface and use to line a 23 cm / 9 inch flan tin. Line the pastry with greaseproof paper and fill with baking beans. Bake for 10 minutes. Remove the paper and beans; cook for 5 minutes. Set aside.

Lower the oven temperature to 140°C / 275°F / gas 1. Arrange the apples in the flan. Sprinkle with 30 ml / 2 tbsp of the cooking liquid and the brown sugar.

In a clean, grease-free bowl, whisk the egg whites until stiff. Whisk in 10 ml / 2 tsp of the caster sugar and spread lightly over the apples. Sprinkle the remaining sugar over. Bake for 1 hour. Serve warm or cold.

SERVES SIX

ALMOND AND APRICOT TARTLETS

10 ml / 2 tsp apricot jam
50 g / 2 oz butter or margarine
50 g / 2 oz sugar
1 egg
15 ml / 1 tbsp plain cake crumbs
15 ml / 1 tbsp ground almonds
3 drops almond essence
10 ml / 2 tsp nibbed almonds
15 ml / 1 tbsp Apricot Glaze (page 134)
10 ml / 2 tsp chopped angelica

SHORT CRUST PASTRY
100 g / 4 oz plain flour
1.25 ml / ¼ tsp salt
50 g / 2 oz margarine (or half butter, half lard)
flour for rolling out

Set the oven at 190°C / 375°F / gas 5. To make the pastry, sift the flour and salt into a bowl, then rub in the margarine until the mixture resembles fine breadcrumbs. Add enough cold water to make a stiff dough. Press the dough together lightly.

Roll out the pastry on a lightly-floured surface and use to line twelve 7.5 cm / 3 inch patty tins. Put a little apricot jam in each. In a bowl, cream the butter or margarine with the sugar until pale and fluffy. Gradually beat in the egg. Stir in the cake crumbs, ground almonds and almond essence. Half fill each pastry case with the mixture and smooth the tops. Sprinkle the nibbed almonds on top.

Bake for 15 minutes or until firm to the touch. Leave the tartlets to cool. Warm the apricot glaze, brush it on top of the tartlets, then sprinkle with the chopped angelica.

MAKES TWELVE

CUSTARD TARTLETS

1 egg
15 ml / 1 tbsp caster sugar
125 ml / 4 fl oz milk
pinch of grated nutmeg

SWEET SHORT CRUST PASTRY
100 g / 4 oz plain flour
1.25 ml / ¼ tsp salt
50 g / 2 oz margarine (or half butter, half lard)
5 ml / 1 tsp caster sugar
flour for rolling out

Set the oven at 180°C / 350°F / gas 4. To make the pastry, sift the flour and salt into a bowl, then rub in the margarine until the mixture resembles fine bread-crumbs. Stir in the caster sugar. Add enough cold water to make a stiff dough. Press the dough together with your fingertips. Roll out and use to line twelve 7.5 cm / 3 inch patty tins.

Beat the egg lightly in a bowl and add the sugar. Warm the milk in a saucepan, then pour it onto the egg. Strain the custard mixture into the pastry cases and sprinkle a little nutmeg on top of each.

Bake for about 30 minutes, until the custard is firm and set. Leave to cool before removing from the tins.

MAKES TWELVE

VARIATION

• **Custard Meringue Tartlets** Make as above, but omit the nutmeg and bake for 15 minutes only. Lower the oven temperature to 140°C / 275°F / gas 1. Whisk 2 egg whites in a clean, grease-free bowl until stiff. Fold in 75 g / 3 oz caster sugar. Pile the meringue on to the tartlets. Bake for about 30 minutes.

VOL-AU-VENT CASES

**Puff Pastry (page 9), using 200 g / 7 oz flour
flour for rolling out
beaten egg for glazing**

Set the oven at 220°C / 425°F / gas 7. Roll out the pastry on a lightly-floured surface about 2 cm / ¼ inch thick (1 cm / ½ inch thick for bouchées). Cut into round or oval shapes as liked. Place on a baking sheet and brush the top of the pastry with beaten egg.

With a smaller, floured cutter, make a circular or oval cut in each case, to form an inner ring cutting through about half the depth of the pastry. Bake for 20–25 minutes until golden brown and crisp.

When baked, remove the inner circular or oval lid, then scoop out the soft inside while still warm to make room for the filling.

**MAKES TWENTY-FOUR 5 CM / 2 INCH
OR TWELVE 7.5 CM / 3 INCH BOUCHEES
OR EIGHT 9 CM / 3½ INCH
OR TWO 15 CM / 6 INCH VOL-AU-VENT CASES**

LARGE DEEP VOL-AU-VENT

The pastry should be prepared as for the previous recipe and the oven preheated. The pastry should be rolled to a thickness of 3.5 cm / 1½ inches. Use a plate to stamp out the vol-au-vent. It is possible to buy large cutters, plain and fluted, from specialist cookshops and catering suppliers. Bake as for small vol-au-vent cases, allowing an extra 5 minutes cooking if necessary.

FILLINGS FOR PASTRY HORNS AND VOL-AU-VENT CASES

- **Seafood Filling** For vol-au-vent cases. Melt 25 g / 1 oz butter in a saucepan. Stir in 25 g / 1 oz plain flour, then cook for 1 minute. Pour in 300 ml / ½ pint milk, stirring all the time, and bring to the boil. Simmer for 3 minutes. Add a 200 g / 7 oz can tuna (drained), 100 g / 4 oz frozen peeled cooked prawns and seasoning to taste. Stir in 30 ml / 2 tbsp chopped parsley and simmer for 3 minutes, stirring occasionally until the prawns are thawed. Spoon into the pastry cases and serve hot.

- **Hot Chicken** Make the sauce as for seafood filling, using half milk and half chicken stock. Instead of adding tuna, add 225 g / 8 oz diced cooked chicken meat and 50 g / 2 oz sliced button mushrooms. Season with a little nutmeg, then simmer gently for 5 minutes. Stir in 60 ml / 4 tbsp single cream and a little chopped tarragon or parsley. Heat gently but do not boil.

- **Ham and Tomato** Mix 50 g / 2 oz diced cooked ham with 2 peeled and diced tomatoes, 1 chopped spring onion and 100 g / 4 oz soft cheese (full-fat soft cheese, ricotta, quark or low-fat soft cheese). Add salt and pepper to taste, then spoon into the cold pastry cases.

- **Chicken Mayonnaise** Dice 100 g / 4 oz cooked chicken and bind with mayonnaise to a creamy mixture. Add 30 ml / 2 tbsp snipped chives and salt and pepper to taste, then spoon the mixture into the cold pastry cases.

- **Spiced Turkey** Dice 100–175 g / 4–6 oz cooked turkey and mix with 15 ml / 1 tbsp mango chutney. Cook ½ chopped onion in 25 g / 1 oz butter until soft, stir in 5 ml / 1 tsp curry powder and cook for 2 minutes. Stir into the turkey, then bind with mayonnaise.

- **Stewed Fruit Filling** Apples, plums or other fresh fruit may be used to fill a large hot dessert vol-au-vent. Heat 50–75 g / 2–3 oz sugar and 300 ml / ½ pint water until the sugar dissolves. Bring to the boil. Add the chosen prepared fruit and cook gently, turning occasionally, until tender. Use a slotted spoon to transfer the fruit to a dish. Boil the syrup until well reduced and thickened. Spoon the fruit into the vol-au-vent, then pour the thick syrup over. Dust the filling with icing sugar and serve at once.

- **Jam and Cream** Place 5 ml / 1 tsp jam in each pastry case, then top with whipped cream. The cream may be flavoured with a little liqueur (such as Grand Marnier) or sherry and sweetened with a little caster or icing sugar before whipping. Sprinkle chopped nuts over the cream filling, if liked.

- **Fruit Horns** Roughly chopped fresh fruit, such as strawberries or peaches, may be mixed with lightly sweetened whipped cream to fill the pastry cases.

- **Chocolate Cream** Stir 45 ml / 3 tbsp boiling water into 15 ml / 1 tbsp cocoa. Add 30 ml / 2 tbsp brandy or chocolate liqueur. Mix in 300 ml / ½ pint double cream and 30 ml / 2 tbsp icing sugar. Whip the cream until it stands in soft peaks. Pipe or spoon it into the pastries.

PARISIAN TARTLETS

50 g / 2 oz butter
50 g / 2 oz caster sugar
1 egg, beaten
15 ml / 1 tbsp cornflour
15 ml / 1 tbsp single cream or milk
25 g / 1 oz ground almonds
25 g / 1 oz plain cake crumbs
2.5 ml / ½ tsp ground cinnamon
10 ml / 2 tsp lemon juice
caster sugar for dredging

SHORT CRUST PASTRY
100 g / 4 oz plain flour
1.25 ml / ¼ tsp salt
50 g / 2 oz margarine (or half butter, half lard)
flour for rolling out

Set the oven at 200°C / 400°F / gas 6. To make the pastry, sift the flour and salt into a bowl, then rub in the margarine until the mixture resembles fine bread-crumbs. Add enough cold water to make a stiff dough. Press the dough together with your fingertips.

Roll out on a lightly-floured surface and use to line twelve 7.5 cm / 3 inch patty tins.

Cream the butter and sugar in a bowl until pale and fluffy. Add the egg and beat well. Blend the cornflour with the cream or milk, then stir this into the creamed mixture. Add the ground almonds, cake crumbs, cinnamon and lemon juice. Fill the pastry cases with the mixture.

Bake for 15–20 minutes until golden brown. Dredge with caster sugar when baked.

MAKES TWELVE

FILBERT TARTLETS

30 ml / 2 tbsp cornflour
60 ml / 4 tbsp single cream or creamy milk
2 eggs
75 g / 3 oz caster sugar
75 g / 3 oz shelled filberts (hazelnuts), skinned and chopped
25 g / 1 oz ground almonds
milk and caster sugar for glazing

SHORT CRUST PASTRY
100 g / 4 oz plain flour
1.25 ml / ¼ tsp salt
50 g / 2 oz margarine (or half butter, half lard)
flour for rolling out

Set the oven at 200°C / 400°F / gas 6. To make the pastry, sift the flour and salt into a bowl, then rub in the margarine until the mixture resembles fine bread-crumbs. Add enough cold water to make a stiff dough. Press the dough together with your fingertips. Roll out on a lightly-floured surface and use to line twelve 7.5 cm / 3 inch patty tins, reserving a little pastry for decoration.

In a saucepan, mix the cornflour to a paste with the cream or milk. Stir over gentle heat until the mixture boils. Remove from the heat.

In a bowl, beat the eggs with the sugar until pale and fluffy. Add the chopped filberts, ground almonds and cornflour mixture. Spoon into the pastry cases. Cut the reserved pastry into strips and place 2 strips across each tartlet in the form of a cross.

Brush the tartlets with milk and dredge with caster sugar. Bake for about 20 minutes or until the pastry is golden brown.

MAKES TWELVE

APPLE & BLACKBERRY PUDDING

fat for greasing
custard to serve

SUET CRUST PASTRY
200 g / 7 oz plain flour
5 ml / 1 tsp baking powder
75 g / 3 oz shredded suet
flour for rolling out

FILLING
350 g / 12 oz cooking apples
75 g / 3 oz sugar
350 g / 12 oz blackberries

Grease a 750 ml / 1¼ pint pudding basin. Prepare a steamer or half fill a large saucepan with water and bring to the boil.

Make the pastry. Sift the flour, baking powder and salt into a mixing bowl. Stir in the suet, then add enough cold water (about 150–175 ml / 5–6 fl oz) to make a soft but not sticky dough. Cut off one quarter of the pastry and set aside for the lid. Roll out the rest on a lightly-floured surface to a round 1 cm / ½ inch larger than the top of the basin, then place the round in the basin. Pressing with the fingers, work the pastry evenly up the sides of the basin to the top.

To make the filling, core and peel the apples and slice into a bowl. Stir in the sugar and blackberries. Spoon the fruit into the pastry-lined basin and add 30 ml / 2 tbsp water. Roll out the reserved pastry to make the lid, dampen the rim and place the lid on top of the filling. Press the rim of the lid against the edge of the lining to seal the crust.

Cover the pudding with a well-floured cloth, greased greaseproof paper or foil and secure with string. Put the pudding in the perforated part of the steamer, or stand it on an old saucer or plate in the pan of boiling water. The water should come halfway up the sides of the basin. Cover the pan tightly and steam the pudding over gently simmering water for 2½–3 hours.

Remove the cooked pudding from the steamer. Serve from the basin or leave to stand for a few minutes, then turn out on to a warmed serving dish. Serve with the custard.

SERVES SIX

MRS BEETON'S
MANCHESTER PUDDING

250 ml / 8 fl oz milk
2 strips lemon rind
75 g / 3 oz fresh white breadcrumbs
2 whole eggs plus 2 egg yolks
50 g / 2 oz butter, softened
45 ml / 3 tbsp caster sugar
45 ml / 3 tbsp brandy
45–60 ml / 3–4 tbsp jam
extra caster sugar for sprinkling

PUFF PASTRY
150 g / 5 oz plain flour
1.25 ml / ¼ tsp salt
150 g / 5 oz butter
2.5 ml / ½ tsp lemon juice
flour for rolling out

Heat the milk in a saucepan with the lemon rind, then remove from the heat and leave to infuse for 30 minutes. Put the breadcrumbs in a bowl, strain the flavoured milk over them and return the mixture to the clean pan. Simmer for 2–3 minutes or until the crumbs have absorbed all the milk.

Beat the eggs and yolks until liquid, then stir into the breadcrumbs with the butter, sugar and brandy. Mix thoroughly; the butter should melt in the warm mixture. Cover the surface with dampened greaseproof paper and leave to cool.

Set the oven at 200°C / 400°F / gas 6. Make the pastry. Sift the flour and salt into a mixing bowl and rub in 50 g / 2 oz of the butter. Add the lemon juice and mix to a smooth dough with cold water.

Shape the remaining butter into a rectangle on greaseproof paper. Roll out the dough on a lightly-floured surface to a strip a little wider than the butter and rather more than twice its length. Place the butter on one half of the pastry, fold the other half over it, and press the edges together with the rolling pin. Leave it in a cool place for 15 minutes to allow the butter to harden.

continued overleaf ...

Roll out the pastry into a long strip. Fold the bottom third up and the top third down, press the edges together with the rolling pin and turn the pastry so that the folded edges are on the right and left. Roll and fold again, cover and leave in a cool place for 15 minutes. Repeat this process until the pastry has been rolled out 6 times.

Line a 750 ml / 1¼ pint pie dish with the pastry. If liked, cut a strip out of the pastry trimmings to fit the rim of the pie dish. Dampen the rim of the lining and fit the extra strip. Wrap any remaining pastry and reserve in the refrigerator for another purpose.

Spread the jam over the base of the pastry. Spoon the cooled breadcrumb mixture into the pastry case and bake for 15 minutes, then lower the heat to 180°C / 350°F / gas 4 and cook for 45–60 minutes more. The pudding should be set in the centre. Leave to cool. Serve cold, sprinkled with caster sugar.

SERVES SIX

GATEAU DE PITHIVIERS

225 g / 8 oz plain flour
1.25 ml / ¼ tsp salt
225 g / 8 oz butter
2.5 ml / ½ tsp lemon juice
flour for rolling out
Apricot Glaze (page 134)

1 egg, beaten with 15 ml / 1 tbsp water
icing sugar

FILLING
50 g / 2 oz butter
50 g / 2 oz caster sugar
1–2 drops almond essence
1 egg
20 ml / 4 tsp plain flour
50 g / 2 oz ground almonds

Start by making the filling. Cream the butter with the sugar in a large bowl, adding the essence. Add the egg and mix until smooth. Mix the flour and ground almonds in a bowl, then add them to the butter mixture to make a smooth pastry cream.

Make the pastry. Sift the flour and salt into a mixing bowl and rub in 50 g / 2 oz of the butter. Add the lemon juice and mix to a smooth dough with cold water.

Shape the remaining butter into a rectangle on greaseproof paper. Roll out the dough on a lightly-floured surface to a strip a little wider than the butter and rather more than twice its length. Place the butter on one half of the pastry, fold the other half over it, and press the edges together with the rolling pin. Leave in a cool place for 15 minutes to allow the butter to harden.

Roll the pastry out into a long strip. Fold the bottom third up and the top third down, press the edges together with the rolling pin and turn the pastry so that the folded edges are on the right and left. Roll and fold again, cover and leave in a cool place for 15 minutes. Repeat this process until the pastry has been rolled out 6 times.

Roll out the pastry again and cut 2 rounds, measuring 18 cm / 7 inches and 20 cm / 8 inches in diameter. Place the smaller round on a baking sheet. Cover with apricot glaze to within 1 cm / ½ inch of the edge. Spread with the glaze and then add the almond cream in an even layer. Moisten the edge of the pastry. Lay the larger round on top and press the edges to seal.

Make 5 curved cuts in the pastry lid, radiating from the centre at equal intervals. Brush the surface with the egg and water mixture. Let the pastry rest for 20 minutes.

Set the oven at 190°C / 375°F / gas 5. Bake the pastry for 30 minutes or until risen and set. Dust the surface with icing sugar and return to the oven for 5 minutes to glaze. Cool on the baking sheet.

SERVES EIGHT TO TEN

CREAM SLICES

Puff Pastry (page 9), using 100 g / 4 oz flour
flour for rolling out
Glacé Icing (page 139), using 225 g / 8 oz icing sugar
30 ml / 2 tbsp smooth seedless jam
125 ml / 4 fl oz sweetened whipped cream

Set the oven at 220°C / 425°F / gas 7. Roll out the pastry 1 cm / ½ inch thick on a lightly-floured surface into a neat rectangle. Cut into 8 oblong pieces, each measuring 10 x 2 cm / 4 x ¾ inch. Place on a baking sheet and spread the tops thinly with half of the icing.

Bake for 20 minutes or until the pastry is well risen and the icing is slightly browned. Leave to cool completely.

When cold, split each pastry in half crossways. Spread the top of each bottom half with jam, and the bottom of each top half with cream; then sandwich the halves together again. Spread a little icing on top of each slice, over the browned icing.

MAKES EIGHT

VARIATION

- **Vanilla Slices** Make as for Cream Slices but without the baked icing. When cold, fill with Confectioners' Custard (page 148) or Crème St Honoré (page 149) instead of cream. Ice the tops with Glacé Icing (page 139).

ECCLES CAKES

Rough Puff Pastry (page 10), using 200 g / 7 oz flour
flour for rolling out
25 g / 1 oz butter or margarine
15 ml / 1 tbsp sugar
75 g / 3 oz currants
25 g / 1 oz chopped mixed peel
1.25 ml / ¼ tsp ground mixed spice
1.25 ml / ¼ tsp ground nutmeg
caster sugar for dusting

Set the oven at 200°C / 425°F / gas 7. Roll out the pastry on a lightly-floured surface to 3 mm / ⅛ inch thick. Cut into rounds using a 10 cm / 4 inch pastry cutter.

Cream the butter or margarine and sugar in a bowl. Add the currants, peel and spices. Place spoonfuls of the mixture in the centre of each pastry round. Gather the edges of each round together to form a ball. With the smooth side uppermost, form into a flat cake. Make 2 cuts in the top of each cake with a sharp knife. Brush with water and dust with caster sugar. Put on a baking sheet and bake for 20 minutes or until golden brown.

MAKES TWELVE TO FOURTEEN

MAIDS OF HONOUR

These cakes are supposed to date back to Elizabethan times,
when they were a great favourite of the court. Orange flower water
is a fragrantly scented flavouring essence. It is prepared by distilling
the spring blossom of the bitter Seville or Bigarade orange.

Puff Pastry (page 9), using 200 g / 7 oz flour
flour for rolling out
200 g / 7 oz ground almonds
100 g / 4 oz caster sugar
2 eggs, beaten
25 g / 1 oz plain flour
60 ml / 4 tbsp single cream
30 ml / 2 tbsp orange flower water

Set the oven at 200°C / 400°F / gas 6. Roll out the pastry on a lightly-floured surface and use to line twenty 7.5 cm / 3 inch patty tins.

Mix the ground almonds and sugar in a bowl. Add the eggs, then mix in the flour, cream and orange flower water. Put the mixture into the pastry cases.

Bake for about 15 minutes or until the filling is firm and golden brown.

MAKES TWENTY

SUET PUDDING

This plain pudding to serve with roast meat may be cooked in a basin if preferred. Slices of cooked pudding may be added to the roasting tin around a joint of meat for 2–5 minutes before serving. Traditionally, the slices of pudding would have been served before the meat to fill up a hungry family.

fat for greasing
350 g / 12 oz plain flour
10 ml / 2 tsp baking powder
2.5 ml / ½ tsp salt
150 g / 5 oz shredded suet
about 150 ml / ¼ pint milk
meat juices or melted butter to serve

Grease a large piece of greaseproof paper and lay it on a large sheet of foil. Sift the flour, baking powder and salt into a mixing bowl. Stir in the suet, then add enough milk to make a soft, but not sticky, dough.

Gently knead the dough into an oblong shape measuring about 25 cm / 10 inches long. Place it on the greaseproof paper. Fold the paper edges together several times, then seal the foil in the same way. Keep the wrapping loose to allow room for the pudding to rise. Twist or fold the ends of the paper and foil to seal them.

Bring a large saucepan or deep roasting tin of water to the boil and add the pudding. Cook for 3 hours, topping up with the water and fresh boiling water as necessary. If using a roasting tin, tent foil over the top of it and seal it on the rim to keep in the steam, and top up the water frequently.

To serve, open the package and slice the pudding. Arrange the slices on a heated serving plate and trickle over meat juices or melted butter. Serve promptly.

SERVES SIX TO EIGHT

DUMPLINGS

100 g / 4 oz self-raising flour
50 g / 2 oz shredded beef suet
salt and pepper

Mix the flour and suet in a bowl. Add salt and pepper to taste and bind with enough cold water to make a soft, smooth dough. With floured hands, divide the dough into 16 portions; roll into balls. Drop into simmering salted water, stock, soup or stew, lower the heat and simmer for 15–20 minutes. Serve with the liquid or with boiled meat, stew or vegetables.

MAKES ABOUT SIXTEEN

VARIATION

- **Herb Dumplings** Add 25 g / 1 oz grated onion and 5 ml / 1 tsp chopped fresh herbs to the flour and suet.

STRAWBERRY TABLE DUMPLINGS

These are great fun. As their name implies, they are cooked at the table.
Guests help themselves to suitable accompaniments.

800 g / 1¼ lb fresh strawberries, hulled
100 g / 4 oz caster sugar
15 ml / 1 tbsp kirsch
1 whole egg, separated, plus 2 egg yolks
salt
about 225 g / 8 oz plain flour
flour for rolling out
extra caster sugar to serve

Prepare the strawberries by spreading them in a shallow dish, covering them with sugar and kirsch and leaving to stand for 1 hour. Drain thoroughly, reserving any syrup. Mash the fruit lightly and put to one side.

continued overleaf ...

Combine all the egg yolks in a bowl and beat lightly with a pinch of salt. Gradually add 100 ml / 3½ fl oz water. Then add the flour, about 50 g / 2 oz at a time, until a light firm dough is formed.

Roll out the dough on a lightly-floured surface and cut into rounds, using a 5 cm / 2 inch cutter. Brush the edges of each round with some of the egg white. Put about 2.5 ml / ½ tsp strawberry filling in the centre of each round, then fold over to make small turnovers. Press the edges of each turnover with a fork, to seal.

At the table, have ready a large saucepan of lightly salted boiling water over a burner or hot tray. Lower the dumplings gently into the water, a few at a time, and cook for about 4 minutes until they rise to the surface. Lift out with a slotted spoon, drain over the pan, and serve on to the diners' plates.

A bowl of caster sugar and a sauce-boat containing the strained fruit syrup should be placed by the pan so that diners may help themselves. Soured or fresh whipped cream may also be offered. The dumplings should be sprinkled with sugar before the fruit syrup is poured over them.

SERVES FOUR TO SIX

CHEESE ECLAIRS

Serve these savoury eclairs as cocktail snacks or at a buffet party.

CHOUX PASTRY
100 g / 4 oz plain flour
50 g / 2 oz butter or margarine
pinch of salt
2 whole eggs plus 1 yolk
salt and pepper
pinch of cayenne pepper

FILLING
25 g / 1 oz butter
25 g / 1 oz plain flour
300 ml / ½ pint milk
75–100 g / 3–4 oz mature Cheddar cheese, grated
pinch of mustard powder

Lightly grease a baking sheet. Set the oven at 220°C / 425°F / gas 7. To make the pastry, sift the flour on to a sheet of greaseproof paper. Put 250 ml / 8 fl oz water in a saucepan and add the butter or margarine with the salt. Heat gently until the fat melts.

When the fat has melted, bring the liquid rapidly to the boil and add all the flour at once. Immediately remove the pan from the heat and stir the flour into the liquid to make a smooth paste which leaves the sides of the pan clean. Set aside to cool slightly.

Add the egg yolk and beat well. Add the whole eggs, one at a time, beating well after each addition. Add salt, pepper and cayenne with the final egg. Continue baking until the paste is very glossy.

Put the pastry into a piping bag fitted with a 1 cm / ½ inch nozzle and pipe it in 5 cm / 2 inch lengths on the prepared baking sheet. Cut off each length with a knife or scissors dipped in hot water.

Bake for 10 minutes, then lower the oven temperature to 180°C / 350°F / gas 4 and bake for 20 minutes, or until risen and browned. Split the eclairs open and cool on a wire rack.

Meanwhile, to make the filling, melt the butter in a saucepan. Stir in the flour and cook over low heat for 2–3 minutes, without colouring. Over very low heat, gradually add the milk, stirring constantly. Bring to the boil, stirring, and simmer for 1–2 minutes until smooth and thickened. Stir in the cheese, mustard and salt and pepper to taste.

Cool the eclairs on a wire rack. Fill with the cheese sauce.

MAKES TWENTY TO TWENTY-FOUR

VARIATIONS
- **Ham and Egg Eclairs** Omit the cheese. Add 2 chopped hard boiled eggs, 15 ml / 1 tbsp chopped tarragon and 75 g / 3 oz diced cooked ham to the sauce for the filling.
- **Smoked Salmon Eclairs** Omit the cheese. Add 75 g / 3 oz roughly chopped smoked salmon and 2.5 ml / ½ tsp grated lemon rind to the sauce for the filling. Smoked salmon offcuts are ideal: up to 100 g / 4 oz may be added, depending on flavour and the saltiness of the salmon.
- **Turkey Eclairs** Omit the cheese. Add 100 g / 4 oz diced cooked turkey and 30 ml / 2 tbsp chopped parsley to the sauce.

CREAM ECLAIRS

fat for greasing
250 ml / 8 fl oz whipping cream
25 g / 1 oz caster sugar and icing sugar, mixed
3–4 drops of vanilla essence

CHOUX PASTRY
100 g / 4 oz plain flour
50 g / 2 oz butter or margarine pinch of salt
2 whole eggs plus 1 yolk

CHOCOLATE GLACE ICING
50 g / 2 oz plain chocolate
10 ml / 2 tsp butter
100 g / 4 oz icing sugar, sifted

Lightly grease a baking sheet. Set the oven at 220°C / 425°F / gas 7. To make the pastry, sift the flour on to a sheet of greaseproof paper. Put 250 ml / 8 fl oz water in a saucepan and add the butter or margarine with the salt. Heat gently until the fat melts.

When the fat has melted, bring the liquid rapidly to the boil and add all the flour at once. Immediately remove the pan from the heat and stir the flour into the liquid to make a smooth paste, which leaves the sides of the pan clean. Set aside to cool slightly.

Add the egg yolk and beat well. Add the whole eggs, one at a time, beating well after each addition. Continue beating until the paste is very glossy.

Put the pastry into a piping bag fitted with a 2 cm / ¾ inch nozzle and pipe it in 10 cm / 4 inch lengths on the prepared baking sheet. Cut off each length with a knife or scissors dipped in hot water.

Bake for 10 minutes. Lower the oven temperature to 180°C / 350°F / gas 4. Bake for a further 20 minutes, or until risen and browned. Remove the eclairs from the oven and split them open. Cool completely on a wire rack.

```
┌─────────────────────────────────────────┐
│              FREEZER TIP                  │
│                                           │
│   When cool, the unfilled choux eclairs or│
│   buns may be packed in sealed polythene  │
│   bags and frozen. Thaw in wrappings for  │
│     1–1½ hours at room temperature, then  │
│     place on baking sheets and crisp in a │
│  180°C / 350°F / gas 4 oven for 5 minutes.│
│      Cool before filling and topping.     │
│                                           │
└─────────────────────────────────────────┘
```

Meanwhile, to make the glacé icing, break the chocolate into a heavy-bottomed pan. Add 15 ml / 1 tbsp water and the butter. Warm gently, stirring until smooth and creamy. Stir in the icing sugar, a little at a time.

Whip the cream until it holds its shape, adding the mixed sugars gradually. Add the vanilla essence while whipping.

Fill the eclairs with the cream and close neatly. Cover the tops with the glacé icing.

MAKES TEN TO TWELVE

VARIATION

- **Cream Buns** Pipe the pastry in 5 cm / 2 inch balls. Fill as above, and sift icing sugar over the tops instead of glacé icing.

CROQUEMBOUCHE

This spectacular gâteau is often used as a wedding cake in France.

1 Madeira cake (page 117) (20 cm / 8 inches in diameter,
6 cm / 2½ inches high)
200 g / 7 oz Almond Paste (page 134)
Apricot Glaze (page 134)
Glacé Icing (page 139)
marzipan flowers, to decorate

CHOUX PUFFS
butter for greasing
Choux Pastry (page 12)
Confectioners' Custard (page 148)

CARAMEL
500 g / 18 oz granulated sugar
juice of 1 lemon

If the Madeira cake is peaked, cut out a thin strip of almond paste and put it around the edge of the cake to level the top. Brush off any loose crumbs, then brush the whole cake with warmed apricot glaze. Roll out the remaining almond paste, and use it to cover the top and sides of the cake. Place the cake on a 30 cm / 12 inch serving board.

Lightly butter a baking sheet. Set the oven at 220°C / 425°F / gas 7. Put the choux pastry into a piping bag fitted with a 5 mm / ¼ inch nozzle and pipe small choux puffs on the prepared baking sheet. Bake for 10 minutes, then reduce the oven temperature to 180°C / 350°F / gas 4 and bake for a further 15 minutes, or until risen, browned and crisp. Split the puffs open and cool on a wire rack. When cold, fill with confectioners' custard.

Make a strong paper cone, from heavy cartridge paper that you have covered with non-stick baking parchment. Tape the parchment to the inside of the cone, around the base, to prevent it from slipping. The cone should measure about 30 cm / 12 inches high and about 15 cm / 6 inches in diameter at the base.

To make the caramel, dissolve the sugar in 300 ml / ½ pint water and the lemon juice in a heavy-bottomed pan, then boil, without stirring, until deep golden. Immediately the caramel colours, plunge the bottom of the pan into iced water to prevent further cooking and darkening.

Stick the filled choux on the cone by dipping each in caramel and pressing it onto the cone. Begin each with a circle of choux at the bottom, and work upwards. At the top, stick on the decorative marzipan flowers, using dabs of caramel.

Leave the caramel to harden; then slide out the paper lining and lift the cone very carefully onto the Madeira cake. Ice the exposed sections of the Madeira cake quickly with glacé icing. Serve on the same day as stacking the choux buns. The caramel softens if left to stand for a longer period and the cone will collapse.

SERVES ABOUT TWENTY

PROFITEROLES

CHOUX PASTRY PUFFS
100 g / 4 oz plain flour
50 g / 2 oz butter or margarine
pinch of salt
2 whole eggs plus 1 yolk

FILLING
250 ml / 8 fl oz double cream, chilled
25 g / 1 oz caster sugar
vanilla essence

TOPPING
200 g / 7 oz icing sugar, sifted
15 ml / 1 tbsp cocoa

Lightly grease 2 baking sheets. Set the oven at 220°C / 425°F / gas 7.

Make the choux pastry. Sift the flour on to a sheet of greaseproof paper. Put 250 ml / 8 fl oz water in a saucepan and add the butter or margarine with the salt. Heat gently until the fat melts.

When the fat has melted, bring the liquid rapidly to the boil and add all the flour at once. Immediately remove the pan from the heat and stir the flour into the liquid to make a smooth paste which leaves the sides of the pan clean. Set aside to cool slightly.

continued overleaf ...

FREEZER TIP

When cool, the unfilled choux puffs may be packed in sealed polythene bags and frozen. Thaw in wrappings for 1–1½ hours at room temperature, then place on baking sheets and crisp in a 180°C / 350°F / gas 4 oven for 5 minutes. Cool before filling and topping.

Add the egg yolk and beat well. Add the whole eggs, one at a time, beating well after each addition. Continue beating until the paste is very glossy.

Put the pastry into a piping bag fitted with a 2 cm / ¾ inch nozzle and pipe it in 2 cm / ¾ inch balls on the baking sheets, leaving room for them to puff up. Bake for 10 minutes, then lower the oven temperature to 180°C / 350°F / gas 4 and bake for 20 minutes more until crisp, golden and puffed.

Remove the puffs from the oven, slit them with a sharp knife, and remove any uncooked paste. If necessary, return them to the oven for a few minutes to dry out. Cool the puffs completely on a wire rack.

Just before serving, whip the cream lightly. Whip in the sugar with a few drops of vanilla essence to taste. Put into a piping bag and fill the choux puffs.

Make the chocolate topping by mixing the icing sugar and cocoa in a bowl with enough warm water (about 15–30 ml / 1–2 tbsp) to form an icing that will coat the back of the spoon. Glaze the tops of the puffs with this mixture, reserving a little for assembling the dish.

Let the icing on the puffs harden, then arrange them in a pyramid, sticking the buns together with small dabs of the remaining icing. Serve 3 or 4 buns per person, with a chocolate sauce, if liked.

SERVES EIGHT

VARIATIONS

- The filling may be varied to taste. Sweetened whipped cream, confectioners' custard or chocolate buttercream may be used. Instead of the icing, melted chocolate may simply be poured over the choux.

BEIGNETS

**oil for deep frying
icing sugar for dredging**

CHOUX PASTRY
**100 g / 4 oz plain flour
50 g / 2 oz butter or margarine
pinch of salt
2 whole eggs plus 1 yolk
vanilla essence**

Start by making the choux pastry. Sift the flour on to a sheet of greaseproof paper. Put 250 ml / 8 fl oz water in a saucepan and add the butter or margarine with the salt. Heat gently until the fat melts.

When the fat has melted, bring the liquid rapidly to the boil and add all the flour at once. Immediately remove the pan from the heat and stir the flour into the liquid to make a smooth paste which leaves the sides of the pan clean. Set aside to cool slightly.

Add the egg yolk and beat well. Add the whole eggs, one at a time, beating well after each addition (see Mrs Beeton's Tip). Continue beating until the paste is very glossy.

Put the oil for frying in a deep wide saucepan. Heat the oil to 185 °C / 360°F or until a bread cube immersed in the oil turns pale brown in 45 seconds.

Flavour the choux pastry with vanilla essence to taste. Dip a metal dessertspoon into the hot oil and use it to drop spoonfuls of the mixture gently into the hot oil, a few at a time, Fry slowly until crisp and golden, then drain on absorbent kitchen paper. Serve dredged in icing sugar.

SERVES FOUR

MRS BEETON'S TIP

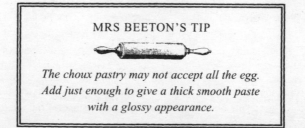

*The choux pastry may not accept all the egg.
Add just enough to give a thick smooth paste
with a glossy appearance.*

GATEAU ST HONORE

This gâteau combines a base of short pastry with a puffed choux pastry topping. It is the traditional birthday cake in France.

SHORT CRUST PASTRY BASE
100 g / 4 oz plain flour
1.25 ml / ¼ tsp salt
50g / 2 oz margarine (or half butter, half lard)
flour for rolling out
2 eggs, beaten, for glazing

CHOUX PASTRY
225 g / 8 oz plain flour
100 g / 4 oz butter or margarine
pinch of salt
4 whole eggs plus 2 yolks

PASTRY CREAM
3 eggs
50 g / 2 oz caster sugar
35 g / 1¼ oz plain flour
25 g / 1 oz cornflour
few drops of vanilla essence
250 ml / 8 fl oz milk

FILLING AND DECORATION
125 ml / 4 fl oz double cream
50 g / 2 oz granulated sugar glacé cherries
angelica

Set the oven at 200°C / 400°F / gas 6. Make the base. Sift the flour into a bowl. then rub in the margarine until the mixture resembles fine breadcrumbs. Add enough cold water to make a stiff dough. Press the dough together with your fingertips. Rest the dough in the refrigerator while making the choux pastry.

Sift the flour for the choux pastry on to a sheet of greaseproof paper. Put 500 ml / 17 fl oz water in a saucepan and add the butter or margarine with the salt. Heat gently until the fat melts.

When the fat has melted, bring the liquid rapidly to the boil and add all the flour at once. Immediately remove the pan from the heat and stir the flour into the liquid to make a smooth paste, which leaves the sides of the pan clean. Set aside to cool slightly.

Add the egg yolks and beat well. Add the whole eggs, one at a time, beating well after each addition. Continue beating until the paste is very glossy.

Roll out the chilled short crust pastry on a lightly-floured surface to a 20 cm / 8 inch round. Place on a baking sheet.

Put the choux pastry into a piping bag fitted with a 1 cm / ½ inch nozzle; pipe a circle of it around the edge of the pastry. Brush with beaten egg.

Use the remaining choux pastry to pipe 18–20 small buns on a separate baking sheet. Bake both pastry round and buns for 15 minutes, then lower the oven temperature to 190°C / 375°F / gas 5 and bake for 10–15 minutes more, until the choux ring is well risen and golden brown. Slit the buns to release the steam, then cool on wire racks.

To make the pastry cream, separate two of the eggs. Reserve the whites. Combine the yolks, whole egg and caster sugar in a bowl and beat well. Stir in the flour, cornflour and vanilla essence. Heat the milk in a saucepan and grad-ually beat it into the egg mixture. Return the mixture to the clean pan and bring to the boil, stirring all the time. Boil for 2–3 minutes. Pour the mixture into a clean bowl. Cover with buttered greaseproof paper and leave until quite cold.

In a bowl, whip the cream until stiff. Place in a piping bag and fill the choux buns. Combine the granulated sugar and 45 ml / 3 tbsp water in a heavy-bottomed saucepan and heat until the sugar has dissolved. Boil until the mixture turns a pale straw colour. Remove from the heat and dip the bottom of each bun quickly in the syrup. Arrange on the choux round. Spoon a little syrup over each choux bun.

Finally, in a clean, grease-free bowl, whisk the reserved egg whites until stiff. Fold into the pastry cream, adding any leftover whipped cream. Fill the centre of the gateau with the pastry cream. Decorate the gateau with glacé cherries and angelica.

SERVES TEN TO TWELVE

PARIS-BREST

A choux pastry ring filled with praline cream,
Paris-Brest is a delectable dessert.

butter for greasing
100 g / 4 oz plain flour
50 g / 2 oz butter or margarine
pinch of salt
2 whole eggs plus 1 yolk

TOPPING
1 egg, beaten with 15 ml / 1 tbsp water
25 g / 1 oz flaked almonds
icing sugar

PRALINE CREAM
50 g / 2 oz hazelnuts, roasted
100 g / 4 oz granulated sugar
125 ml / 4 fl oz double cream
125ml / 4 fl oz single cream

Lightly grease a baking sheet. Set the oven at 220°C / 425°F / gas 7.

Make the choux pastry. Sift the flour on to a sheet of greaseproof paper. Put 250 ml / 8 fl oz water in a saucepan and add the butter or margarine with the salt. Heat gently until the fat melts.

When the fat has melted, bring the liquid rapidly to the boil and add all the flour at once. Immediately remove the pan from the heat and stir the flour into the liquid to make a smooth paste which leaves the sides of the pan clean. Set aside to cool slightly.

Add the egg yolk and beat well. Add the whole eggs, one at a time, beating well after each addition. Continue beating until the paste is very glossy.

Put the pastry into a piping bag fitted with a 1 cm / ½ inch nozzle and pipe an 18 cm / 7 inch ring on the prepared baking sheet. Brush the top of the ring with beaten egg, then sprinkle liberally with the flaked almonds. Bake for 10 minutes, then reduce the oven temperature to 180°C / 350°F / gas 4 and bake for 25–30 minutes, or until the ring is risen, browned and crisp. Split horizontally into 2 layers and cool on a wire rack.

Make the praline cream. Rub off any loose skins from the hazelnuts. Heat the sugar with 30 ml / 2 tbsp water in a heavy-bottomed saucepan, stirring until the sugar dissolves. Bring to the boil and cook until the mixture is a light golden brown. Stir in the nuts. Pour on to an oiled marble or metal surface and leave to harden. When cool and hard, crush the praline finely. In a bowl, whip the double cream until very stiff, gradually whip in the single cream, then fold in the praline.

Fill the ring with the praline cream. The cream will stand up above the pastry casing. Gently put the halves together so that the gâteau resembles a sandwich with a very thick filling. Dust the almond-topped surface of the cake with icing sugar. Serve at once.

SERVES SIX

FILO AND FETA TRIANGLES

225 g / 8 oz feta cheese
5 ml / 1 tsp dried oregano
1 spring onion, chopped
pepper
4 sheets of filo pastry
50 g / 2 oz butter, melted

Set the oven at 190°C / 375°F / gas 5. Mash the feta with the oregano in a bowl, then mix in the spring onion and pepper to taste.

Lay a sheet of filo pastry on a clean, dry surface and brush it with melted butter. Cut the sheet widthways into 9 strips. Place a little feta mixture at one end of the first strip, leaving the corner of the pastry without filling. Fold the corner over the feta to cover it in a triangular shape, then fold the mixture over and over to wrap it in several layers of pastry, making a small triangular-shaped pasty.

continued overleaf ...

Repeat with the other strips of pastry. Cut and fill the remaining sheets in the same way to make 36 triangular pastries. Place these on baking sheets and brush any remaining butter over them.

Bake for about 10 minutes, until the filo pastry is crisp and golden. Transfer the triangles to a wire rack to cool. They are best served warm.

MAKES 36

SHAPES AND FILLINGS

The feta filling used in the triangles is a Greek speciality. A variety of other fillings may be used and the pastry shaped in other ways.

- Instead of cutting strips, the pastry may be cut into squares (about 6 per sheet). The filling should be placed in the middle of the squares, and the pastry may be gathered up to form a small bundle. The butter coating keeps the bundle closed when the filo is pressed together. For strength, the filo may be used double.
- Alternatively, squares of filo may be filled and folded into neat oblong parcels. Oblong pieces of filo (about 4 per sheet) may be folded into neat squares.

FILLINGS

- **Spinach and Cheese** Thoroughly drained, cooked spinach may be used with or without the cheese. Flavour plain spinach with chopped spring onion and grated nutmeg.
- **Sardine** Mashed canned sardines in tomato sauce make a good filling for filo triangles.
- **Chicken or Ham** Chopped cooked chicken or ham are both tasty fillings for filo. Combine them with a little low-fat soft cheese.
- **Apricot** Apricot halves (drained canned or fresh) topped with a dot of marmalade make good sweet filo pastries. Dust them with icing sugar after baking.
- **Apple and Almond** Mix some ground almonds into cold, sweetened apple purée. Use to fill triangles or squares.

LINZERTORTE

Linzertorte improves in flavour if kept for two to three days before cutting.

100 g / 4 oz butter
75 g / 3 oz caster sugar
1 egg yolk
1.25 ml / ¼ tsp almond essence
grated rind of 1 small lemon
juice of ½ lemon
100 g / 4 oz plain flour
5 ml / 1 tsp ground cinnamon
50 g / 2 oz ground almonds flour for rolling out
200 g / 7 oz raspberry jam
15 ml / 1 tbsp icing sugar

In a mixing bowl, cream the butter with the sugar until pale and fluffy. Beat in the egg yolk, almond essence, lemon rind and juice. Add the flour, cinnamon and ground almonds and mix to a smooth dough. Wrap in foil and chill for 1 hour.

Set the oven at 160°C / 325°F / gas 3. Roll out three quarters of the pastry on a lightly-floured surface and use to line an 18 cm / 7 inch flan tin. Spread the jam over the base.

Roll out the remaining pastry to a rectangle 18 cm / 7 inches long and cut into strips about 5 mm / ¼ inch wide. Arrange the strips in a lattice on top of the jam. Bake for about 1 hour or until the pastry is golden brown. Leave to cool.

Remove from the flan tin, dredge with icing sugar and serve cold, with whipped cream.

SERVES SIX

APPLE STRUDEL

Anyone who has ever watched an Austrian pastry-cook at work will know that the best strudel is coaxed out to the correct size by hand. Using a rolling pin is no disgrace, however, and the recipe below gives very good results.

200 g / 7 oz plain flour
1.25 ml / ¼ tsp salt
30 ml / 2 tbsp oil
1 egg
flour for rolling out

FILLING
450 g / 1 lb cooking apples
50 g / 2 oz butter
50 g / 2 oz soft light brown sugar
5 ml / 1 tsp ground cinnamon
50 g / 2 oz sultanas

To make the strudel pastry, sift the flour and salt into a mixing bowl. Add the oil and egg, with 60 ml / 4 tbsp warm water. Mix to a firm dough, cover with foil and leave in a warm place for about an hour. Set the oven at 190°C / 375°F / gas 5.

Peel and core the apples. Chop them finely and put them into a bowl. Melt the butter in a small saucepan. Have the brown sugar, cinnamon and sultanas ready.

Lightly flour a clean tablecloth or sheet, placed on a work surface. Place the pastry on the cloth and roll it out very thinly to a rectangle measuring 50 x 25 cm / 20 x 10 inches.

Brush the strudel pastry with some of the melted butter and sprinkle with the brown sugar, cinnamon and sultanas. Top with the chopped apple. Starting from a long side, roll the strudel up like a Swiss roll using the sheet as a guide. Slide the strudel on to a large baking sheet, turning it to a horseshoe shape if necessary. Position it so that the join is underneath. Brush the top with more melted butter.

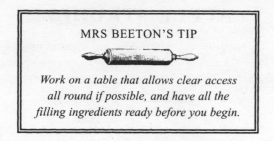

MRS BEETON'S TIP

*Work on a table that allows clear access
all round if possible, and have all the
filling ingredients ready before you begin.*

Bake for 40 minutes or until golden brown. To serve, cut the strudel in wide diagonal slices. It tastes equally good hot or cold, with or without cream.

SERVES EIGHT

VARIATIONS

- Filo pastry may be used for a quick strudel. Brush each sheet generously with melted butter, covering any filo not in use with a clean damp tea-towel or cling film to prevent it from drying out.

- **Savoury Strudel** Savoury fillings may be used instead of apples in the strudel. Chopped onion, cooked in oil or butter until soft, with shredded cabbage, a little grated carrot and grated eating apple is tasty. Diced cooked ham or lean bacon may be added and the mixture may be seasoned with a little grated nutmeg.

- Alternatively, drained cooked spinach with lightly toasted pine nuts, cooked onion and crumbled Lancashire or Wensleydale cheese is delicious. A few sultanas or raisins may be added to the spinach, which may be spiced with a good sprinkle of ground coriander.

Baked Cheesecakes

The cheesecakes that are popular today tend to be American-style concoctions. Try these European baked cheesecakes – zesty with lemon, fruity with sultanas, delicate and creamy with ricotta cheese – and you will be converted.

CLASSIC BAKED CHEESECAKE

BASE
75 g / 3 oz butter
150 g / 5 oz fine dried white breadcrumbs
50 g / 2 oz caster sugar
7.5 ml / 3 tsp ground cinnamon

FILLING
3 eggs, separated
100 g / 4 oz caster sugar
375 g / 13 oz full-fat soft cheese
grated rind and juice of 1 lemon
125 ml / 4 fl oz soured cream
icing sugar for dusting

Set the oven at 180°C / 350°F / gas 4. Make the base. Melt the butter in a frying pan and stir in the breadcrumbs. Cook over gentle heat, stirring until the crumbs are golden. Remove from the heat; stir in the sugar and cinnamon. Press the crumbs over the base of a loose-bottomed 18 cm / 7 inch cake tin.

Beat the egg yolks in a mixing bowl until liquid. Add the sugar to the egg yolks, beating until creamy. Rub the cheese through a sieve into the bowl, then work in lightly. Add the lemon rind and juice to the mixture with the soured cream.

In a clean, grease-free bowl, whisk the egg whites to soft peaks. Stir 30 ml / 2 tbsp into the cheese mixture, then fold in the rest lightly. Turn the mixture gently on to the prepared base in the tin. Bake for 45 minutes. Cover loosely with foil and bake for a further 15 minutes. Cool in the tin. Serve dusted with icing sugar.

SERVES TEN

ALMOND CHEESECAKE

fat for greasing
75 g / 3 oz curd cheese
50 g / 2 oz butter, melted
2 eggs, separated
grated rind and juice of ½ lemon
50 g / 2 oz ground almonds
50 g / 2 oz caster sugar
30 ml / 2 tbsp self-raising flour

Line and grease a 15 cm / 6 inch sandwich cake tin. Set the oven at 220°C / 425°F / gas 7.

Rub the curd cheese through a sieve into a mixing bowl. Add the melted butter, egg yolks, lemon rind and juice, almonds and caster sugar and mix thoroughly. Sift the flour over the mixture and fold in.

In a clean, grease-free bowl, whisk the egg whites until stiff. Fold into the almond mixture. Spoon the mixture into the prepared tin and bake for 10 minutes.

Lower the oven temperature to 180°C / 350°F / gas 4 and cook for about 15 minutes more. Test to see whether the cake is cooked (see Mrs Beeton's Tip). If necessary, return the cake to the oven for a few minutes, covering the surface loosely with foil or greaseproof paper to prevent overbrowning.

SERVES FOUR

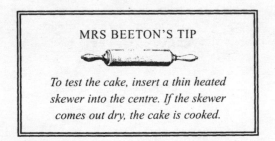

MRS BEETON'S TIP

To test the cake, insert a thin heated skewer into the centre. If the skewer comes out dry, the cake is cooked.

APPLE CHEESECAKE

This is not a cheesecake in the modern sense, but a tart filled
with apple cheese (or apple curd). It is refreshing and delicious.

350 g / 12 oz puff pastry, thawed if frozen
450 g / 1 lb cooking apples, peeled, cored and sliced
100 g / 4 oz caster sugar
100 g / 4 oz butter, melted
grated rind and juice of 1 lemon
2 eggs plus 2 egg yolks

Set the oven at 200°C / 400°F / gas 6. Roll out the pastry and use to line a 25 cm / 10 inch flan dish or tin. Prick the pastry all over, then chill for 20 minutes in the bottom of the refrigerator or 10 minutes in the freezer. Bake for 20 minutes. Remove the pastry case from the oven. Reduce the oven temperature to 180°C / 350°F / gas 4.

Place the apples in a saucepan and add 30 ml / 2 tbsp water. Cook over medium heat, stirring, until the fruit begins to soften. Allow to simmer gently and cover the pan. Stir occasionally until the apples are reduced to a pulp, then press them through a sieve into a bowl.

Stir the sugar, butter and lemon rind and juice into the apples. Beat the eggs and yolks together, then strain them through a fine sieve into the apple mixture. Beat well and pour the mixture into the pastry case. Bake for 25–30 minutes, until the apple filling is set.

Leave to cool, then serve with fresh cream or fromage frais.

SERVES TWELVE

CHEDDAR CHEESECAKE

BASE
175 g / 6 oz plain flour
75 g / 3 oz margarine
1 egg yolk
flour for rolling out

FILLING
1 egg, separated, plus 1 white
grated rind and juice of 1 lemon
75 ml / 5 tbsp plain yogurt
25 g / 1 oz self-raising flour
75 g / 3 oz caster sugar
150 g / 5 oz Cheddar cheese, grated

Set the oven at 200°C / 400°F / gas 6. To make the pastry base, sift the flour into a bowl, then rub in the margarine until the mixture resembles fine breadcrumbs. Add the egg yolk and enough water (about 15–30 ml / 1–2 tbsp) to mix the ingredients into a short pastry. Press the pastry together gently with your fingertips.

Roll out the pastry on a lightly-floured surface and use to line a 20 cm / 8 inch flan ring or dish. Bake 'blind' (see Mrs Beeton's Tip). Lower the oven temperature to 160°C / 325°F / gas 3.

In a mixing bowl, combine the egg yolk, lemon rind and juice, yogurt, flour and sugar. Mix well, then fold in the grated cheese.

In a clean, grease-free bowl, whisk both egg whites until stiff. Stir 15 ml / 1 tbsp of the beaten egg whites into the cheese mixture to lighten it, then gently fold in the remaining egg white. Turn into the prepared pastry case.

Bake for 35–45 minutes or until firm in the centre and lightly browned. Serve cold.

SERVES SIX TO EIGHT

MRS BEETON'S TIP

To bake blind, prick the base of the pastry case with a fork, then cover with a piece of greaseproof paper. Fill the pastry case with dried beans, bread crusts or rice and bake at 200°C / 400°F / gas 6 for 10 minutes. Remove the paper and beans or other dry filling and return the case to the oven for 5 minutes to dry out the inside before adding the chosen filling and returning the case to the oven. If a fully cooked pastry case is required, as when a cold filling is to be added, bake the pastry case blind for 20–30 minutes, and dry out for 5–7 minutes.

VARIATIONS

- **Cheshire Cheesecake** Substitute Cheshire cheese for the Cheddar. Either grate it finely or crumble the Cheshire cheese, then crush it with a fork until it breaks down into fine crumbs. Cheshire is milder and slightly more tangy than Cheddar.
- **Apple and Cheddar Cheesecake** Spread a layer of stewed apples or sweetened apple purée in the pastry case before adding the cheese filling.
- **Glacé Fruit Cheesecake** Sprinkle a mixture of glacé and candied fruit and peel over the pastry case before adding the cheese mixture. Chopped angelica, cherries, candied peel and crystallized ginger are suitable.
- **Individual Cheesecakes** Make individual cheesecakes in patty tins.

TORTA DI RICOTTA

BASE
100 g / 4 oz butter or margarine
75 g / 3 oz icing sugar
2 egg yolks
pinch of ground cinnamon
250 g / 9 oz plain flour
flour for rolling out

FILLING
675 g / 1½ lb ricotta cheese
25 g / 1 oz grated Parmesan cheese
2 eggs
25 g / 1 oz plain flour
45 ml / 3 tbsp plain yogurt
50 g / 2 oz caster sugar
grated rind and juice of 1 lemon
pinch of salt
few drops of lemon essence

DECORATION AND SAUCE
225 g / 8 oz fresh raspberries
15 ml / 1 tbsp arrowroot
100 g / 4 oz raspberry jam
60 ml / 4 tbsp maraschino liqueur
125 ml / 4 fl oz sweet red vermouth

Make the pastry. Cream the butter or margarine with the sugar in a mixing bowl until light and fluffy. Blend in the egg yolks, cinnamon and flour. Knead the mixture lightly and roll into a ball. Chill for 20 minutes.

Set the oven at 200°C / 400°F / gas 6. Roll out the pastry on a lightly-floured surface to line a 25 cm / 10 inch flan ring set on a baking sheet (see Mrs Beeton's Tip). Prick the base with a fork and chill for 30 minutes. Line with greaseproof paper and sprinkle with baking beans or dried peas. Bake for 20 minutes; remove paper and beans or peas. Lower the oven temperature to 180°C / 350°F / gas 4.

MRS BEETON'S TIP

*To line the flan ring, place on the baking sheet and roll
the pastry to a round at least 5 cm / 2 inches larger than
the ring. The pastry should be about 3 mm / ⅛ inch thick.
Lift the pastry round over a rolling pin to prevent it
breaking and stretching, and lay it in the flan ring. Press
the pastry gently down on the baking sheet and into the
base of the ring. Working from the centre outwards, press
the pastry into the base and up the sides, making sure it
fits snugly into the flutes, if present, and is of even
thickness all round. Trim off any surplus pastry by rolling
across the top of the ring with the rolling pin.*

For the filling, rub the ricotta through a sieve, then beat it with the Parmesan in
a bowl and gradually beat in the rest of the filling ingredients. Spoon into the
partially cooked flan case, level the surface and bake for about 50 minutes.
Cover loosely with foil if the top becomes too dark. The filling should be firmly
set when cooked. Leave to cool in the tin.

Decorate the cooled flan with the raspberries, and chill while making the sauce.
Put the arrowroot in a small bowl and mix to a thin cream with 125 ml / 4 fl oz
water. Melt the jam in a saucepan. When it boils, stir in the arrowroot mixture
to thicken it. Flavour with the maraschino liqueur and vermouth. Remove from
the heat and when cold, pour a little of the sauce over the raspberries. Serve the
rest separately.

SERVES EIGHT

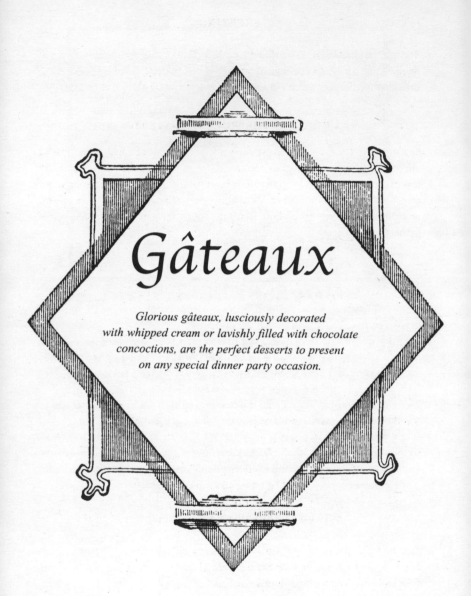

Gâteaux

*Glorious gâteaux, lusciously decorated
with whipped cream or lavishly filled with chocolate
concoctions, are the perfect desserts to present
on any special dinner party occasion.*

FREEZING

For best results, freeze the unfilled gateau, separating the layers with sheets of freezer film. These do not have to be thawed before being filled and decorated, provided the finished gateau is set aside for some time before it is served.

COATING THE SIDE OF A GATEAU

Gâteaux are often covered completely in cream, with chopped nuts, grated chocolate or vermicelli used to decorate the sides. To coat the sides, the layers must first be sandwiched together. The coating ingredient should be spread out on a sheet of greaseproof paper. Spread the side of the gâteau thinly with cream, or a similar covering. Using both hands to support the gâteau on its side, roll it in the chosen coating.

MOUSSELINE CAKE

fat for greasing
caster sugar for dusting
50 g / 2 oz plain flour
50 g / 2 oz cornflour
4 eggs, separated
100 g / 4 oz caster sugar
vanilla essence or grated rind of 1 lemon

DECORATION
125 ml / 4 fl oz double cream
100 g / 4 oz strawberries
100 g / 4 oz icing sugar
5–10 ml / 1-2 tsp orange-flavoured liqueur

Base line and grease two 18 cm / 7 inch sandwich cake tins. Dust with caster sugar, tapping out the excess. Set the oven at 190°C / 375°F / gas 5. Sift the flour and cornflour together into a bowl and set aside.

In a large heatproof bowl, whisk the egg yolks with the sugar until thick, creamy and pale, adding the essence or grated lemon rind. Whisk the egg

continued overleaf...

FREEZER TIP

*The cooked, cooled cakes may be frozen. Wrap
them in foil or pack them in a freezer bag,
placing a sheet of foil between them. Unwrap
the cakes and leave at room temperature until
softened before filling and decorating as above.*

---

whites in a clean, grease-free bowl until they form soft peaks, then add to the
yolk mixture.

Set the bowl of mixture over gently simmering water and whisk until the
volume is greatly increased and the mixture is thick enough to hold the mark of
a trail for 2–3 seconds. Remove the bowl from the heat and continue whisking
until the mixture is cold.

Fold the sifted flours into the cold cake mixture. Divide between the prepared
sandwich tins and bake for 20–25 minutes until well risen and browned. Leave
in the tins for 1–2 minutes, then turn out on to wire racks to cool.

To decorate the cake, whip the cream in a bowl. Put one third of the cream into
a piping bag fitted with a star nozzle. Set aside 4 of the best strawberries. Chop
the rest and add to the remaining cream. Mix lightly, then spread over one layer
of the cake. Add the top layer.

In a small bowl. mix the icing sugar with enough of the liqueur to form a glacé
icing. Warm the icing by placing the bowl in a basin of hot water, if necessary.

Pipe whirls of whipped cream around the top edge of the cake. Carefully spoon
the liqueur icing over the top of the cake to form an even coating. Cut the
reserved strawberries in half or in slices and decorate the top of the cake. Serve
as soon as possible.

SERVES SIX

VARIATIONS

- Ring the changes with different fresh or well-drained canned fruit.
  Raspberries, pineapple, peaches or nectarines are good. Flavour the cream
  with a complementary liqueur. The exotic combination of kiwi fruit and
  cream flavoured with advocaat is delicious and looks striking.

COFFEE GATEAU

fat for greasing
20 ml / 4 tsp instant coffee
150 g / 5 oz butter
150 g / 5 oz caster sugar
3 eggs, beaten
150 g / 5 oz self-raising flour

COFFEE BUTTERCREAM
30 ml / 2 tbsp instant coffee
150 g / 5 oz butter
450 g / 1 lb icing sugar

DECORATION
50–75 g / 2–3 oz walnuts, chopped
10–12 walnut halves

Line and grease two 20 cm / 8 inch sandwich tins. Set the oven at 160°C / 325°F / gas 3. In a cup, mix the instant coffee with 20 ml / 4 tsp boiling water. Set aside to cool.

In a mixing bowl, cream the butter with the sugar until light and fluffy. Beat in the cooled coffee. Add the eggs gradually, beating well after each addition. If the mixture shows signs of curdling, add a little of the flour.

Sift the flour and fold it into the creamed mixture, using a metal spoon. Divide between the tins and bake for 35–40 minutes or until well risen, firm and golden brown. Leave in the tins for 2–3 minutes, then cool on a wire rack. Make the buttercream. In a cup, mix the instant coffee with 30 ml / 2 tbsp boiling water and leave to cool. Cream the butter with half the icing sugar in a bowl. Beat in the cooled coffee, then beat in the rest of the icing sugar.

Using about a quarter of the buttercream, sandwich the cake layers together. Spread about half the remaining buttercream on the sides of the cake, then roll in the chopped walnuts. Spread most of the remaining buttercream on top of the cake and mark with a fork in a wavy design. Spoon any remaining buttercream into a piping bag fitted with a small star nozzle and pipe 10–12 rosettes on top of the cake. Decorate each rosette with a walnut half.

SERVES EIGHT TO TWELVE

APRICOT GATEAU

fat for greasing
75 g / 3 oz plain flour
pinch of salt
50 g / 2 oz margarine
3 eggs
75 g / 3 oz caster sugar

FILLING AND TOPPING
30 ml / 2 tbsp sherry
22–24 sponge fingers
1 (540 g / 18 oz) can unsweetened apricot
halves in natural juice
1 (142 g / 5 oz) packet lemon jelly
30 ml / 2 tbsp smooth apricot jam
600 ml / 1 pint double cream
25 g / 1 oz caster sugar
angelica (see method)

Line and grease a 15 cm / 6 inch round cake tin. Set the oven at 180°C / 350°F / gas 4.

Sift the flour and salt into a bowl and put in a warm place. Melt the margarine in a saucepan without letting it get hot. Set aside.

Whisk the eggs lightly in a heatproof bowl. Add the sugar and place the bowl over a saucepan of hot water. Whisk for 10–15 minutes until thick. Take care that the bottom of the bowl does not touch the water. Remove from the heat and continue whisking until at blood-heat. The melted margarine should be at the same temperature.

Sift half the flour over the eggs, then pour in half the melted margarine in a thin stream. Fold in gently. Repeat, using the remaining flour and fat. Spoon gently into the prepared tin and bake for 30–40 minutes. Cool the cake on a wire rack.

To assemble the gâteau, place the sponge on a serving plate and sprinkle the sherry over. Trim the sponge fingers to a length of about 7.5 cm / 3 inches. The base of each sponge finger should be level, so that it will stand straight. Drain the apricots, reserving 125 ml / 4 fl oz juice.

Heat the reserved apricot juice, add the lemon jelly and stir until dissolved. Pour into a shallow bowl and leave to cool but not set. Heat the apricot jam in the saucepan.

Brush the sugar-free side of each trimmed sponge finger with apricot jam to a depth of 2.5 cm / 1 inch. Dip one long side of each finger into the liquid jelly and attach to the sponge cake. The sponge fingers should touch each other, with the jam-coated sides facing inwards and the jelly sealing each to its neighbour. They should extend above the cake to form a shell. When all the sponge fingers are in place, tie a 2 cm / ¾ inch wide ribbon around the finished cake, if liked, to hold the fingers in position. Place in a cool place until set.

Reserve 6 apricot halves for decoration and chop the rest. Put the cream in a bowl and whip until just stiff; stir in the sugar. Spoon 45 ml / 3 tbsp of the cream into a piping bag fitted with a small star nozzle. Keep in the refrigerator until required. Stir the chopped apricots and the rest of the liquid jelly into the remaining cream. Chill until on the point of setting, then spoon on top of the cake, filling the cavity formed by the wall of sponge fingers.

Return the gâteau to the refrigerator for 1 hour until set, then arrange the reserved apricot halves on top. Pipe the reserved cream on top of the gâteau in a decorative border. Alternatively, the cream may be piped between the fruit. Decorate with angelica.

SERVES EIGHT TO TEN

MICROWAVE TIP

If the jelly sets while you are working, simply warm it for a few seconds in the microwave on High.

DEVIL'S FOOD CAKE

In America, it is often the custom to serve a cake as a dessert.
Devil's Food Cake is an excellent choice to follow a simple main course.

fat for greasing
plain flour for dusting
100 g / 4 oz butter
350 g / 12 oz granulated sugar
5 ml / 1 tsp vanilla essence
3 eggs, separated
250 g / 9 oz plain flour
50 g / 2 oz cocoa
7.5 ml / 1½ tsp bicarbonate of soda
5 ml / 1 tsp salt

FROSTING
100 g / 4 oz soft light brown sugar
60 ml / 4 tbsp golden syrup
1 egg white
pinch of cream of tartar
pinch of salt
5 ml / 1 tsp vanilla essence

Grease and lightly flour three 20 cm / 8 inch sandwich tins. Tap out excess flour. Set the oven at 180°C / 350°F / gas 4.

In a mixing bowl, cream the butter with 225 g / 8 oz of the sugar until light, then add the vanilla essence. Beat in the egg yolks, one at a time, alternately with 275 ml / 9 fl oz cold water. Beat well after each addition. Beat in the flour, cocoa, soda and salt.

In a clean, grease-free bowl, whisk the egg whites to soft peaks, add the remaining sugar and continue whisking until stiff peaks form. Fold the egg whites into the chocolate mixture lightly but thoroughly.

Gently pour one third of the mixture into each prepared tin. Bake for 30–35 minutes until each layer is firm in the centre and has shrunk from the sides of the tin. Cool lightly, then transfer to wire racks. Set aside until cold.

Meanwhile make the frosting. Combine all the ingredients except the vanilla essence in the top of a double saucepan. Set the pan over boiling water and cook, beating constantly with an electric whisk or rotary whisk until the mixture thickens and stands in peaks.

Remove the pan from the heat and add the vanilla essence. Continue to beat until the mixture is thick and forms swirls. Use the icing immediately to fill and cover the cake.

SERVES EIGHT

MRS BEETON'S TIPSY CAKE

1 (15 cm / 6 inch) sponge cake
30 ml / 2 tbsp redcurrant jelly
75 ml / 3 fl oz brandy
50 g / 2 oz whole blanched almonds
375 ml / 13 fl oz milk
125 ml / 4 fl oz single cream
8 egg yolks
75 g / 3 oz caster sugar
extra redcurrant jelly to decorate

Put the cake in a glass bowl or dish 16 cm / 6½ inches in diameter and slightly deeper than the cake. Spread the cake thinly with jelly, then pour over as much brandy as the cake can absorb. Cut the almonds lengthways into spikes and stick them all over the top of the cake.

Mix the milk and cream in a bowl. In a second, heatproof, bowl beat the yolks until liquid, and pour the milk and cream over them. Stir in the sugar. Transfer the mixture to the top of a double saucepan and cook over gently simmering water for about 20 minutes or until the custard thickens, stirring all the time. Let the custard cool slightly, then pour it over and around the cake. Cover with dampened greaseproof paper. When cold, refrigerate the tipsy cake for about 1 hour. Decorate with small spoonfuls of redcurrant jelly and serve.

SERVES FOUR TO SIX

BLACK FOREST GATEAU

fat for greasing
150 g / 5 oz butter or margarine
150 g / 5 oz caster sugar
3 eggs, beaten
few drops of vanilla essence
100 g / 4 oz self-raising flour or plain flour
5 ml / 1 tsp baking powder
25 g / 1 oz cocoa
pinch of salt

FILLING AND TOPPING
250 ml / 8 fl oz double cream
125 ml / 4 fl oz single cream
1 (540 g / 18 oz) can Morello cherries
kirsch (see method)
25 g / l oz plain chocolate, grated

Line and grease a 20 cm / 8 inch cake tin. Set the oven at 180°C / 350°F / gas 4.

In a mixing bowl, cream the butter or margarine with the sugar until light and fluffy. Add the eggs gradually, beating well after each addition. Stir in the vanilla essence.

Sift the flour, cocoa, salt and baking powder, if used, into a bowl. Stir into the creamed mixture, lightly but thoroughly, until evenly mixed.

Spoon into the tin and bake for 40 minutes. Cool on a wire rack. When quite cold, carefully cut the cake into three layers, brushing all loose crumbs off the cut sides.

Make the filling. Combine the creams in a bowl and whip until stiff. Place half the whipped cream in another bowl.

Drain the cherries, reserving the juice. Set aside 11 whole cherries and halve and stone the remainder. Gently fold the halved cherries into one of the bowls of cream. Set aside. Strain the reserved cherry juice into a measuring jug and add kirsch to taste.

Prick the cake layers and sprinkle with the cherry juice and kirsch until well saturated. Sandwich the layers together with the whipped cream and cherries. When assembled, cover with the remaining plain cream and use the whole cherries to decorate the top. Sprinkle the grated chocolate over the cream.

SERVES TEN TO TWELVE

AUSTRIAN HAZELNUT LAYER

fat for greasing
200 g / 7 oz hazelnuts
5 eggs, separated
150 g / 5 oz caster sugar
grated rind of 1 lemon
flour for dusting

FILLING
250 ml / 8 fl oz double cream
vanilla essence

DECORATION
whole hazelnuts
grated chocolate

Grease and flour two 25 cm / 10 inch springform or loose-bottomed cake tins. Set the oven at 180°C / 350°F / gas 4.

Spread the hazelnuts out on a baking sheet and roast for 10 minutes or until the skins start to split. While still warm, rub them in a rough cloth to remove the skins. Grind the nuts in a nut mill or process briefly in a blender.

Combine the egg yolks and sugar in a bowl and beat until light and creamy. Mix in the ground nuts and lemon rind. Whisk the egg whites in a clean, grease-free bowl until stiff but not dry. Fold the egg whites quickly and gently into the nut mixture. Divide between the prepared tins and bake for 1 hour. Test that the cakes are cooked (see Mrs Beeton's Tip, overleaf), then cool the layers on wire racks, removing the sides and bases of the tins after a few minutes.

continued overleaf ...

MRS BEETON'S TIP

When the cakes are ready, a warmed skewer pushed into the centre of each layer should come out dry. The sides of the cake should have begun to shrink slightly from the edges of the tin.

To make the filling, whip the cream with a few drops of vanilla essence until stiff. When the cake layers are cold, sandwich them together with some of the cream, and cover the top with the remainder. Decorate with a few whole hazelnuts and a sprinkling of grated chocolate.

SERVES TWELVE

SACHER TORTE

Invented by Franz Sacher, this is one of the most delectable (and calorific) cakes imaginable. Serve it solo, or with whipped cream. The icing owes its gloss to glycerine, which is available from chemists.

butter for greasing
175 g / 6 oz butter
175 g / 6 oz icing sugar
6 eggs, separated
175 g / 6 oz plain chocolate, in squares
2–3 drops of vanilla essence
150 g / 5 oz plain flour, sifted
about 125 ml / 4 fl oz apricot jam, warmed
and sieved, for filling and glazing

ICING
150 g / 5 oz plain chocolate, in squares
125 g / 4 oz icing sugar, sifted
12.5 ml / 2½ tsp glycerine

Line and grease a 20 cm / 8 inch loose-bottomed cake tin. Set the oven at 180°C / 350°C / gas 4.

In a mixing bowl, beat the butter until creamy. Add 100 g / 4 oz of the icing sugar, beating until light and fluffy. Add the egg yolks, one at a time, beating after each addition.

Melt the chocolate with 30 ml / 2 tbsp water in a heatproof bowl over hot water. Stir into the cake mixture with the vanilla essence.

In a clean, grease-free bowl, whisk the egg whites to soft peaks. Beat in the remaining icing sugar and continue beating until stiff but not dry. Fold into the chocolate mixture alternately with the sifted flour, adding about 15 ml / 1 tbsp of each of a time.

Spoon the mixture into the prepared cake tin and set the tin on a baking sheet. With the back of a spoon, make a slight depression in the centre of the cake to ensure even rising. Bake for 1–1¼ hours or until a skewer inserted in the centre of the cake comes out clean.

Leave the cake in the tin for a few minutes, then turn out on to a wire rack. Cool to room temperature.

Split the cake in half and brush the cut sides with warmed apricot jam. Sandwich the layers together again and glaze the top and sides of the cake with apricot jam. Set aside.

Make the icing. Melt the chocolate with 75 ml / 5 tbsp water in a heatproof bowl over hot water. Stir in the icing sugar and whisk in the glycerine, preferably using a balloon whisk.

Pour the icing over the cake, letting it run down the sides. If necessary, use a metal spatula, warmed in hot water, to smooth the surface. Avoid touching the icing too much at this stage, or the gloss will be lost. Serve when the icing has set.

SERVES TWELVE

MRS BEETON'S TIP

Do not refrigerate this cake after baking; chilling would spoil the glossy appearance of the icing.

CHOCOLATE ROULADE

This cake is best baked the day before it is to be served.

oil and butter for greasing
150 g / 5 oz plain dessert chocolate, in squares
4 eggs, separated
100 g / 4 oz caster sugar
15 g / ½ oz icing sugar, plus extra for dusting
about 175 ml / 6 fl oz double cream
few drops of vanilla essence

Brush a 42 x 30 cm / 17 x 12 inch Swiss roll tin with oil. Line with a piece of greaseproof paper, letting the paper overlap the edge a little. Cut out a second sheet of greaseproof paper to the same size, to cover the cooked roulade, and have ready a damp clean tea-towel with which to cover the paper-topped roulade. Set the oven at 190°C / 375°F / gas 5.

Heat a saucepan of water. Place the chocolate in a heatproof bowl. When the water boils, remove the pan from the heat and set the bowl over it. Leave to melt, stirring occasionally.

Combine the egg yolks and caster sugar in a bowl and beat briskly until the mixture is pale and creamy. Add 45 ml / 3 tbsp hot water to the melted chocolate and beat until well blended. Stir the chocolate into the egg yolk mixture, then whisk thoroughly.

In a clean, grease-free bowl, whisk the egg whites until fairly stiff. Using a metal spoon, fold them carefully into the chocolate mixture. Tip into the prepared Swiss roll tin and bake for 20 minutes until the roulade is firm.

Butter the remaining sheet of greaseproof paper. Remove the tin from the oven and immediately cover the cake with the buttered paper and the damp tea-towel. Leave to stand for several hours or overnight.

Next day, remove the cloth. Turn the paper buttered side up, sprinkle with icing sugar and replace sugared side down. Grip the paper and tin and invert both together so that the roulade is upside-down. Lay it down on the paper and remove the tin. Peel off the lining paper.

In a bowl, whip the cream until very stiff, stir in the vanilla essence and spread evenly over the surface of the roulade. Roll the roulade up from one long side,

MRS BEETON'S TIP

Do not worry too much if cracks appear in the roulade during rolling. The mixture does not include any flour so that the baked roulade is rich and sweet with a fragile texture. Dusting with icing sugar disguises the cracks.

using the paper as a guide. Place on a serving plate, with the join underneath, dust with extra icing sugar and chill for several hours before serving.

SERVES SIX

SAVOY CAKE WITH GINGER CREAM

This light sponge may be used as a base for making fruit and cream gâteaux or for trifles. Originally, the ginger cream was set in a mould to be served on its own as a rich dessert. Combined, the cake and cream make an irresistible dessert duo.

6 eggs, separated
15 ml / 1 tbsp orange flower water or rose water
grated rind of 1 lemon
175 g / 6 oz caster sugar
175 g / 6 oz plain flour

GINGER CREAM
15 ml / 1 tbsp gelatine
4 egg yolks
600 ml / 1 pint double cream
75 g / 3 oz preserved stem ginger, finely sliced
15 ml / 1 tbsp syrup from preserved ginger
icing sugar for dredging

continued overleaf ...

Set the oven at 180°C / 350°C / gas 4. Grease and flour a 20 cm / 8 inch round deep cake tin.

Cream the egg yolks with the orange flower water or rose water, lemon rind and sugar until pale and thick. In a clean, grease-free bowl, whisk the egg whites until stiff, then fold them into the yolks.

Sift the flour over the mixture and fold it in gently. Turn the mixture into the prepared tin and bake for about 45 minutes, until the cake is risen, browned and firm. Turn the cake out on to a wire rack to cool.

To make the ginger cream, sprinkle the gelatine over 30 ml / 2 tbsp cold water in a heatproof basin and set aside for 15 minutes, until spongy. Place over a saucepan of hot water and stir until dissolved completely.

Beat the yolks in a heatproof bowl. Stir in the cream, ginger and syrup. Place over a saucepan of hot water and stir until the mixture has thickened sufficiently to thinly coat the back of a spoon.

Stir a little of the cream into the gelatine, then pour it into the main batch of mixture and stir well. Leave to cool, stirring often. Chill well.

To serve, dredge the top of the cake thickly with icing sugar. Serve each slice of cake topped with a generous spoonful of ginger cream; offer the remaining ginger cream separately.

SERVES TEN

HAZELNUT MERINGUE GATEAU

75 g / 3 oz hazelnuts
3 egg whites
150 g / 5 oz caster sugar
2–3 drops of vinegar
2–3 drops of vanilla essence

FILLING AND TOPPING
125 ml / 4 fl oz double cream
5–10 ml / 1–2 tsp caster sugar

Reserve a few hazelnuts for decorating the gâteau. Bake the rest in a preheated 180°C / 350°F / gas 4 oven for 10 minutes. Rub off the skins. Chop the nuts very finely or process briefly in a blender or food processor. Set aside. Do not turn off the oven.

Line two baking sheets with greaseproof paper or non-stick baking parchment. Draw a 15 cm / 6 inch circle on each and very lightly oil the greaseproof paper, if used.

Combine the egg whites and caster sugar in a heatproof bowl. Set over a saucepan of gently simmering water and whisk until the meringue is very thick and holds its shape. Add the vinegar, vanilla essence and chopped nuts.

Spread the meringue inside the marked circles or place it in a piping bag with a 1 cm / ½ inch plain nozzle. Starting from the middle of one circle, pipe round and round to form a coiled, flat round 15 cm / 6 inches in diameter. Pipe a similar round on the other sheet. Bake for 35–40 minutes, until each layer is crisp and lightly browned. Leave to cool.

Whip the cream in a bowl until it stands in stiff peaks, then stir in caster sugar to taste. Place one of the meringue rounds on a serving plate and spread with most of the cream. Put the second meringue round on top and decorate with the rest of the cream and hazelnuts.

SERVES FOUR TO SIX

STRAWBERRY MERINGUE TORTE

4 egg whites
pinch of salt
100 g / 4 oz granulated sugar
100 g / 4 oz caster sugar

FILLING
450 g / 1 lb fresh strawberries, hulled
juice of 1 lemon
30 ml / 2 tbsp caster sugar
125 ml / 4 fl oz double cream or whipped cream flavoured with brandy or kirsch

Line a baking sheet with greaseproof paper or non-stick baking parchment. Draw a 15 cm / 6 inch circle on the paper and very lightly oil the greaseproof paper if used. Set the oven at 110°C / 225°F / gas ¼.

Combine the egg whites, salt and sugars in a heatproof bowl. Set over a saucepan of gently simmering water and whisk until the mixture is very thick and holds its shape.

Spread some of the meringue all over the circle to form the base of a meringue case. Put the rest of the mixture into a piping bag fitted with a large star nozzle. Pipe three quarters of the mixture around the edge of the ring to make a 5 cm / 2 inch rim or border. Use the remaining mixture to pipe small meringue shapes. Bake the case for 3–4 hours; the small shells for 1½–2 hours. Leave to cool.

Make the filling. Put the strawberries in a bowl and sprinkle with the lemon juice and caster sugar. Chill in the refrigerator until the meringue case is cool. Reserve a few choice berries for decoration. Drain and halve the rest and put them into the meringue case. In a bowl, whip the cream (or use the liqueur-flavoured cream) and cover the fruit. Decorate with the meringues and strawberries. Serve at once.

SERVES FOUR

PAVLOVA

3 egg whites
150 g / 5 oz caster sugar
2.5 ml / ½ tsp vinegar
2.5 ml / ½ tsp vanilla essence
10 ml / 2 tsp cornflour
glacé cherries and angelica to decorate

FILLING
250 ml / 8 fl oz double cream
caster sugar (see method)
2 peaches, skinned and sliced

Line a baking sheet with greaseproof paper or non-stick baking parchment. Draw a 20 cm / 8 inch circle on the paper and very lightly grease the greaseproof paper, if used. Set the oven at 150°C / 300°F / gas 2.

In a large bowl whisk the egg whites until very stiff. Continue whisking, gradually adding the sugar until the mixture stands in stiff peaks. Beat in the vinegar, vanilla and cornflour.

Spread the meringue over the circle, piling it up at the edges to form a rim, or pipe the circle and rim from a piping bag fitted with a large star nozzle.

Bake for about 1 hour or until the pavlova is crisp on the outside and has the texture of marshmallow inside. It should be pale coffee in colour. Leave to cool then carefully remove the paper. Put the pavlova on a large serving plate.

Make the filling by whipping the cream in a bowl with caster sugar to taste. Add the sliced peaches and pile into the cold pavlova shell. Decorate with glacé cherries and angelica and serve as soon as possible.

SERVES FOUR

Large
Plain
Cakes &
Fruit
Cakes

PLAIN CAKE

fat for greasing
200 g / 7 oz self-raising flour
or 200 g / 7 oz plain flour and 10 ml / 2 tsp baking powder
1.25 ml / ¼ tsp salt
75 g / 3 oz margarine or blended white cooking fat, diced
75 g / 3 oz sugar
2 small eggs
about 125 ml / 4 fl oz milk

Line and grease a 15 cm / 6 inch cake tin. Set the oven at 180°C / 350°F / gas 4.

Mix the flour and salt together in a mixing bowl. Rub in the margarine or cooking fat until the mixture resembles fine breadcrumbs. Add the baking powder, if used, and the sugar.

In a bowl, beat the eggs with some of the milk and stir into the flour mixture. Add a little more milk if necessary to give a consistency which just drops off the end of the wooden spoon.

Spoon the mixture into a prepared tin and bake to 1–1½ hours or until cooked through. Cool on a wire rack

MAKES ONE 15 CM / 6 INCH CAKE

ONE-STAGE FRUIT CAKE

fat for greasing
225 g / 8 oz self-raising flour
5 ml / 1 tsp mixed spice (optional)
100 g / 4 oz soft margarine
100 g / 4 oz glacé cherries, chopped
100 g / 4 oz currants
75 g / 3 oz sultanas
25 g / 1 oz cut mixed peel
100 g / 4 oz soft light brown sugar
2 eggs
75 ml / 3 fl oz milk

Line and grease an 18cm / 7 inch round cake tin. Set the oven at 180°C / 350°F / gas 4. Mix the flour and spice, if used.

Put all the ingredients in a bowl, stir, then beat until smooth, allowing 2–3 minutes by hand or 1–1½ minutes with an electric mixer. Spoon the mixture into the prepared tin and bake for 2 hours. Cool on a wire rack.

MAKES ONE 18 CM / 7 INCH CAKE

VICTORIA SANDWICH CAKE

The original Victoria Sandwich was oblong, filled with jam or marmalade and cut into fingers or sandwiches. Now, the basic mixture is used with many different flavourings and fillings and is served as a single, round cake. For a softer-centred cake bake the mixture in a 20 cm / 8 inch round cake tin, then split and fill. All loose crumbs must be brushed off before filling. Keep the filling fairly firm – if it is too moist, it will seep into the cake.

fat for greasing
150 g / 5 oz butter or margarine
150 g / 5 oz caster sugar
3 eggs, beaten
150 g / 5 oz self-raising flour or plain flour
5 ml / 1 tsp baking powder
pinch of salt
raspberry or other jam for filling
caster sugar for dredging

Line and grease two 18 cm / 7 inch sandwich tins. Set the oven at 180°C / 350°F / gas 4.

In a mixing bowl cream the butter or margarine with the sugar until light and fluffy. Add the eggs gradually, beating well after each addition. Sift the flour, salt and baking powder, if used, into a bowl. Stir into the creamed mixture, lightly but thoroughly, until evenly mixed.

Divide between the tins and bake for 25–30 minutes. Cool on a wire rack, then sandwich together with jam. Sprinkle the top with caster sugar or spread with Glacé Icing (page 139).

MAKES ONE 18 CM / 7 INCH CAKE

ONE-STAGE
VICTORIA SANDWICH

fat for greasing
150 g / 5 oz self-raising flour
pinch of salt
150 g / 5 oz soft margarine
150 g / 5 oz caster sugar
3 eggs

Line and grease two 18 cm / 7 inch sandwich tins. Set the oven at 180°C / 350°F / gas 4.

Put all the ingredients in a mixing bowl and stir. Beat until smooth, allowing 2–3 minutes by hand or 1–1½ minutes with an electric mixer.

Divide the mixture evenly between the tins; level each surface. Bake for 25–30 minutes. Cool on a wire rack, then fill and top as desired.

MAKES ONE 18 CM / 7 INCH CAKE

continued overleaf ...

FLAVOURING AND FILLING FOR VICTORIA SANDWICH CAKES

- **Chocolate Sandwich Cake** Substitute 60 ml / 4 tbsp of cocoa for an equal quantity of the flour. Sift the cocoa with the flour and continue as in the main recipe. Sandwich the cooled cakes together with chocolate spread and sift a little icing sugar over the top of the chocolate cake.
- **Cinnamon and Apple Sandwich Cake** Add 10 ml / 2 tsp of ground cinnamon to the flour. Continue as in the main recipe. Peel, core and slice a large cooking apple, then cook it with a little sugar until it is reduced to a pulp. Press the pulp through a sieve, return it to the saucepan and add 10 ml / 2 tsp of cornflour blended with 30 ml / 2 tbsp of milk. Bring to the boil, stirring, and cook until thickened. Sweeten the purée to taste, then leave it to cool. Gradually fold in 50 ml / 2 fl oz of whipped double cream, then use this apple cream to sandwich the cooled cakes together.
- **Coffee Sandwich Cake** Dissolve 30 ml / 2 tbsp of instant coffee in 30 ml / 2 tbsp boiling water and leave to cool. Fold this into the mixture last. Whip 150 ml / ¼ pint double cream with 5 ml / 1 tsp of instant coffee dissolved in 15 ml / 1 tbsp of boiling water and 30 ml / 2 tbsp of icing sugar. Sandwich the cooled cakes with this coffee cream.
- **Ginger Sandwich Cake** The combination of ground ginger and lemon rind makes a delicious cake. Add the grated rind of 1 lemon to the fat and sugar. Sift 15 ml / 1 tbsp of ground ginger with the flour. Prepare and bake the cake as in the main recipe. When cool, sandwich the layers with ginger marmalade.
- **Harlequin Sandwich Cake** Make the cake mixture as in the main recipe, then put half in one sandwich tin. Add pink food colouring to the second portion of mixture, making it a fairly strong colour. Put the second portion in the other sandwich tin and bake the cake. When cool, cut both cakes into rings: cut a 5 cm / 2 inch circle from the middle of each cake, then cut a 10 cm / 4 inch circle around it. Either use plain pastry cutters or cut out circles of paper and use a pointed knife to cut around them. You should have three rings of each cake. Carefully put the rings of cake together alternating the colours to make two layers. Sandwich the layers together with raspberry jam. Spread warmed raspberry jam over the top of the cake and sift icing sugar over it. Alternatively, fill the cake with whipped cream and swirl more whipped cream over the top. When slices are cut the pattern will show.
- **Lemon Sandwich Cake** Add the grated rind of 1 large lemon to the fat and sugar. Continue as in the main recipe, then sandwich the cooled cakes together with lemon curd.

- **Mocha Sandwich Cake** Substitute 30 ml / 2 tbsp of cocoa for an equal quantity of flour and sift it with the flour. Prepare the mixture as in the main recipe. Dissolve 10 ml / 2 tsp of instant coffee in 15 ml / 1 tbsp of boiling water and add it to the mixture. Sandwich the cooled cakes together with chocolate spread.
- **Orange Sandwich Cake** Add the grated rind of 1 large orange to the fat and sugar, then continue as in the main recipe. Sandwich the cooled cakes together with orange marmalade.

GENOESE SPONGE OR PASTRY

fat for greasing
100 g / 4 oz plain flour
2.5 ml / ½ tsp salt
275 g / 3 oz clarified butter or margarine
4 eggs
100 g / 4 oz caster sugar

Line and grease a 30 x 20 cm / 12 x 8 inch Swiss roll tin. Set the oven at 180°C / 350°F / gas 4.

Sift the flour and salt into a bowl and put in a warm place. Melt the clarified butter or margarine without letting it get hot.

Whisk the eggs lightly in a mixing bowl. Add the sugar and place the bowl over a saucepan of hot water. Whisk for 1–15 minutes until thick. Take care that the base of the bowl does not touch the water. Remove from the heat and continue whisking until at blood-heat. The melted butter should be at the same temperature.

Stir half the flour over the eggs, then pour in half the melted butter or margarine in a thin stream. Fold in gently. Repeat, using the remaining flour and fat. Spoon gently into the prepared tin and bake for 30–40 minutes. Cool on a wire rack.

MAKES ONE 30 X 20 CM / 12 X 8 INCH CAKE

PLAIN CHOCOLATE LOAF

*Serve this simple loaf sliced, with a chocolate
and hazelnut spread for those who like to gild the lily.*

fat for greasing
175 g / 6 oz plain flour
50 g / 2 oz cocoa
10 ml / 2 tsp baking powder
2.5 ml / ½ tsp bicarbonate of soda
1.25 ml / ¼ tsp salt
150 g / 5 oz sugar
2 eggs, beaten
75 g / 3 oz butter or margarine, melted
250 ml / 8 fl oz milk

Line and grease a 23 x 13 x 7.5 cm / 9 x 5 x 3 inch loaf tin. Set the oven at 180°C / 350°F / gas 4. Sift the flour, cocoa, baking powder, bicarbonate of soda and salt into a mixing bowl. Stir in the sugar.

In a second bowl beat the eggs with the melted butter or margarine and milk. Pour the milk mixture into the dry ingredients and stir lightly but thoroughly.

Spoon into the prepared tin and bake for 40–50 minutes until cooked through and firm to the touch. Cool on a wire rack.

MAKES ONE 23 X 13 X 7.5 CM / 9 X 5 X 3 INCH LOAF

VARIATIONS

- **Chocolate Layer Loaf** The simplest way to enrich the loaf cake is to cut it horizontally into three layers and sandwich them together with chocolate and hazelnut spread. If you like, coat the top of the cake with melted chocolate softened with a knob of butter, and top with toasted hazelnuts.
- **Chocolate Orange Split** Add the grated rind of 1 orange to the dry ingredients, then continue as in the main recipe. Beat 225 g / 8 oz curd cheese with enough orange juice to make it soft and creamy, then add icing sugar to taste. Stir 50 g / 2 oz of finely grated plain chocolate. Split the loaf vertically along its length into four slices. Sandwich the slices together with the cheese

mixture and spread a thin layer over the top of the loaf. Sprinkle the top with extra grated chocolate.

- **Chocolate Walnut Loaf** Add 100 g / 4 oz of finely chopped walnuts to the dry ingredients, then continue as in the main recipe. Melt 50 g / 2 oz of plain chocolate with 25 g / 1 oz of chopped walnuts. Top the loaf with this mixture.

PLAIN ALMOND CAKE

fat for greasing
100 g / 4 oz butter or margarine
100 g / 4 oz caster sugar
275 g / 10 oz plain flour
10 ml / 2 tsp baking powder
3 eggs
200 ml / 7 fl oz milk
2.5 ml / ½ tsp almond essence

Line and grease a 15 cm / 6 inch round cake tin. Set the oven at 160°C / 325°F / gas 3.

In a mixing bowl, cream the butter or margarine with the sugar until light and fluffy. Into another bowl, sift the flour and baking powder. In a measuring jug, beat the eggs with the milk.

Add the dry ingredients to the creamed mixture in 3 parts, alternately with the egg and milk mixture. Beat well after each addition. Lightly stir in the almond essence and the flaked almonds.

Spoon lightly into the prepared tin and bake for 1¼–1½ hours until cooked through and firm to the touch. Cool on a wire rack.

MAKES ONE 15 CM / 6 INCH CAKE

DATE AND WALNUT CAKE

fat for greasing
200 g / 7 oz self-raising flour
or 200 g / 7 oz plain flour and 10 ml / 2 tsp baking powder
pinch of grated nutmeg
75 g / 3 oz margarine
75 g / 3 oz dates, stoned and chopped
25 g / 1 oz walnuts, chopped
75 g / 3 oz soft light brown sugar
2 small eggs
About 125 ml / 4 fl oz milk

Line and grease a 15 cm / 6 inch tin. Set the oven at 180°C / 350°F / gas 4.

Mix the flour and nutmeg in a mixing bowl, and rub in the margarine until the mixture resembles fine breadcrumbs. Add the dates and walnuts with the sugar and baking powder, if used.

In a bowl, beat the eggs with the milk and stir into the dry ingredients. Mix well.

Spoon the mixture into the cake tin and bake for 1¼–1½ hours or until cooked through and firm to the touch. Cool on a wire rack.

MAKES ONE 15 CM / 6 INCH CAKE

BANANA AND WALNUT CAKE

fat for greasing
200 g / 7 oz plain flour
1.25 ml / ¼ tsp baking powder
3.75 ml / ¾ tsp bicarbonate of soda
pinch of salt
100 g / 4 oz butter
150 g / 5 oz caster sugar
3 large bananas, mashed
2 eggs, beaten
45 ml / 3 tbsp soured milk
50 g / 2 oz walnuts, finely chopped

Line and grease either a 20 cm / 8 inch ring tin, or two 23 cm / 9 inch sandwich tins. Set the oven at 180°C / 350°F / gas 4. Sift the flour, baking powder, bicarbonate of soda and salt into a bowl.

In a mixing bowl, cream the butter and sugar until light and creamy. Mix in the mashed banana at once, blending well. Add the eggs, one at a time, beating well after each addition. Add the dry ingredients, one-third at a time, alternately with the soured milk, beating well after each addition.

Stir in the walnuts and spoon into the prepared tin. Bake the ring cake for about 40 minutes; the sandwich cakes for about 30 minutes. Cool on a wire rack.

**MAKES ONE 20 CM / 8 INCH RING CAKE
OR TWO 23 CM / 9 INCH LAYERS**

OATMEAL GINGERBREAD

fat for greasing
100 g / 4 oz plain flour
1.25 ml / ¼ tbsp ground ginger
5 ml / 1 tsp bicarbonate of soda
100 g / 4 oz fine oatmeal
50 g / 2 oz butter or margarine
50 g / 2 oz soft light brown sugar
20 ml / 4 tsp black treacle
1 egg
75 ml / 5 tbsp milk or soured milk

Line and grease an 18 cm / 7 inch square tin. Set the oven at 180°C / 350°F / gas 4. Sift the flour, salt, ginger and bicarbonate of soda into a mixing bowl. Add the oatmeal.

Heat the butter or margarine with the sugar and treacle gently in a saucepan until the fat has melted.

In a bowl, beat the egg and milk together. Add the melted mixture to the dry ingredients with the beaten egg and milk mixture. Stir well. Pour into the prepared tin and bake for 1–1¼ hours until cooked through and firm to the touch. Cool on a wire rack.

MAKES ONE 18 CM / 7 INCH CAKE

GINGERBREAD

fat for greasing
200 g / 7 oz plain flour
1.25 ml / ¼ tsp salt
10–15 ml / 2–3 tsp ground ginger
2.5 ml / ½ tsp bicarbonate soda
75 g / 3 oz lard
50 g / 2 oz soft light brown sugar
50 g / 2 oz black treacle
1 egg
milk (see method)

Line and grease a 15 cm / 6 inch square tin. Set the oven at 160°C / 325°F / gas 3.

Sift the flour, salt, ginger and bicarbonate of soda into a mixing bowl. Warm the lard, sugar, syrup and treacle in a saucepan until the fat has melted. Do not let the mixture become hot.

In a measuring jug, beat the egg lightly and add enough milk to make up to 125 ml / 4 fl oz. Add the melted mixture to the dry ingredients with the beaten egg and milk mixture. Stir thoroughly; the mixture should run easily off the spoon.

Pour into the prepared tin and bake for 1¼–1½ hours until firm to the touch. Cool the gingerbread on a wire rack.

MAKES ONE 15 CM / 6 INCH SQUARE CAKE

RICH GINGERBREAD

fat for greasing
225 g / 8 oz plain flour
1.25 ml / ¼ tsp salt
10 ml / 2 tsp ground ginger
2.5 –5 ml / ½–1 tsp ground cinnamon or grated nutmeg
5 ml / 1 tsp bicarbonate of soda
100 g / 4 oz butter
100 g / 4 oz soft light brown sugar
100 g / 4 oz golden syrup
1 egg
45 ml / 3 tbsp plain yogurt
30 ml / 2 tbsp ginger preserve

Line and grease a 20 cm / 8 inch square tin. Set the oven at 160°C / 325°F / gas 3.

Sift the flour, salt, spices and bicarbonate of soda into a mixing bowl. Heat the butter, sugar and syrup gently in a saucepan until the butter has melted.

In a bowl, beat the egg and yogurt together. Add to the dry ingredients, with the melted mixture, to give a soft, dropping consistency. Stir in the preserve.

Spoon into the prepared tin and bake for 50–60 minutes until cooked through and firm to the touch. Cool on a wire rack.

MAKES ONE 23 CM / 9 INCH CAKE

APPLE AND GINGER CAKE

fat for greasing
175 g / 6 oz plain flour
1.25 ml / ¼ tsp salt
2.5 ml / ½ tsp bicarbonate of soda
5 ml / 1 tsp baking powder
5 ml / 1 tsp ground ginger
100 g / 4 oz crystallized ginger, chopped
100 g / 4 oz butter or margarine
150 g / 5 oz caster sugar
2 eggs, beaten
250 ml / 8 fl oz sieved apple purée

Line and grease an 18 cm / 7 inch square tin. Set the oven at 180°C / 350°F / gas 4. Sift the flour, salt, bicarbonate of soda, baking powder and ground ginger into a bowl. Stir in the crystallized ginger and mix well. Set aside.

Place the butter or margarine in a mixing bowl and beat until very soft. Add the sugar and cream together until light and fluffy. Add the beaten eggs gradually, beating well after each addition. If the mixture shows signs of curdling, add a little of the flour mixture. Stir in the apple purée. Fold in the dry ingredients lightly but thoroughly. Spoon into the prepared tin, smooth the surface and make a slight hollow in the centre.

Bake for 30 minutes, then reduce the oven temperature to 160°C / 325°F / gas 3 and bake for 15 minutes more until firm to the touch. Cool on a wire rack.

MAKES ONE 18 CM / 7 INCH CAKE

CHERRY CAKE

fat for greasing
200 g / 7 oz plain flour
1.25 ml / ¼ tsp salt
2.5 ml / ½ tsp baking powder
100 g / 4 oz glacé cherries, washed, dried and quartered
150 g / 5 oz butter or margarine
150 g / 5 oz caster sugar
4 eggs, beaten
15 ml / 1 tbsp milk (optional)

Line and grease a 15 cm / 6 inch cake tin. Set the oven at 180°C / 350°F / gas 4. Sift the flour, salt and baking powder into a bowl. Add the cherries and mix well. Set aside.

Place the butter or margarine in a mixing bowl and beat until very soft. Add the sugar and cream together until light and fluffy. Add the beaten eggs gradually, heating well after each addition. If the mixture shows signs of curdling, add a little of the flour mixture.

Fold in the dry ingredients lightly but thoroughly, adding the milk if too stiff.

Spoon into the prepared tin, level the surface and make a slight hollow in the centre. Bake for 30 minutes, then reduce the oven temperature to 160°C / 325°F / gas 3 and bake for 50 minutes more until cooked through and firm to the touch. Cool on a wire rack.

MAKES ONE 15 CM / 6 INCH CAKE

FESTIVAL FRUIT CAKE

fat for greasing
225 g / 8 oz plain flour
1.25 ml / ¼ tsp salt
2.5 ml / ½ tsp baking powder
50 g / 2 oz currants
50 g / 2 oz sultanas
50 g / 2 oz glacé cherries, washed, dried and chopped
50 g / 2 oz cut mixed peel
150 g / 5 oz butter or margarine
150 g / 5 oz caster sugar
2 eggs, beaten
15 ml / 1 tbsp milk (optional)

Line and grease an 18 cm / 7 inch cake tin. Set the oven at 180°C / 350°F / gas 4. Sift the flour, salt and baking powder into a bowl. Stir in the dried fruit and mixed peel and mix well. Set aside.

Place the butter or margarine in a mixing bowl and beat until very soft. Add the sugar and cream together until light and fluffy. Add the beaten eggs gradually, beating well after each addition. If the mixture shows signs of curdling, add a little of the flour mixture.

Fold in the dry ingredients lightly but thoroughly, adding the milk if too stiff.

Spoon into the prepared tin, smooth the surface and make a slight hollow in the centre. Bake for 30 minutes, then reduce the oven temperature to 160°C / 325°F / gas 3 and bake for 40 minutes more until firm to the touch. Cool on a wire rack.

MAKES ONE 18 CM / 7 INCH CAKE

COUNTESS SPICE CAKE

fat for greasing
100 g / 4 oz plain flour
100 g / 4 oz cornflour
2.5 ml / ½ tsp ground ginger
3.75 ml / ¾ grated nutmeg
3.75 ml / ¾ ground cinnamon
1.25 ml / ¼ tsp salt
75 g / 3 oz margarine
10 ml / 2 tsp baking powder
75 g / 3 oz sugar
2 small eggs
about 125 ml / 4 fl oz milk
50 g / 2 oz currants
50 g / 2 oz seedless raisins

Line and grease a 15 cm / 6 inch tin. Set the oven for 180°C / 350°F / gas 4.

Mix the flour, cornflour, spices and salt in a mixing bowl. Rub in the margarine until the mixture resembles fine breadcrumbs. Add the baking powder and the sugar.

In a bowl, beat the eggs with 50 ml / 2 fl oz of the milk and stir into the flour mixture. Add more milk, if necessary, to give a consistency which just drops off the end of a wooden spoon. Stir in the currants and raisins.

Spoon the mixture into the prepared cake tin and bake for 1–1½ hours or until cooked through. Cool on a wire rack.

MAKES ONE 15 CM / 6 INCH CAKE

Special Cakes

*A special cake is an essential feature
of any celebration, whether the occasion
is a birthday tea, an informal gathering
of friends, or a grand party.*

CHRISTMAS CAKE

fat for greasing
200 g / 7 oz plain flour
1.25 ml / ¼ tsp salt
5–10 ml / 1–2 tsp mixed spice
200 g / 7 oz butter
200 g / 7 oz caster sugar
6 eggs, beaten
30–60 ml / 2–4 tbsp brandy or sherry
100 g / 4 oz glacé cherries, chopped
50 g / 2 oz preserved ginger, chopped
50 g / 2 oz walnuts, chopped
200 g / 7 oz currants
200 g / 7 oz sultanas
150 g / 5 oz seedless raisins
75 g / 3 oz cut mixed peel

COATING AND ICING
Almond Paste (page 134)
Royal Icing (page 143)

Line and grease a 20 cm / 8 inch round cake tin. Use doubled greaseproof paper. Set the oven at 160°C / 325°F / gas 3.

Stir the flour, salt and spice into a bowl. In a mixing bowl, cream the butter and sugar together until light and fluffy. Gradually beat in the eggs and the brandy or sherry, adding a little flour if the mixture starts to curdle. Add the cherries, ginger and walnuts. Stir in the dried fruit, peel and flour mixture. Spoon into the prepared tin and make a slight hollow in the centre.

Bake for 45 minutes then reduce the oven temperature to 150°C / 300°F / gas 2 and bake for a further hour. Reduce the temperature still further to 140°C / 275°F / gas 1, and continue cooking for 45–60 minutes until cooked though and firm to the touch. Cool in the tin. Cover the cake with almond paste and decorate with royal icing.

MAKES ONE 20 CM / 8 INCH CAKE

TWELFTH NIGHT CAKE

*The tradition of the Twelfth Night Cake goes back to the days
of the early Christian Church and beyond. In the Middle Ages,
whoever found the bean in his cake became the 'Lord of Misrule' or
'King' for the festivities of Twelfth Night, with the finder of the pea
as his 'Queen'. Finding the bean was thought to bring luck. The
tradition survived until near the end of the nineteenth century.*

fat for greasing
150 g / 5 oz margarine
75 g / 3 oz soft dark brown sugar
3 eggs
300 g / 11 oz plain flour
60 ml / 4 tbsp milk
5 ml / 1 tsp bicarbonate of soda
30 ml / 2 tbsp golden syrup
2.5 ml / ½ tsp mixed spice
2.5 ml / ½ tsp ground cinnamon
pinch of salt
50 g / 2 oz currants
100 g / 4 oz sultanas
100 g / 4 oz cut mixed peel
1 dried bean (see above)
1 large dried whole pea (see above)

Line and grease a 15 cm / 6 inch round cake tin. Set the oven at 180°C / 350°F / gas 4.

In a mixing bowl, cream the margarine and sugar until light and fluffy. Beat in the eggs, one at a time, adding a little flour with each. Warm the milk, add the bicarbonate of soda and stir until dissolved. Add the syrup.

Mix the spices and salt with the remaining flour in a bowl. Add this to the creamed mixture alternately with the flavoured milk. Lightly stir the dried fruit and peel. Spoon half the cake mixture into the prepared tin, lay the bean and pea in the centre, then cover with the rest of the cake mixture. Bake for about 2 hours. Cool on a wire rack.

MAKES ONE 15 CM / 6 INCH CAKE

PINEAPPLE UPSIDE-DOWN CAKE

Serve this delicious cake with cream as a dessert, or cold for afternoon tea.

1 (227 g / 8 oz) can pineapple rings
100 g / 4 oz butter
275 g / 10 oz soft dark brown sugar
8 maraschino or glacé cherries
450 g / 1 lb self-raising flour
5 ml / 1 tsp ground cinnamon
5 ml / 1 tsp ground nutmeg
2 eggs
250 ml / 8 fl oz milk

Drain the pineapple rings, reserving the syrup. Melt 50 g / 2 oz of the butter in a 20 cm / 8 inch square baking tin. Add 100 g / 4 oz of the sugar and 15 ml / 1 tbsp pineapple syrup and mix well. Arrange the pineapple rings in the even pattern on the base of the tin, and place a cherry in the centre of each ring. Set the oven at 180°C / 350°F / gas 4.

Sift the flour, cinnamon and nutmeg into a mixing bowl. In a second bowl, beat the eggs with the remaining brown sugar. Melt the remaining butter in a saucepan, and add to the eggs and sugar with the milk; stir into the spiced flour and mix well.

Pour this mixture carefully over the fruit in the baking tin without disturbing it. Bake for 45–50 minutes. Remove the tin from the oven and at one turn upside-down on to a plate; allow the caramel to run over the cake before removing the baking tin.

MAKES ONE 20 CM / 8 INCH CAKE

VARIATIONS

- **Apricot Upside-down Cake** Substitute canned apricot halves for the pineapple, placing them rounded-side down in the tin. Arrange the cherries between the apricots.
- **Plum Upside-down Cake** Arrange halved and stoned fresh plums in the bottom of the tin instead of pineapple. Use orange juice instead of pineapple syrup and place the plums cut side down. Omit the cherries.
- **Pear Upside-down Cake** Use canned pears instead of the pineapple. If you like, substitute ground ginger for the nutmeg.

SIMNEL CAKE

fat for greasing
200 g / 7 oz plain flour
2.5 ml / ½ tsp baking powder
1.25 ml / ¼ tsp salt
150 g / 5 oz butter
150 g / 5 oz caster sugar
4 eggs
100 g / 4 oz glace cherries, halved
150 g / 5 oz currants
150 g / 5 oz sultanas
100 g / 4 oz seedless raisins
50 g / 2 oz cut mixed peel
50 g / 2 oz ground almonds
grated rind of 1 lemon

DECORATION
Double quantity Almond Paste (page 134) or 450 ml / 1 lb marzipan
30 ml / 2 tbsp smooth apricot jam (see method)
1 egg, beaten
Glace Icing (page 139) using 50 g / 2 oz icing sugar
Easter decorations

Line and grease a 18 cm / 7 inch cake tin. Set the oven at 180°C / 350°F / gas 4.

Sift the flour, baking powder and salt into a bowl. In a mixing bowl, cream the butter and sugar together well and beat in the eggs, adding a little of the flour mixture if necessary. Fold the flour mixture, cherries, dried fruit, peel and ground almonds into the creamed mixture. Add the lemon rind and mix well.

Spoon half the mixture into the prepared tin. Cut off one third of the almond paste and roll it to a pancake about 1 cm / ½ inch thick and slightly smaller than the circumference of the tin. Place it gently on top of the cake mixture and spoon them remaining cake mixture on top.

Bake for 1 hour, then reduce the oven temperature to 160°C / 325°F / gas 3 and bake for 1½ hours more. Cool in the tin, then turn out on a wire rack.

Warm, then sieve the apricot jam. When the cake is cold, divide the remaining almond paste in half. Roll one half to a round of a slightly smaller diameter than the top of the cake. Brush the top of the cake with apricot jam and press the almond paste lightly on to it. Trim the edge neatly.

Make 11 small balls with the remaining paste and place them around the edge of the cake. Brush the balls with the beaten egg and brown under the grill. Pour the glacé icing into the centre of the cake and decorate with chickens and Easter eggs.

MAKES ONE 18 CM / 7 INCH CAKE

CHOCOLATE LAYER CAKE

fat for greasing
150 g / 5 oz butter or margarine
150 g / 5 oz caster sugar
3 eggs, beaten
few drops of vanilla essence
100 g / 4 oz self-raising flour or plain flour and 5 ml / 1 tsp baking powder
25 g / 1 oz cocoa
Chocolate Fudge Icing (page 138) for filling
caster sugar for dredging

Line and grease two 18 cm / 7 inch sandwich tins. Set the oven at 180°C / 350°F / gas 4.

In a mixing bowl cream the butter or margarine with the sugar until light and fluffy. Add the eggs gradually, beating will after each addition and adding a little of the flour if the mixture shows signs of curdling. Stir in the vanilla essence.

Sift the flour, cocoa, salt and baking powder, if used, into a bowl. Stir into the creamed mixture, lightly but thoroughly, until evenly mixed.

Divide between the tins and bake for 25–30 minutes. Cool on a wire rack, then sandwich together with the buttercream. Sprinkle the top of the cake with caster sugar.

MAKES ONE 18 CM / 7 INCH CAKE

SWISS ROLL

fat for greasing
3 eggs
75 g / 3 oz caster sugar
75 g / 3 oz plain flour
2.5 ml / ½ tsp baking powder
pinch of salt
about 60 ml / 4 tbsp jam for filling
caster sugar for dusting

Line and grease a 30 x 20 cm / 12 x 8 inch Swiss roll tin. Set the oven at 220°C / 425°F / gas 7.

Combine the eggs and sugar in a heatproof bowl. Set the bowl over a pan of hot water, taking care that the bottom of the bowl does not touch the water. Whisk for 10–15 minutes until thick and creamy, then remove from the pan. Continue whisking until the mixture is cold.

Sift the flour, baking powder and salt into a bowl, then lightly fold into the egg mixture. Pour into the prepared tin and bake for 10 minutes. Meanwhile warm the jam in a small saucepan.

When the cake is cooked, turn it on to a large sheet of greaseproof paper dusted with caster sugar. Peel off the lining paper. Trim off any crisp edges. Spread the cake with the warmed jam and roll up tightly from one long side. Dredge with caster sugar and place on a wire rack, with the join underneath, to cool.

MAKES ONE 30 CM / 12 INCH SWISS ROLL

VARIATIONS

- **Chocolate Ice Roll** Make chocolate roll, using 65 g / 2 ½ flour, 30 ml / 2 tbsp cocoa and Chocolate Fudge Icing (page 138) instead of jam. Leave to cool completely. Using a shallow spoon, scoop flat portions of ice cream and place them on a baking sheet lined with cling film. Replace them in the freezer till firmly frozen. Just before the cake is to be served, unroll it and fill with the ice cream. Quickly re-roll the cake and sprinkle with icing sugar. Serve at once, with whipped cream.

- **Chocolate Rum Roll** Make this luscious, rich, rolled cake for special occasions. Prepare chocolate roll, as for Chocolate Ice Roll (page 108), and allow it to cool. Soak 50 g / 2 oz of seedless raisins in 60 ml / 4 tbsp of rum for 30 minutes. Drain the raisins and add the rum to 150 ml / ¼ pint of double cream. Add 15 ml / 1 tbsp of icing sugar to the cream and lightly whip it. Fold in the raisins and 30 ml / 2 tbsp of chopped maraschino cherries. Spread this cream over the unrolled cake and re-roll.

- **Easter Almond Roll** Make the Swiss Roll following the recipe on the left. Leave to cool completely. Roll out 350 g / 12 oz marzipan or almond paste into an oblong the same width as the length of the roll, and long enough to wrap around the roll. Brush the outside of the Swiss Roll with warmed apricot jam and place it on the rolled out marzipan or almond paste. Wrap the paste around the roll, trimming off excess and making sure that they join underneath. Decorate the top of the roll with miniature chocolate Easter eggs.

- **Ginger Cream Roll** Make the plain Swiss Roll following the recipe on the left. Roll up with a sheet of greaseproof paper in the hot cake instead of jam, then leave it to cool completely. Remove the paper. Whip 300 ml / ½ pint of double cream with 45 ml / 3 tbsp of ginger wine. Mix 30 ml / 2 tbsp of finely chopped crystallized ginger into half the cream and spread this over the unrolled cake, then re-roll it. Cover the outside with a thin layer of the remaining cream and pipe rosettes of cream along the top. Decorate the roll with crystallized ginger.

- **Raspberry Meringue Roll** Make a plain Swiss Roll as left, rolling it up with a sheet of greaseproof paper instead of spreading it with jam. Remove the paper when the roll is cold. Whip 150 ml / ¼ pint of double cream with 30 ml / 2 tbsp of icing sugar, then fold in 175 g / 6 oz of raspberries. Spread this over the unrolled cake and roll it up again. Whisk 2 egg whites until stiff, then whisk in 100 g / 4 oz caster sugar. Continue whisking until the mixture is smooth, stiff and glossy. Swirl or pipe this meringue all over the roll. Brown the meringue under a moderately hot grill. Decorate with a few raspberries.

- **St Clement's Roll** Make a Swiss Roll as left, adding the grated rind of 1 orange to the eggs and sugar. Instead of jam, use lemon curd to fill the cake.

- **Walnut and Orange Roll** Make a Swiss Roll following the recipe on the left and adding the grated rind of 1 orange to the eggs and sugar. Roll the cake with a sheet of greaseproof paper instead of adding the jam, then leave it to cool. Remove the paper. Finely chop 100 g / 4 oz of fresh walnuts. Beat 15–30 ml / 1–2 tbsp of honey, to taste, into 100 lb / 4 oz of soft cheese. Stir in the nuts and spread this mixture over the cake before re-rolling it.

ALMOND MACAROON CAKE

fat for greasing
150 g / 5 oz self-raising flour
pinch of salt
150 g / 5 oz butter or margarine
150 g / 5 oz caster sugar
3 eggs
100 g / 4 oz ground almonds
grated rind of 1 lemon
25 g / 1 oz blanched split almonds to decorate

MACAROON
1 egg white
50 g / 2 oz ground almonds
75 g / 3 oz caster sugar
5 ml / 1 tsp ground rice
few drops of almond essence

Line and grease a 15 cm / 6 inch loose-bottomed cake tin. Set the oven at 180°C / 350°F / gas 4. Start by making the macaroon mixture; whisk the egg white in a bowl until frothy, then add the rest of the ingredients, beating well.

Make the cake mixture. Mix the flour and salt in a bowl. In a mixing bowl, cream the butter or margarine and sugar. Add the eggs, one at a time with a spoonful of flour. Stir in, then beat well. Fold in the remaining flour and the ground almonds. Add the lemon rind.

Spread a 2 cm / ¾ inch layer of the cake mixture on the base of the prepared tin. Divide the macaroon mixture into two equal portions; put half in the centre of the cake mixture. Add the rest of the mixture and spread the rest of the macaroon mixture on top. Cover with the blanched split almonds.

Bake for 1¼ hours, covering the top with greaseproof paper as soon as it is pale brown. Cool on a wire rack.

MAKES ONE 15 CM / 6 INCH CAKE

BATTENBURG CAKE

fat from greasing
100 g / 4 oz self-raising flour
pinch of salt
100 g / 4 oz butter or margarine
100 g / 4 oz caster sugar
2 eggs
pink food colouring
Apricot Glaze (page 134)
200 g / 7 oz Almond Paste (page 134)

Line and grease a 23 x 18 cm / 9 x 7 inch Battenburg tin, which has a metal divider down the centre; or use a 23 x 18 cm / 9 x 7 inch tin and cut double greaseproof paper to separate the mixture into 2 parts. Set the oven at 190°C / 375°F / gas 5. Mix the flour and salt in a bowl.

In a mixing bowl, cream the butter or margarine and sugar together until light and fluffy. Add the eggs, one at time, with a little flour. Stir in, then beat well. Stir in the remaining flour lightly but thoroughly.

Place half the mixture in one half of the tin. Tint the remaining mixture pink, and place it in the other half of the tin. Smoothe both mixtures away from the centre towards the outside of the tin.

Bake for 25–30 minutes. Leave the cakes in the tin for a few minutes, then transfer them to a wire rack and peel off the paper. Leave to cool completely.

To finish the Battenburg, cut each slab of cake lengthways into 3 strips. Trim off any crisp edges and rounded surfaces so that all 6 strips are neat and of the same size. Arrange 3 strips with 1 pink strip in the middle. Where the cakes touch, brush with the glaze and press together lightly. Make up the other layer in the same way, using 2 pink with 1 plain strip in the middle. Brush glaze over the top of the base layer and place the second layer on top.

Roll out the almond paste thinly into a rectangle the same length as the strips and wide enough to wrap around them. Brush it with glaze and place the cake in the centre. Wrap the paste around the cake and press the edges together lightly. Turn so that the join is underneath; trim the ends. Mark the top of the paste with the back of a knife to make a criss-cross pattern.

MAKES ONE 23 X 18 CM / 9 X 7 INCH CAKE

MARBLE CAKE

fat for greasing
175 g / 6 oz butter or margarine
175 g / 6 oz caster sugar
3 eggs, beaten
few drops of vanilla essence
225 g / 8 oz self-raising flour
pinch of salt
30 ml / 2 tbsp milk
30 ml / 2 tbsp strong black coffee
50 g / 2 oz chocolate, broken into chunks
Chocolate Fudge Icing (page 138)
15 ml / 1 tbsp grated chocolate

Line and grease a 20 cm / 8 inch round cake tin. Set the oven at 180°C / 350°F / gas 4.

In a mixing bowl cream the butter or margarine with the sugar until light and fluffy. Add the eggs gradually, beating well after each addition. Stir in the vanilla.

Sift the flour and salt into a bowl. Stir into the creamed mixture, lightly but thoroughly, until evenly mixed. Place half the mixture in a second bowl and beat in the milk.

Combine the coffee and chocolate in a bowl set over a saucepan of simmering water. Heat gently until the chocolate melts. Stir thoroughly, then add to the cake mixture in the mixing bowl, beating well.

Put alternative spoonfuls of plain and chocolate mixture into the prepared cake tin. Bake for 45–60 minutes, until firm to the touch. Cool on a wire rack. Top with the buttercream and grated chocolate.

MAKES ONE 20 CM / 8 INCH CAKE

VARIATION

- **Three-tone Marble Cake** This is a popular with children. Divide the cake mixture into three equal parts, leaving one plain, flavouring one with chocolate and tinting the third pink with food colouring. Combine and bake as suggested above.

MRS BEETON'S BRIDE CAKE

900 g / 2 lb plain flour
7.5 ml / 1½ tsp baking powder
7.5ml / 1½ tsp grated nutmeg
7.5 ml / 1½ tsp ground mace
2.5 ml / ½ tsp ground cloves
350 g / 12 oz ground almonds
900 g / 2 lb currants
350 g / 12 oz good quality candied citron and orange peel, chopped
675 g / 1½ lb butter
575 g / 1¼ lb caster sugar
11 eggs (size 3)
75 ml / 3 fl oz brandy
75 ml / 3 fl oz port or medium sherry

Line and grease a 30 cm / 12 inch round tin. Set the oven at 150°C / 300°F / gas 2. Sift the flour, baking powder and spices together, then stir in the ground almonds. In a separate bowl, mix the currants with the candied peel.

Cream the butter and sugar until the mixture is pale and soft. Beat the eggs together, then gradually beat them into the creamed mixture, adding spoonfuls of the flour mixture from curdling. Continue alternating additions of egg and flour until both are fully incorporated.

Mix in the currants and candied peel, brandy and port or sherry. Turn the mixture into the prepared tin and bake for about 4½ hours, or until the cake is cooked through. Test by inserting a skewer into the middle of the cake – if it comes out free of mixture the cake is cooked.

Leave the cake to cool in the tin for 1–2 hours, then turn it out on a wire rack to cool completely. Leave the greaseproof paper on the cake, wrap it in a clean covering of paper and store in an airtight container for at least a month. Ice and decorate as desired.

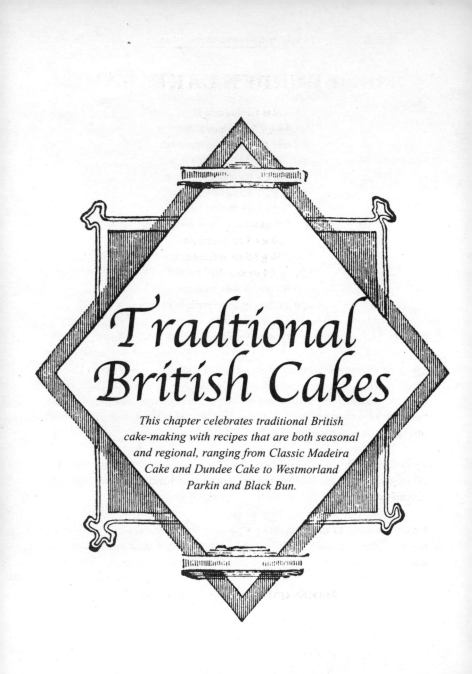

Tradtional British Cakes

This chapter celebrates traditional British cake-making with recipes that are both seasonal and regional, ranging from Classic Madeira Cake and Dundee Cake to Westmorland Parkin and Black Bun.

DUNDEE CAKE

fat for greasing
200 g / 7 oz plain flour
2.5 ml / ½ tsp baking powder
1.25 ml / ¼ tsp salt
150 g / 5 oz butter
150 g / 5 oz caster sugar
4 eggs, beaten
100 g / 4 oz glacé cherries, quartered
150 g / 5 oz currants
150 g / 5 oz sultanas
100 g / 4 oz seedless raisins
50 g / 2 oz cut mixed peel
50 g / 2 oz ground almonds
grated rind of 1 lemon
50 g / 2 oz blanched split almonds

Line and grease an 18 cm / 7 inch ground cake tin. Set the oven at 180°C / 350°F / gas 4. Sift the flour, baking powder and salt into a bowl. In a mixing bowl, cream the butter and sugar together well, and beat in the eggs. Fold the flour mixture, cherries, dried fruit, peel and ground almonds into the creamed mixture. Add the lemon rind and mix well.

Spoon into the prepared tin and make a slight hollow in the centre. Bake for 20 minutes, by which time the hollow should have filled in. Arrange the split almonds on top.

Return the cake to the oven, bake for a further 40–50 minutes, then reduce the temperature to 160°C / 325°F / gas 3 and bake for 1 hour more. Cool on a wire rack.

MAKES ONE 18 CM / 7 INCH CAKE

BLACK BUN

*A rich cake, encased in pastry, from the Highlands of Scotland, served either
on Twelfth Night (traditionally) or at Hogmanay to celebrate the new year.*

400 g / 14 oz plain flour
100 g / 4 oz blanched whole almonds, roughly chopped
675 g / 1½ lb muscatel raisins, seeded
675 g / 1½ lb currants
100 g / 4 oz cut mixed peel
200 g / 7 oz caster sugar
30 ml / 2 tbsp ground ginger
30 ml / 2 tbsp ground cinnamon
30 ml / 2 tbsp mixed spice
2.5 ml / ½ tsp freshly ground black pepper
10 ml / 2 tsp bicarbonate of soda
5 ml / 1 tsp cream of tartar
350 ml / 12 fl oz milk
15 ml / 1 tbsp brandy

PASTRY
450 g / 1 lb plain flour
225 g / 8 oz butter
5 ml / 1 tsp baking powder
flour for rolling out
beaten egg for glazing

Sift the flour into a large bowl. Add the almonds, fried fruit, peel, sugar and
spices and mix well. Stir in the bicarbonate of soda and the cream of tartar, then
moisten with the milk and brandy. Set the oven at 200°C / 400°F / gas 6.

Make the pastry. Put the flour into a mixing bowl. Rub in the butter until the
mixture resembles fine breadcrumbs, then add the baking powder. Stir in
enough water (about 125 ml / 4 fl oz) to form a stiff dough. Leave the dough to
rest for a few minutes, then roll out on a lightly-floured surface to a thickness
of about 5 mm / ¼ inch. Using three-quarters of the pastry, line a 23 cm / 9 inch
round cake tin (about 10 cm / 4 inches deep), leaving a border around the edges
for overlap. Roll out the remaining pastry for the lid.

Fill the pastry-lined tin with the cake mixture, and turn the edges of the pastry over it. Moisten the edges with water, put on the lid and seal. Decorate the pastry with any trimmings, prick with a fork all over the top and brush with egg.

Bake for 1 hour, then lower the oven temperature to 160°C / 325°F / gas 3, cover the top of the bun loosely with paper or foil and continue baking for 2 hours more.

Leave the bun to cool in the tin for 20 minutes, then remove it from the tin and cool completely. Keep for 1 month in an airtight tin before using.

MAKES ONE 23 CM / 9 INCH CAKE

CLASSIC MADEIRA CAKE

fat for greasing
150 g / 5 oz butter or margarine
150 g / 5 oz caster sugar
4 eggs, beaten
200 g / 7 oz plain flour
10 ml / 2 tsp baking powder
pinch of salt
grated rind of 1 lemon
caster sugar for dredging
1 thin slice of candied glacé citron peel

Line and grease a 15 cm / 6 inch round cake tin. Set the oven at 180°C / 350°F / gas 4.

In a mixing bowl, cream the butter or margarine with the sugar until light and fluffy. Gradually add the eggs, beating well after each addition. Sift the flour, baking powder and salt together into a second bowl, then fold into the creamed mixture. Stir in the lemon rind and mix well. Spoon into the prepared tin. Dredge the top with caster sugar.

Bake for 20 minutes, then lay the slice of peel on top. Bake for a further 45–50 minutes or until cooked through and firm to the touch. Cool on a wire rack.

MAKES ONE 15 CM / 6 INCH CAKE

WESTMORLAND PARKIN

This makes a dense, dark parkin with excellent keeping qualities.

fat for greasing
200 g / 7 oz butter or clarified dripping
450 g / 1 lb black treacle
450 g / 1 lb fine oatmeal
200 g / 7 oz plain flour
5 ml / 1 tsp ground ginger
2.5 ml / ½ tsp salt
10 ml / 2 tsp baking powder
200 g / 7 oz demerara sugar
100 ml / 3½ fl oz milk
5 ml / 1 tsp bicarbonate of soda

Line and grease two 20 cm / 8 inch square tins. Set the oven at 160°C / 325°F / gas 3.

Heat the butter or dripping and treacle gently in a saucepan, stirring until the fat has melted. Mix all the dry ingredients, except the bicarbonate of soda, in a mixing bowl and make a well in the centre.

Warm the milk in a saucepan over a low heat till hand-hot. Stir in the bicarbonate of soda until dissolved. Pour into the dry ingredients and mix well. Stir in the melted butter and treacle.

Spoon the mixture into the prepared tins and bake for about 1¼ hours or until cooked through and firm to the touch. Cool in the tins, then cut into squares.

MAKES TWO 20 CM / 8 INCH CAKES (ABOUT 32 SQUARES)

OLD ENGLISH CIDER CAKE

fat for greasing
225 g / 8 oz plain flour
7.5 ml / 1½ tsp grated nutmeg
1.25 ml / ¼ tsp ground cinnamon
5 ml / 1 tsp baking powder
pinch of salt
100 g / 4 oz butter or margarine
100 g / 4 oz caster sugar
2 eggs
125 ml / 4 fl oz dry still cider

Line and lightly grease a shallow 20 cm / 8 inch square cake tin. Set the oven at 180°C / 350°F / gas 4.

Sift the flour into a bowl with the spices, baking powder and salt. Cream the butter or margarine with the sugar until light and fluffy, then beat in the eggs. Beat half the flour mixture into the creamed mixture. Beat in half the cider. Repeat using the remaining flour and cider.

Spoon the mixture into the prepared tin and bake for 50–55 minutes until the cake is cooked through and firm to the touch. Cool the cake on a wire rack.

MAKES ONE 20 CM / 8 INCH CAKE

PATTERDALE PEPPER CAKE

Store this traditional British cake for at least a week before cutting.

fat for greasing
450 g / 1 lb self-raising flour
15 ml / 1 tbsp ground ginger
1.25 ml / ¼ tsp ground cloves
2.5 ml / ½ tsp freshly ground black pepper
100 g / 4 oz butter
200 g / 7 oz caster sugar
100 g / 4 oz seedless raisins
100 g / 4 oz currants
25 g / 1 oz golden syrup, warmed
2 large eggs, lightly beaten
125 ml / 4 fl oz skimmed milk

Line and grease a deep 18 cm / 7 inch square cake tin or a somewhat shallower 20 cm / 8 inch cake tin.

Set the oven at 160°C / 325°F / gas 3. Sift the flour, spices and black pepper into a mixing bowl. Rub in the butter until the mixture resembles fine breadcrumbs. Stir in the sugar, and add the fruit and peel. Make a well in the flour mixture, pour in the syrup, eggs and milk, and beat lightly.

Spoon the mixture into the prepared tin and bake for 2½ hours or until cooked through and firm to the touch. Cool on a wire rack.

MAKES ONE 18 CM / 7 INCH CAKE

SHEARING CAKE

*In Welsh this simple cake is known as 'Cacen Gneifio' and traditionally
it was prepared to serve with tea for all the farm workers who gathered
to help on days when the sheep were sheared and dipped.*

**butter for greasing
400 g / 14 oz plain flour
pinch of salt
10 ml / 2 tsp baking powder
200 g / 7 oz butter
225 g / 8 oz soft light brown sugar
grated rind of ½ lemon
20 ml / 4 tsp caraway seeds
5 ml / 1 tsp grated nutmeg or to taste
2 eggs
200 ml / 7 fl oz milk**

Line and grease a 20 cm / 8 inch round cake tin. Set the oven at 180°C / 350°F / gas 4.

Sift the flour, salt and baking powder into a mixing bowl. Rub in the butter until the mixture resembles breadcrumbs, then stir in the sugar, lemon rind and spices.

In a second bowl, beat the eggs lightly with the milk, then stir the liquid gradually into the dry ingredients.

Spoon the mixture into the prepared tin and back for 1½ hours or until cooked through and firm to the touch, covering the surface with a piece of greased paper or foil if it browns too quickly. Cool for 10 minutes in the tin, then invert on a wire rack to cool completely.

MAKES ONE 20 CM / 8 INCH CAKE

SEED CAKE

fat for greasing
200 g / 7 oz plain flour
1.25 ml / ¼ tsp salt
2.5 ml / ½ tsp baking powder
15 ml / 1 tbsp caraway seeds
150 g / 5 oz butter or margarine
150 g / 5 oz caster sugar
4 eggs, beaten
15 ml / 1 tbsp milk (optional)

Line and grease a 15 cm / 6 inch cake tin. Set the oven at 180°C / 350°F / gas 4. Sift the flour, salt and baking powder into a bowl. Stir in the caraway seeds and mix well. Set aside.

Place the butter or margarine in a mixing bowl and beat until very soft. Add the sugar and cream together until light and fluffy. Add the beaten eggs gradually, beating well after each addition. If the mixture shows signs of curdling, add a little of the flour mixture.

Fold in the dry ingredients lightly but thoroughly, adding the milk if too stiff.

Spoon into the prepared tin, smooth the surface and make a slight hollow in the centre. Bake for 30 minutes, then reduce the oven temperature to 160°C / 325°F / gas 3 and bake for a further 50 minutes until firm to the touch. Cool the cake on a wire rack.

MAKES ONE 15 CM / 6 INCH CAKE

GUY FAWKES GINGERBREAD

*Make this gingerbread at least a week before eating
and store in an airtight tin. It is best eaten sliced and spread
lightly with butter. An excellent treat for November 5th!*

fat for greasing
200 g / 7 oz plain flour
1.25 ml / ¼ tsp salt
15 ml / 1 tsp ground ginger
50 g / 2 oz soft light brown sugar
50 g / 2 oz butter or margarine
100 g / 4 oz black treacle
75 ml / 5 tbsp milk
5 ml / 1 tsp bicarbonate of soda
1 egg, beaten

Line and grease an 18 cm / 7 inch square tin or a 23 x 13 x 7.5 cm / 9 x 5 x 3 inch
loaf tin. Set the oven at 180°C / 350°F / gas 4.

Sift the flour, salt and ginger into a mixing bowl. Add the sugar. Heat the butter
or margarine, treacle, and most of the milk gently in a saucepan until the fat has
melted.

In a second saucepan, warm the remaining milk and stir in the bicarbonate of
soda until dissolved. Pour the melted mixture into the dry ingredients. Add the
beaten egg with the milk and soda mixture and beat well.

Pour into the prepared tin and bake for 20 minutes. Reduce the oven temperature to 150°C / 300°F / gas 2 and bake for a further 30–40 minutes until cooked
through and firm to the touch.

**MAKES ONE 18 CM / 7 INCH SQUARE CAKE
OR ONE 23 X 13 X 7.5 CM / 9 X 5 X 3 INCH LOAF**

Small Cakes

Small cakes can be simple or special.
Whether you intend to batch bake
for the freezer or prepare a treat for tea,
small cakes are quick to make
and easy to serve.

BASIC BUNS

These small buns may be baked in paper cases or greased patty tins
if preferred, in which case the consistency should be softer than when the
buns are put on a baking sheet. The mixture should drop off the spoon with
a slight shake, so increase the egg and milk mixture to about 150 ml / ¼ pint.
If baked in the patty tins, the mixture will make 14 to 16 buns.

fat for greasing
200 g / 7 oz self-raising flour
1.25 ml / ¼ tsp salt
75 g / 3 oz margarine
75 g / 3 oz sugar
1 egg
milk (see method)
Glacé Icing (page 139), to decorate (optional)

Thoroughly grease two baking sheets. Set the oven at 200°C / 400°F / gas 6.

Sift the flour and salt into mixing bowl. Rub in the margarine until the mixture resembles fine breadcrumbs. Stir in the sugar. Put the egg into a measuring jug and add enough milk to make up to 125 ml / 4 fl oz. Add the liquid to the dry ingredients and mix with a fork to a sticky, stiff mixture that will support the fork.

Divide the mixture into 12–14 portions. Form into rocky heaps on the prepared baking sheets, allowing about 2 cm / ¾ inch between each for spreading. Bake for 15–20 minutes or until each bun is firm to the touch on the base. Cool on a wire rack, then coat with glacé icing if liked.

MAKES TWELVE TO FOURTEEN

VARIATIONS

- **Chocolate Buns** Add 50 g / 2 oz cocoa to the flour and 5 ml / 1 tsp vanilla essence with the milk.
- **Chocolate Chip Buns** Add 100 g / 4 oz of chocolate chips with the sugar.
- **Coconut Buns** Add 75 g / 3 oz desiccated coconut with the flour and an extra 10 ml / 2 tsp milk.

continued overleaf...

- **Fruit Buns** Add 75 g / 3 oz mixed dried fruit with the sugar.
- **Seed Buns** Add 15 ml / 1 tbsp caraway seeds with the sugar.
- **Spice Buns** Add 5 ml / 1 tsp mixed spice or 2.5 ml / ½ tsp ground cinnamon and 2.5 ml / ½ tsp grated nutmeg with flour.
- **Walnut Orange Buns** Add the grated rind of 1 orange to the flour. Stir in 100 g / 4 oz finely chopped walnuts with the sugar.

GINGER BUNS

fat for greasing (optional)
150 g / 5 oz self-raising flour
pinch of salt
5 ml / 1 tsp ground ginger
1.25 ml / ¼ tsp ground cinnamon
75 g / 3 oz butter or margarine
50 g / 2 oz soft light brown sugar
25 g / 1 oz blanched almonds, chopped
1 egg
20 ml / 4 tsp black treacle
20 ml / 4 tsp golden syrup
30 ml / 2 tbsp milk

Grease 18–20 bun tins or arrange an equivalent number of paper cake cases on baking sheets. Set the oven at 190°C / 375°F / gas 5.

Sift the flour, salt and spices into a mixing bowl. Rub in the butter or margarine until the mixture resembles fine breadcrumbs. Stir in the sugar and almonds.

Put the egg into a jug and add the treacle, syrup and milk. Mix well. Add the liquid to the dry ingredients and beat until smooth.

Divide the mixture between the prepared bun tins or paper cases. Bake for 15–20 minutes or until well risen and cooked through. Cool on a wire rack.

MAKES EIGHTEEN TO TWENTY

BUTTERFLY CAKES

fat for greasing
100 g / 4 oz self-raising flour
pinch of salt
100 g / 4 oz butter or margarine
100 g / 4 oz caster sugar
2 eggs, beaten

DECORATION
150 ml / ¼ pint double cream
5 ml / 1 tsp caster sugar
1.25 ml / ¼ tsp vanilla essence
icing sugar for dusting

Grease 12–14 bun tins. Set the oven at 180°C / 350°F / gas 4. Mix the flour and salt in a bowl.

In a mixing bowl, cream the butter or margarine with the sugar until light and fluffy. Beat in the eggs, then lightly stir in the flour and salt. Divide the mixture evenly between the prepared bun tins, and bake for 15–20 minutes until golden brown. Cool on a wire rack.

In a bowl, whip the cream with the caster sugar and vanilla essence until stiff. Transfer to a piping bag fitted with a large star nozzle.

When the cakes are cold, cut a round off the top of each. Cut each round in half to create two 'butterfly wings'. Pipe a star of cream on each cake, then add the 'wings', placing them cut side down and slightly apart. Dust with icing sugar.

MAKES TWELVE TO FOURTEEN

CHOCOLATE SPICE SQUARES

The combination of chocolate and cinnamon makes these
delicious tray-bake cakes a bit different. If you want to
make them extra special, top them with melted chocolate.

fat for greasing
225 g / 8 oz margarine
225 g / 8 oz soft light brown sugar
4 eggs
225 g / 8 oz self-raising flour
30 ml / 2 tbsp cocoa
10 ml / 2 tsp cinnamon

Base-line and grease a roasting tin, measuring about 30 x 25 cm / 12 x 10 inches. Set the oven at 180°C / 350°F / gas 4.

Cream the margarine and sugar together until soft and light. Beat in the eggs. Sift the flour with the cocoa and the cinnamon, then fold these dry ingredients into the mixture.

Turn the mixture into the prepared tin and smooth it out evenly. Bake for about 1 hour, until the mixture is evenly risen and firm to the touch. Leave to cool in the tin for 15 minutes, then cut the cake into 5 cm / 2 inch squares and transfer them to a wire rack to cool completely.

MAKES 30

A VARIETY OF TRAY BAKES

By baking a large quantity of cake mixture in a roasting tin or large baking tin, then cutting it into squares, you can make a good batch of individual cakes very speedily. It is a good idea to set aside a roasting tin specifically for baking cakes. Use the mixture for the Chocolate Spice Squares as a base and try some of the ideas given here.

- **Fruit 'n' Nut Squares** Omit the cocoa from the mixture. Instead, fold in 225 g / 8 oz of chopped nuts – walnuts, hazelnuts or mixed nuts – and 100 g / 4 oz of mixed dried fruit.
- **Almond Squares** Omit the cocoa from the Chocolate Spice Squares. Add a few drops of almond essence to the fat and sugar. Fold in 225 g / 8 oz of ground almonds with the flour. Sprinkle 100 g / 4 oz of flaked almonds over the mixture once it is smoothed in the tin.

- **Coconut Squares** The chocolate can be omitted if liked, or it can be left in the mixture as its flavour is complementary to the coconut. Add 225 g / 8 oz of desiccated coconut after the flour is folded in. Soften the mixture with 60 ml / 4 tbsp of milk or orange juice. The cooked squares can be spread with apricot or raspberry jam and sprinkled with desiccated or long-thread coconut.
- **Marbled Squares** Prepare the mixture, omitting the cocoa. Divide it into two portions and flavour one half with cocoa. Add a little grated orange rind and juice to the second portion. Drop small spoonfuls of the mixture into the prepared tin and drag the point of the knife through just once. Do not over-swirl the two flavours or they will blend into one during cooking. Top the cooked cakes with melted chocolate.
- **Marmalade Squares** Make up the cake mixture, creaming 60 ml / 4 tbsp of marmalade with the fat and sugar and omitting the cocoa. Glaze the cakes with warmed marmalade.

HONEY BUNS

fat for greasing (optional)
200 g / 7 oz self-raising flour
pinch of salt
75 g / 3 oz butter or margarine
25 g / 1 oz caster sugar
1 egg
30 ml / 2 tbsp liquid honey
30 ml / 2 tbsp milk

Grease 18–20 bun tins or arrange an equivalent number of paper cake cases on baking sheets. Set the oven at 190°C / 375°F / gas 5.

Sift the flour and salt into a mixing bowl. Rub in the butter margarine until the mixture resembles fine breadcrumbs. Stir in the sugar.

Put the egg into a jug and add the honey and milk. Mix well. Add the liquid to the dry ingredients and beat until smooth.

Divide the mixture between the prepared bun tins or paper cases. Bake for 15–20 minutes or until well risen and cooked through. Cool on a wire rack.

MAKES EIGHTEEN TO TWENTY

ENGLISH MADELEINES

fat for greasing
100 g / 4 oz self-raising flour
pinch of salt
100 g / 4 oz butter or margarine
100 g / 4 oz caster sugar
2 eggs, beaten

DECORATION
45 ml / 3 tbsp smooth apricot jam
25 g / 1 oz desiccated coconut
glacé cherries, halved
20 angelica leaves

Thoroughly grease 10 dariole moulds. Set the oven at 180°C / 350°F / gas 4. Mix the flour and salt in a bowl.

In a mixing bowl, cream the butter or margarine with the sugar until light and fluffy. Beat in the eggs, then lightly stir in the flour and salt. Divide the mixture evenly between the prepared mould, and bake for 15–20 minutes until golden brown. Cool on a wire rack.

Trim off the rounded ends of the cakes, if necessary, and stand upright. Warm the jam in a small saucepan, then brush the cakes all over. Toss in the coconut. Decorate the top of each madeleine with a glacé cherry or angelica leaves or both.

MAKES TEN

BUTTERSCOTCH BROWNIES

Rich, gooey and delightfully chewy, these are bound to prove popular.

fat for greasing
75 g / 3 oz butter
175 g / 6 oz soft light brown sugar
1 egg, beaten
5 ml / 1 tsp vanilla essence
75 g / 3 oz plain flour
5 ml / 1 tsp baking powder
1.25 ml / ¼ tsp salt
50 g / 2 oz dates, chopped
50 g / 2 oz blanched almonds, chopped

Line and grease an 18 cm / 7 inch square tin. Set the oven at 160°C / 325°F / gas 3.

Combine the butter and sugar in a large heavy-bottomed saucepan and heat gently until all the sugar has dissolved, stirring occasionally. Remove from the heat, cool slightly, then blend in the egg and vanilla essence.

Sift the flour, baking powder and salt into a bowl. Add the dates and mix to coat in flour. Stir the flour mixture into the pan with the almonds and mix well.

Spoon the mixture into the prepared tin and bake for 20–30 minutes. Cool in the tin. When cold, cut into squares.

MAKES TWENTY

ROCK CAKES

fat for greasing
200 g / 7 oz self-raising flour
1.25 g / ¼ tsp salt
1.25 g / ¼ tsp grated nutmeg
75 g / 3 oz margarine
75 g / 3 oz sugar
75 g / 3 oz mixed dried fruit (currants, sultanas, mixed peel, glacé cherries)
1 egg
milk (see method)

Thoroughly grease two baking sheets. Set the oven at 200°C / 400°F / gas 6.

Sift the flour and salt into a mixing bowl. Add the nutmeg. Rub in the margarine until the mixture resembles fine breadcrumbs. Stir in the sugar and dried fruit.

Put the egg into a measuring jug and add enough milk to make up to 125 ml / 4 fl oz. Add the liquid to the dry ingredients and mix with a fork to a sticky stiff mixture that will support the fork.

Divide the mixture into 12–14 portions. Form into rocky heaps on the prepared baking sheets, allowing about 2 cm / ¾ inch between each for spreading. Bake for 15–20 minutes or until each bun is firm to the touch on the base. Cool on a wire rack.

MAKES TWELVE TO FOURTEEN

VARIATION

- **Coconut Cakes** Omit the dried fruit. Stir in 50 g / 2oz desiccated coconut instead. Bake as above.

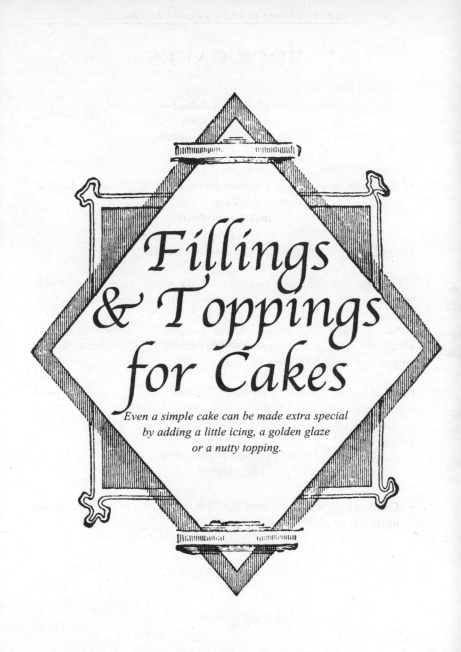

Fillings & Toppings for Cakes

Even a simple cake can be made extra special
by adding a little icing, a golden glaze
or a nutty topping.

APRICOT GLAZE

Brush this glaze over a cake before applying the marzipan.
Any yellow jam or marmalade may be used.

225 g / 8 oz apricot jam

Warm the jam with 30 ml / 2 tbsp water in a small saucepan over a low heat until the jam has melted. Sieve the mixture and return the glaze to the clean pan. Bring slowly to the boil allow to cool slightly before use.

SUFFICIENT TO COAT THE TOP AND SIDES
OF ONE 20 CM / 8 INCH CAKE

ALMOND PASTE

This recipe makes a pale, creamy yellow-coloured paste that can be used to cover and decorate cakes, as well as for a base coat before applying icing.

225 g / 8 oz ground almonds
100 g / 4 oz caster sugar
100 g / 4 oz icing sugar
5 ml / 1 tsp lemon juice
few drops of almond essence
1 egg, beaten

Using a coarse sieve, sift the almonds, caster sugar and icing sugar into a mixing bowl. Add the lemon juice, almond essence and sufficient egg to bind the ingredients together. Knead lightly with the fingertips until smooth.

Wrap in cling film and overwrap in foil or a plastic bag to prevent the paste drying out. Store in a cool place until required.

MAKES ABOUT 450 G / 1 LB

ALMOND PASTE AND MARZIPAN

Either almond paste or marzipan may be used to cover a Battenburg cake, to fill a Simnel cake or as a base for royal icing on a Christmas or wedding cake. Both almond paste and marzipan provide a flat, even surface over which icing will flow in a smooth glossy sheet, and as a bonus, will prevent crumbs from the cake spoiling the appearance of the icing. Marzipan resembles almond paste, but is smoother and more malleable. It is easier to use than almond paste when making moulded decorations or petits fours.

MARZIPAN

1 egg
1 egg white
200 g / 7 oz icing sugar, sifted
200 g / 7 oz ground almonds
5 ml / 1 tsp lemon juice
few drops of almond essence

Whisk the egg, egg white and icing sugar in a heatproof bowl over hot water until thick and creamy. Add the ground almonds with the lemon juice and almond essence and mix well. Work in more lemon juice, if necessary. When cool enough to handle, knead lightly until smooth. Use as for almond paste.

MAKES ABOUT 400 G / 14 OZ

GLAZE FOR SWEET FLANS

This slightly thickened glaze is useful for coating fruit as a decoration for light gâteaux. It can also be used with fresh fruit to top a plain cheesecake.

5 ml / 1 tsp arrowroot
150 ml / ¼ pint fruit syrup from canned or bottled fruit
or 150 ml / ¼ pint water and 25 g / 1 oz sugar
1–3 drops of food colouring
lemon juice (see method)

continued overleaf...

In a bowl, mix the arrowroot to a paste with a little of the cold fruit syrup or water. Pour the remaining syrup into a saucepan and bring to the boil. If using water, add the sugar and bring to the boil, stirring constantly until all the sugar has dissolved. Pour on to the arrowroot mixture, stir well, then return to the pan. Bring to the boil, stirring constantly. Add the appropriate food colouring, then stir in lemon juice to taste. Use at once.

SUFFICIENT TO GLAZE ONE 18 CM / 7 INCH FRUIT FLAN OR TWELVE TO SIXTEEN TARTLETS

COOKED ALMOND PASTE

This makes a smoother and more malleable paste than the uncooked mixture. Use it for moulding decorations and for covering wedding cakes.

450 g / 1 lb granulated sugar
1.25 ml / ¼ tsp cream of tartar
300 g / 11 oz ground almonds
2 egg whites
5 ml / 1 tsp almond essence
50 g / 2 oz icing sugar

Place the sugar with 150 ml / ¼ pint water in a saucepan over moderate heat. Stir occasionally until all the sugar had dissolved, then bring the syrup to the boil.

In a cup, dissolve the cream of tartar in 5 ml / 1 tsp water and stir in into the syrup. Boil, without stirring, until the syrup registers 115°C / 240°F on a sugar thermometer, the soft ball stage.

Remove the pan from the heat and immediately stir in the ground almonds followed by the unbeaten egg whites and almond essence. Return the pan to low heat and cook, stirring constantly, for 2 minutes. Set the pan aside until the mixture is cool enough to handle.

Sift the icing sugar on to a clean work surface, place the almond paste in the centre and knead with the fingertips until the sugar is absorbed. If the almond paste is sticky, leave to cool for longer and then add a little more icing sugar, if necessary. Cover lightly until cold, then wrap and store in a cool place, as for uncooked almond paste.

MAKES ABOUT 900 G / 2 LB

BUTTERCREAMS AND FUDGE ICINGS

These are soft icings made with butter and icing sugar, which may be used for filling or covering lighter cakes and gâteaux. On drying, an outer crust forms, but the icing remains soft underneath. The iced cake should be stored away from heat or direct sunlight.

Use unsalted butter if possible and flavour the icing as required. Soften the butter before using or try using a butter mixture that spreads easily even when chilled – these usually contain vegetable oil and therefore little or no extra liquid will be required when mixing the icing.

When adding food colouring to butter-based icings, do not expect clear colours. Avoid adding blue, as the yellow in the butter will turn it green. If a clear colour is essential, use white vegetable fat instead of butter.

All these icings may be spread with a palette knife or piped using a nozzle.

RICH BUTTERCREAM

This buttercream is enriched by the addition of an egg yolk.
Use only very fresh eggs and make sure that all utensils
used to prepare the buttercream are perfectly clean.

1 egg yolk
200 g / 7 oz icing sugar, sifted
100 g / 4 oz butter, softened
flavouring

Beat the egg yolk in a mixing bowl, adding the sugar gradually until the mixture is smooth. Beat in the butter, a little at a time with the flavouring.

SUFFICIENT TO FILL AND COAT THE TOP
OF ONE 20 CM / 8 INCH CAKE

BUTTERCREAM

100 g / 4 oz butter, softened
15 ml / 1 tbsp milk or fruit juice
225 g / 8 oz icing sugar, sifted
100 g / 4 oz butter, softened
flavouring

In a mixing bowl, cream the butter with the milk or juice and gradually work in the icing sugar. Beat the icing until light and fluffy. Alternatively, work all the ingredients in a food processor, removing the plunger for the final mixing to allow air to enter the buttercream mixture.

SUFFICIENT TO FILL AND COAT THE TOP
OF ONE 20 cm / 8 INCH CAKE

CHOCOLATE FUDGE ICING

100 g / 4 oz plain chocolate, broken into pieces
50 g / 2 oz butter, cut up
1 egg, beaten
175 g / 6 oz icing sugar, sifted

Combine the chocolate and butter in a heat-proof bowl. Set over hot water until the chocolate has melted. Beat in the egg, then remove the bowl from the heat and stir in half the icing sugar. Beat in the remaining sugar and continue beating until the icing is smooth and cold. Use immediately.

SUFFICIENT TO FILL AND COAT THE TOP
OF ONE 20 CM / 8 INCH CAKE

VARIATIONS

- **Chocolate Walnut Fudge Icing** Add 50 g / 2 oz of finely chopped walnuts to the icing just before spreading it on the cake.
- **Chocolate Rum Fudge Icing** Add 30 ml / 2 tbsp of rum to the icing with the egg and continue as in the main recipe.
- **Chocolate Orange Fudge Icing** Add the grated rind of 1 orange to the chocolate and butter. Continue as in the main recipe. This icing is excellent on a Victoria Sandwich Cake which has the grated rind of 1 orange added to the mixture.

GLACE ICING

Glacé icing is mainly used as a covering for light cakes. It is quick and easy to make and therefore ideal for simple, informal cakes. This icing can also be used to coat plain biscuits.

The consistency of the icing is all important; it should be stiff enough to coat the back of a spoon thickly. It should also be used immediately, and if left to stand, even for a short while, must be covered with cling film. Any decorations should be placed as soon as the cake is iced, or the surface may crack. Crystallized flower petals, chocolate decorations and small sweets which will shed colour should not be used.

GLACE ICING

This simple basic icing is quickly prepared and is ideal for topping
a plain sponge cake or a batch of small cakes. Make the icing just before
it is to be used and keep any extra decorations to the minimum.

100 g / 4 oz icing sugar, sifted
food colouring, optional

Place the icing sugar in a bowl. Using a wooden spoon gradually stir in sufficient water (about 15 ml / 1 tbsp) to create icing of a consistency that will thickly coat the back of the spoon. Take care not to add too much liquid or the icing will be too runny. At first the icing will seem quite stiff, but it slackens rapidly as the icing sugar absorbs the water. Stir in 1–2 drops of food colouring, if required.

SUFFICIENT TO COVER THE TOP OF ONE 18 CM / 7 INCH CAKE

VARIATIONS

- **Lemon or Orange Glacé Icing** Use 15 ml / 1 tbsp strained lemon or orange juice instead of the water.
- **Chocolate Glacé Icing** Combine 50 g / 2 oz plain chocolate, a knob of butter and 15 ml / 1 tbsp water in a heatproof bowl. Set over hot water until the chocolate and butter melt. Stir the mixture, gradually adding 100 g / 4 oz icing sugar. Stir in a little more water if required. This icing sets particularly quickly; use at once.
- **Coffee Glacé Icing** Dissolve 5 ml / 1 tsp instant coffee in 15 ml / 1 tbsp warm water and add instead of the water in the main recipe.
- **Liqueur-flavoured Glacé Icing** Replace half the water with the liqueur of your choice.

FROSTINGS

Frosting is usually spread thickly all over a cake, covering the sides as well as the top. When set, it is crisper than glacé icing, because the sugar is heated or boiled when making it. It should have a soft, spreading consistency when applied. Have the cake ready before starting to make the frosting.

AMERICAN FROSTING

225 g / 8 oz granulated sugar
pinch of cream of tartar
1 egg white
2.5 ml / ½ tsp vanilla essence or a few drops of lemon juice

Combine the sugar and cream of tartar in a small saucepan. Add 60 ml / 4 tbsp water. Place over low heat, stirring occasionally until the sugar has melted. Heat, without stirring, until the syrup registers 115°C / 240°F, the soft ball stage, on a sugar thermometer. Remove from the heat.

In a large grease-free bowl whisk the egg white until stiff. Pour on the syrup in a thin stream, whisking continuously. Add the flavouring and continue to whisk until the frosting is thick and glossy and stands in peaks.

Quickly spread over the cake. As the frosting cools, it may be swirled with a knife.

SUFFICIENT TO COVER THE TOP AND SIDES
OF ONE 18 CM / 7 INCH CAKE

QUICK AMERICAN FROSTING

175 g / 6 oz caster sugar
1 egg white
pinch of cream of tartar
pinch of salt

Heat a mixing bowl over a large saucepan of simmering water. Remove the bowl and place all the ingredients in it. Add 30 ml / 2 tbsp water and whisk with the rotary or electric whisk until the ingredients are well mixed.

Remove the pan of simmering water from the heat, place the bowl, over the water, and whisk until the frosting forms soft peaks. Use immediately.

SUFFICIENT TO COVER THE TOP AND SIDES
OF ONE 18 CM / 7 INCH CAKE

CARAMEL FROSTING

350 g / 12 oz soft light brown sugar
1.25 ml / ¼ tsp cream of tartar
2 egg whites
pinch of salt
5 ml / 1 tsp vanilla essence

Heat a mixing bowl over a large saucepan of boiling water. Remove the bowl and add all the ingredients except the vanilla essence. Add 150 ml / ¼ pint water and whisk with a rotary or electric whisk until well mixed.

Place the bowl over the water and continue to whisk until the frosting forms soft peaks. Remove the bowl from the water, add the essence and whisk the frosting for about 2 minutes more, until it reaches a spreading consistency. Use immediately.

SUFFICIENT TO FILL AND COVER THE TOP AND SIDES
OF ONE 18 CM / 7 INCH CAKE

TRADITIONAL FONDANT

Not to be confused with moulding icing or sugar paste icing, traditional fondant is poured over the cake. It sets to a dry, shiny finish that remains soft inside. It is widely used by commercial confectioners for petits fours and is also used as a filling for chocolates or to make sweets. Some specialist shops sell fondant icing in powdered form. This is a boon because small quantities may be made up by adding water or stock syrup. To use fondant, dilute with stock syrup. You will need a sugar thermometer to make fondant.

**450 g / 1 lb caster or lump sugar
20 ml / 4 tsp liquid glucose**

Put the sugar in a heavy-bottomed saucepan which is absolutely free from grease. Add 150 ml / ¼ pint water and heat gently until the sugar has completely dissolved. Stir very occasionally and use a wet pastry brush to wipe away any crystals that form on the side of the pan. When the sugar has dissolved add the liquid glucose and boil to 115°C / 240°F, the soft ball stage, without stirring. Keep the sides of the pan clean by brushing with the wet brush when necessary. Remove from the heat and allow the bubbles in the mixture to subside.

Pour the mixture slowly into the middle of a wetted marble slab and allow to cool a little. Work the sides to the middle with a sugar scraper or palette knife to make a smaller mass.

With a wooden spatula in one hand and the scraper in the other, make a figure of eight with the spatula, keeping the mixture together with the scraper. Work until the whole mass is completely white.

Break off small amounts and knead well, then knead together to form a ball.

Store in a screw-topped jar, or wrap closely in several layers of polythene. When required, dilute with stock syrup (opposite).

MAKES ABOUT 450 G / 1 LB FONDANT

STOCK SYRUP

Use this syrup when diluting fondant. It may also be kneaded into commercially made almond paste to make the paste more pliable.

150 g / 5 oz granulated sugar

Put the sugar in a saucepan and add 150 ml / ¼ pint water. Heat, stirring occasionally, until the sugar had dissolved; boil without stirring for 3 minutes. Use a spoon to remove any scum that rises to the surface.

Allow the syrup to cool, then strain into a screw-topped jar; close the jar tightly. If not required immediately, store in a cool place (not the refrigerator) for up to 2 months.

MAKES ABOUT 200 ML / 7 FL OZ

ROYAL ICING

Royal icing is used for special celebration cakes, especially for wedding cakes, because the icing has sufficient strength when it sets hard to hold the tiers. The icing cannot be applied directly to the cake because it would drag the crumbs and discolour badly, so rich fruit cakes are usually covered with a layer of almond paste or marzipan before the royal icing is applied.

ROYAL ICING QUANTITIES

Quick guide to quantities required to cover cakes (sufficient for 3 coats):

ROUND	ROYAL ICING
15 cm / 6 inch	575 g / 1¼ lb
18 cm / 7 inch	675 g / 1½ lb
20 cm / 8 inch	800 g / 1¾ lb
23 cm / 9 inch	900 g / 2 lb
25 cm / 10 inch	1 kg / 2¼ lb
28 cm / 11 inch	1.25 kg / 2¾ lb
30 cm / 12 inch	1.4 kg / 3 lb

SQUARE	ROYAL ICING
15 cm / 6 inch	675 g / 1½ lb
18 cm / 7 inch	800 g / 1¾ lb
20 cm / 8 inch	900 g / 2 lb
23 cm / 9 inch	1 kg / 2¼ lb
25 cm / 10 inch	1.25 kg / 2¾ lb
28 cm / 11 inch	1.4 kg / 3 lb
30 cm / 12 inch	1.5 kg / 3¼ lb

ROYAL ICING

It is vital to ensure that the bowl is clean and free from grease.
Use a wooden spoon kept solely for the purpose and do not be tempted
to skimp on the beating – insufficient beating will produce an
off-white icing with a heavy, sticky texture.

2 egg whites
450 g / 1 lb icing sugar, sifted

Place the egg whites in a bowl and break them up with a fork. Gradually beat in about two-thirds of the icing sugar with a wooden spoon and continue beating for about 15 minutes until the icing is pure white and forms soft peaks. Add the remaining icing sugar, if necessary, to attain this texture. Cover the bowl with cling film and place a dampened tea-towel on top. Place the bowl inside a polythene bag if storing overnight or for longer.

Before use, lightly beat the icing to burst any air bubbles that have risen to the surface. Adjust the consistency for flat icing or piping.

SUFFICIENT TO COAT THE TOP AND SIDES
OF ONE 20 CM / 8 INCH CAKE

SUGAR PASTE

Since the introduction of this versatile and easy-to-use icing from the humid regions of Australia and South Africa, where royal icing does not dry well, cake decorating has been revolutionized. Sugar paste, also known as decorating icing or mallow paste, resembles commercially made marzipan in its properties, texture and application (although not in colour or flavour). Sometimes it is referred to as fondant icing but it must not be confused with a traditional, pouring fondant. It is rolled out and moulded over the cake. In many cases this makes a base layer of marzipan unnecessary. It is, therefore, widely used on sponge cakes and because it can be easily coloured, makes wonderful novelty cakes and plaques.

If well wrapped in polythene the paste will keep for several weeks in a cupboard. Do not store it in the refrigerator as it would lose its elasticity and become difficult to work.

Sugar paste is malleable and may be moulded into shapes and petals for flowers. When worked into very thin pieces, it will dry hard and brittle.

As a general rule, it is best not to freeze a whole cake covered in this icing, especially if different colours have been used. This is because the icing becomes wet and the colours may run into each other. If only a small area of the cake has sugar paste icing, as in a novelty cake covered in buttercream with moulded icing features, the cake can be frozen. When required, it must be taken out of the freezer, all wrappings removed and left at room temperature for 4–5 hours to allow the icing to dry off.

SUGAR PASTE

675 g / 1½ lb icing sugar, sifted
2 medium egg whites
30 ml / 2 tbsp warmed liquid glucose
5 ml / 1 tsp glycerine

Place the icing sugar in a clean, grease-free bowl. Add the remaining ingredients and work together with either a clean wooden spoon or the fingertips. Place the rough mixture on a clean surface dusted with icing sugar and knead hard for several minutes until smooth, pliable and not sticky, adding a little extra icing sugar if necessary. Wrap the sugar paste in polythene and leave to rest for 24 hours before using.

SUFFICIENT TO COVER THE TOP AND SIDES
OF ONE 20 CM / 8 INCH CAKE
SUGAR PASTE QUANTITIES

Quick guide to quantities required to cover cakes:

ROUND	SUGAR PASTE
15 cm / 6 inch	450 g / 1 lb
18 cm / 7 inch	575 g / 1¼ lb
20 cm / 8 inch	675 g / 1½ lb
23 cm / 9 inch	800 g / 1¾ lb
25 cm / 10 inch	900 g / 2 lb
28 cm / 11 inch	1 kg / 2¼ lb
30 cm / 12 inch	1.1 kg / 2½ lb

SQUARE	SUGAR PASTE
15 cm / 6 inch	575 g / 1¼ lb
18 cm / 7 inch	675 g / 1½ lb
20 cm / 8 inch	800 g / 1¾ lb
23 cm / 9 inch	900 g / 2 lb
25 cm / 10 inch	1 kg / 2¼ lb
28 cm / 11 inch	1.1 kg / 2½ lb
30 cm / 12 inch	1.4 kg / 3 lb

CREAM FILLINGS

Fresh cream is still a prime favourite as a filling for gâteaux and afternoon tea cakes. Double cream has the best flavour and may be whipped and piped in much the same way as royal icing. Once whipped, it may be frozen on the decorated gâteau and will not lose its shape when thawed. To reduce the risk of over-whipping, which might cause the cream to separate in hot weather, add 15 ml / 1 tbsp milk to each 150 ml / ¼ pint cream with single cream. There is no need to add sugar to whipped cream.

TO WHIP THE CREAM

Choose a cool area of the kitchen in which to work and chill the bowl and whisk before use, by placing them in a refrigerator or freezer for a few minutes. A small wire balloon whisk is the best utensil, but for large quantities a hand-held electric whisk may be used with care.

Stand the bowl on a wet cloth or a non-slip surface, add the cream and tip the bowl. While whipping, incorporate as much air as possible. If using an electric whisk, start on high and reduce speed to low as the cream begins to thicken. Be very careful not to overwhip. Stop whipping as soon as the cream will stand in soft peaks and has doubled in volume.

The cream will continue to thicken slightly on standing and when piped, so stop whipping just before you think the cream is ready. It should be smooth and shiny in appearance. Overwhipped cream will 'frill' at the edges when piped.

For best results, use the whipped cream immediately, or cover the bowl and store in the refrigerator until required, giving it a gentle stir before use.

If the finished gâteau is to stand in a warm room for any length of time, whip in 5 ml / 1 tsp gelatine dissolved in 10 ml / 2 tsp warm water, and cool.

FLAVOURINGS

Add any flavouring to cream when it has been whipped to soft peaks. Lemon or orange juice, liqueur or sherry may be used and should be added gradually during the final whipping. Once the cream has been whipped, finely-chopped nuts, glacé fruits or grated citrus rind may be added.

REDUCING THE FAT CONTENT

For a low-fat whipped cream, replace up to one third with low- or full-fat plain yogurt. This will not only make the cream less rich, but will prevent overwhipping and keep the cream smooth and shiny.

FREEZING

Cakes decorated with cream should be frozen and stored in a large plastic box. Alternatively, open freeze and then cocoon carefully in a dome of foil. Label well to avoid other items being inadvertently placed on top.

To thaw, remove the wrappings and thaw the cakes in a cool place, refrigerator or microwave (following the manufacturer's directions).

Small quantities of leftover cream may be whipped with a little caster sugar and piped in small stars on non-stick baking parchment for freezing. They may then be lifted off and placed, still frozen, on desserts and gâteaux for instant decoration.

MRS BEETON'S TIP

These light fillings, thickened with eggs, go very well with light sponge cakes and gâteaux that are filled or decorated with fresh fruit. They can also be used to decorate cheesecakes. This type of filling should not be frozen as it tends to curdle.

CUSTARD FILLINGS

Confectioners' Custard, sometimes called Crème Pâtissière, makes an excellent filling for cakes. Thickened with eggs, flour or cornflour, the custard sets to a thick cream when cold. Mock Cream is a simple filling based on milk thickened with cornflour and enriched with butter, while Quick Diplomat Cream is richer still, with double cream used as its base.

Unless using a double saucepan, it is easier to make these custards with yolks rather than whole eggs as the whites cook more quickly and lumps of cooked egg white may spoil the texture.

Vanilla sugar may be used instead of caster sugar in the recipes that follow. The vanilla pod or essence should then be omitted.

To prevent the formation of a skin on the cooked custard, press a dampened piece of greaseproof paper lightly on the surface. Do not use plasticized cling film for this purpose when the custard is hot.

CONFECTIONERS' CUSTARD

300 ml / ½ pint milk
1 vanilla pod or a few drops of vanilla essence
2 egg yolks
50 g / 2 oz caster sugar
25 g / 1 oz plain flour

Place the milk and vanilla pod, if used, in a small saucepan and bring to the boil over low heat. Remove from the heat and leave to one side, adding the vanilla essence, if used.

Whisk the egg yolks with the sugar in a bowl until thick and creamy, then add the flour. Remove the vanilla pod and very gradually add the milk to the egg mixture, beating constantly until all has been incorporated. Pour the mixture back into the pan and stir over low heat for 1–2 minutes to cook the flour. The custard should thickly coat the back of the wooden spoon and be smooth and shiny.

Pour the custard into a clean bowl, cover and leave to cool. Beat well, then cover again and chill until required.

MAKES ABOUT 300 ML / ½ PINT

VARIATIONS
- **Chocolate Custard** Stir 25 g / 1 oz grated chocolate into the custard while still hot.
- **Crème St Honore** Whisk 2 egg whites with 10 ml / 2 tsp of caster sugar until stiff. Fold into cold custard. Use for choux pastry or as an alternative cream for gâteaux.
- **Crème Frangipane** Omit the vanilla flavouring. Add 40 g / 1½ oz finely chopped butter to final cooking. When cold, fold in 75 g / 3 oz crushed almond macaroons or 50 g / 2 oz ground almonds and a few drops of almond essence.

MOCK CREAM

10 ml / 2 tsp cornflour
150 ml / ¼ pint milk
50 g / 2 oz butter, softened
50 g / 2 oz icing or caster sugar
few drops of vanilla or almond essence

Mix the cornflour with a little milk in a small saucepan. Gradually stir in the remaining milk and cook over low heat, stirring constantly until the mixture thickens. Cover and leave until tepid.

Cream the butter and sugar together in a bowl until light and fluffy. Gradually add the custard mixture to the butter, beating well between each addition. Beat in the essence, cover the bowl and chill.

SUFFICIENT FOR TWO LAYERS IN ONE 18 CM / 7 INCH CAKE

QUICK DIPLOMAT CREAM

15 ml / 1 tbsp custard powder
10 ml / 2 tsp caster sugar
150 ml / ¼ pint milk
150 ml / ¼ pint double cream
few drops of vanilla essence

Mix the custard powder and sugar with a little milk in a small saucepan. Gradually stir in the remaining milk and stir over low heat for 1 minute until thick. Transfer the mixture to a bowl, cover and leave to cool. Beat well then cover again and chill.

In a clean bowl, whip the cream with the vanilla essence until thick. Beat the custard until smooth and lightly fold in the cream until well blended. Chill until required.

MAKES ABOUT 300 ML / ½ PINT

VARIATIONS
- **Orange or Lemon** Fold in 5 ml / 1 tsp finely grated orange or lemon rind.
- **Chocolate** Stir 50 g / 2 oz grated chocolate into the hot custard.
- **Liqueur** Replace the essence with brandy or liqueur.

TOPPINGS

These simple toppings may be prepared in advance and used to decorate and finish a cake or gâteau quickly. Most toppings can be stored in a screw-topped jar or in a cardboard box for several months. A wide variety of simple decorations are available from grocers, supermarkets and sweet shops. The choice includes chocolate vermicelli and buttons, crystallized flowers and fruits, dragees, liquorice sweets, sugar strands and sugared almonds.

COCONUT

Coconut has an interesting texture and makes a good topping on plain cakes. Choose good-quality desiccated coconut with large strands and use plain or colour as follows: Place about 50 g / 2 oz coconut in a screw-topped jar, leaving at least 2.5 cm / 1 inch space at the top. Add a few drops of food colouring (liquid colours are best), screw on the lid and shake the jar vigorously for a few minutes until the coconut is evenly coloured. Use the same day or spread the coconut out on a piece of greaseproof paper and leave in a warm place to dry before storing in a dry screw-topped jar.

Toasted coconut is prepared in the same way as Toasted Nuts (opposite).

COLOURED SUGAR CRYSTALS

Use either granulated sugar or roughly crushed sugar lumps and colour and dry in the same way as the coloured coconut above.

TOASTED NUTS

Whole flaked or chopped nuts may be lightly tasted to improve both colour and flavour. Almonds and hazelnuts are the most commonly used varieties.

To toast nuts, remove the rack from the grill pan and line the pan with a piece of foil. Spread the nuts over the foil. Heat the grill and toast the nuts under a medium heat, stirring occasionally until evenly browned. This will only take a few seconds. Lift out the foil carefully and leave the nuts to cool. This method may also be used to remove the skins from hazelnuts. Roast them under the grill, then rub the skins off while still hot.

Toasted nuts are best used on the same day, alternatively, store when cold in a screw-topped jar for a few days.

PRALINE

This is a fine powder of crushed nuts and caramel used to flavour creams and fillings. Crushed roughly, it may be used as a cake decoration.

oil for greasing
100 g / 4 oz caster sugar
100 g / 4 oz blanched almonds, toasted

Brush a baking sheet with oil. Place the sugar in a small heavy-bottomed saucepan with 15 ml / 1 tbsp water. Heat slowly until the sugar dissolved, stirring occasionally. Continue cooking until the sugar turns from pale golden in colour to deep golden. Stir in the toasted blanched almonds. Quickly pour the mixture on to the prepared baking sheet and leave until cold.

Crush the caramel to a fine powder with a rolling pin or pestle and mortar. Alternatively, break it up roughly and crush in a blender. Store the powder in a dry screw-topped jar for up to 3 months.

MAKES ABOUT 225 G / 8 OZ

CHOCOLATE AND ITS USES

Dark and bitter, smooth and milky or pale and creamy – there are many types of chocolate available now and they can be put to a wide variety of uses.

Chocolate is a blend of cocoa solids and cocoa butter to which varying quantities of vegetable fats, milk and sugar have been added. The quantity of added fat determines the hardness or softness of the chocolate.

A block of chocolate can be finely or coarsely grated, chopped, slivered and curled for decorating or coating the sides and tops of cakes.

Melted chocolate is malleable; it dries to a smooth, glossy film. It flavours and provides texture, as well as setting quality, to icings and fillings. Melted chocolate has many other uses: it can be poured over cakes, or fruits or marzipan and nuts can be dipped in it. Chocolate leaves are made by coating real leaves. Chocolate curls, known as caraque, are a widely used decoration. Melted chocolate can also be set in a thin sheet, then cut into shapes, for example squares, triangles or shaped using cutters. The melted chocolate can also be piped.

Milk and Plain Chocolate Milk chocolate has added milk products and is paler and softer in texture than plain chocolate which is darker and more brittle. The quantity of added sugar determines the sweetness. Milk chocolate contains more sugar than plain chocolate which is available as bitter, semi-sweet or plain. The quality of the product varies widely, particularly with plain chocolate.

Chocolate-flavoured Cake Covering This is not true chocolate. In this product the cocoa butter is replaced by other fats which make it more malleable. The resulting flavour is poor and the texture waxy. It is useful for inexpensive, everyday cakes but it should not be applied when a good result is required.

White Chocolate This is made from cocoa butter, sugar and milk and does not contain any of the cocoa solids or non-fat parts of the cocoa-bean. Quality varies, with some bars of white chocolate having a poor, very sweet flavour. This is best bought from a good cake decorating supplier.

Carob This is manufactured from the pulp of the carob or locust bean to resemble chocolate in appearance. It is naturally sweeter than cocoa so less sugar is added; also, it is caffeine-free. It is available in powder form for cooking and in block form for eating uncooked. Carob can be used instead of chocolate for some of the following decorations but it is waxy in consistency and does not have such a glossy appearance as chocolate.

STORING CHOCOLATE DECORATIONS

Store chocolate decorations in a cool, dry atmosphere for the shortest possible time, and no longer than seven to ten days. Chocolate will sweat if it is kept in a warm room. On very hot days keep the chocolate in the refrigerator but bring it to room temperature before melting it.

MELTED CHOCOLATE

Break up or roughly chop the chocolate and place it in a bowl that fits over a saucepan. Place about 5 cm / 2 inches of water in the pan and bring it to the boil, then remove the pan from the heat and stand the bowl over it. Leave for a few minutes, then stir the chocolate until it has melted and is smooth and glossy. If you leave the pan on the heat, the chocolate will overheat and white streaks may appear in it when it sets again.

DIPPING FOOD IN CHOCOLATE

Biscuits, choux buns, nuts, marzipan shapes, real leaves and fruits such as maraschino cherries, grapes, raisins, dates, strawberries and slices of banana can all be dipped in melted chocolate. They can be part-dipped or fully dipped according to the effect required. Special dipping forks have two long prongs that are bent at the ends to stop the food falling off when dipped. Alternatively, use a corn-on-the-cob fork, cocktail stick or two fine skewers, one on either side of the food. For larger pieces of food such as choux buns, or hard foods such as almonds, it is best to use your fingers to dip the ingredients.

Melt the chocolate following the instructions left. For dipping food the consistency should be thick enough to coat the back of a spoon. If the chocolate is too thin, remove the bowl from the pan and leave it to cool slightly, until the chocolate thickens. Keep the chocolate arm (over the saucepan of water), which you are working. If the chocolate becomes too thick, remove the bowl, reheat the water, then replace the bowl. Stir the chocolate occasionally as you are dipping the food; this gives you a glossy finish.

You will need a good depth of melted chocolate to dip food successfully; it should be at least 5 cm / 2 inches deep. (When the chocolate becomes too shallow for successful dipping, do not discard it; stir the excess into buttercream or similar icings to avoid wastage).

Line a baking sheet or wire rack with a sheet of waxed paper or non-stick baking parchment. Have ready all the food to be dipped and start with firm items, such as nuts and marzipan. Finish with soft foods, such as fruits. Plunge the food into the chocolate to the depth required, then quickly withdraw it at the same angle at which it was plunged. Do not rotate part-dipped food in the chocolate or the top line of chocolate will be uneven. Gently shake the food to allow the excess chocolate to fall back into the bowl, then place it on the prepared sheet or rack to dry.

TO DIP LEAVES

Select clean, undamaged leaves such as rose leaves. Thoroughly wash the leaves, rubbing them to remove any dust, dirt or sap. Dry well and brush the underside to each leaf over the surface of the chocolate. Dry the leaves chocolate side uppermost, then carefully peel away the leaf, leaving the impression of the leaf on the chocolate.

PIPING CHOCOLATE

When adding chocolate decoration to the top of a cake, melted chocolate is difficult to pipe because it begins to set in the nozzle. Mixing a little icing sugar with it will make it more malleable; this is not suitable for piping shapes that have to set hard.

25 g / 1 oz icing sugar, sifted
100 g / 4 oz chocolate, melted

Stir the icing sugar into the melted chocolate with a few drops of water to make a mixture of a thick piping consistency that drops from the spoon.

PIPING WITH CHOCOLATE

The chocolate should be of a thin, flowing consistency. Very little pressure is required to pipe the chocolate as it should flow slowly out of the bag without any encouragement.

TO PIPE MOTIFS AND SHAPES

Trace a design on to thick white card and cover it with waxed paper, taping both securely on to a board. Alternatively, work freehand on to the waxed paper.

Place 30–45 ml / 2–3 tbsp melted chocolate in an icing bag made of baking parchment (or purchased from cake decorating suppliers) and snip off the end. Start with a fine hole until you have checked the size of the piping. It is a good idea to practice piping beads and buttons on the paper first. Pipe the shapes, making sure that all the lines of piping are joined somewhere in the design. Shapes may be filled in using a different coloured chocolate, such as milk chocolate or white chocolate with plain chocolate. Leave the shapes to dry hard.

CHOCOLATE CURLS OR SCROLLS (CARAQUE)

Whether you are making curls or frills the chocolate is prepared in the same way: pour melted chocolate over a clean, dry surface, such as a marble slab or a clean smooth area of work surface. Spread the chocolate backwards and forwards with a large palette knife until it is smooth, fairly thin and even. Leave to dry until almost set; do not allow the chocolate to set hard.

Hold a long, thin-bladed knife at an acute angle to the chocolate. Hold the top of the knife with the other hand and pull the knife towards you with a gentle sawing action, scraping off a thin layer of chocolate which curls into a roll.

CHOCOLATE FRILLS

Starting at the edge of the chocolate, hold the tip of a small palette knife at an angle of 45 degrees or lower to the surface, and push the palette knife away from you. A thin layer of chocolate will fill as you push. Place the frills on waxed paper as you make them.

TO CUT CHOCOLATE SHAPES

Spread the melted chocolate on to waxed paper or non-stick baking parchment paper. Use petits fours cutters or small biscuit cutters, to stamp shapes out of the chocolate, cutting them as close together as possible. Leave to set hard before peeling away the paper. The excess chocolate can be finely chopped for decorations or melted for use in making more shapes.

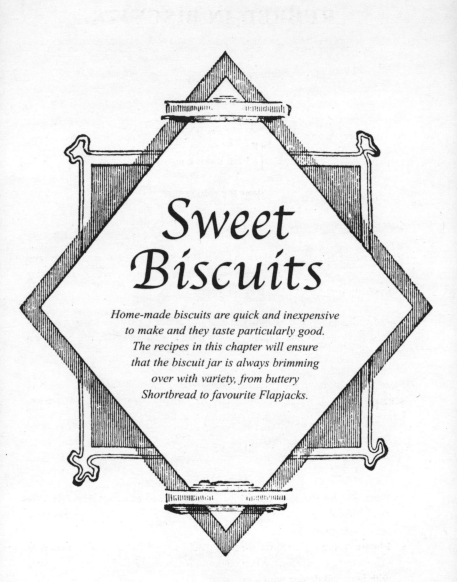

Sweet Biscuits

*Home-made biscuits are quick and inexpensive
to make and they taste particularly good.
The recipes in this chapter will ensure
that the biscuit jar is always brimming
over with variety, from buttery
Shortbread to favourite Flapjacks.*

RUBBED-IN BISCUITS

This simple method may be used for making a wide variety of biscuits.

fat for greasing
200 g / 7 oz plain flour
1.25 ml / ¼ tsp salt
75–100 g / 3–4 oz butter or margarine
50 g / 2 oz caster sugar
5 ml / 1 tsp baking powder
1 egg yolk
flour for rolling out

Grease two baking sheets. Set the oven at 180°C / 350°F / gas 4.

In a mixing bowl, mix the flour and salt. Rub in the butter or margarine until the mixture resembles fine breadcrumbs, then stir in the sugar and baking powder. Bind to a stiff paste with the egg yolk.

Knead well and roll our to a thickness of just under 1 cm / ¼ inch on a lightly-floured surface. Cut into rounds with a 5 cm / 2 inch cutter. Re-roll and re-cut any trimmings.

Place the biscuits on the prepared baking sheets, pricking the top of each in several places. Bake for 12–15 minutes or until firm and pale golden brown. Leave to stand for a few minutes, then cool on a wire rack.

MAKES 20–26

VARIATIONS

- **Plain Mocha Biscuits** Add 50 g / 2 oz powdered drinking chocolate with the flour and 10 ml / 2 tsp instant coffee dissolved in 7.5 ml / 1½ tsp boiling water with the eggs.
- **Plain Cinnamon or Spice Biscuits** Add 5 ml / 1 tsp ground cinnamon or mixed spice to the flour. When cold, sandwich the biscuits together in pairs with jam, and dredge with icing sugar.
- **Plain Coconut Biscuits** Use 150 g / 5 oz flour and 50 g / 2 oz desiccated coconut. As soon as the biscuits are cooked, brush with warm Apricot Glaze (page 134) and sprinkle with coconut.

SIMPLE BISCUITS

The mixture for these plain biscuits is simply rolled into balls,
which are then flattened slightly on the baking sheet.

fat for greasing
100 g / 4 oz butter
100 g / 4 oz soft light brown sugar
1 egg, beaten
grated rind of 1 lemon
225 g / 8 oz self-raising flour

Grease two or more baking sheets. Set the oven at 160°C / 325°F / gas 3. Cream the butter and sugar together until soft and creamy. Beat in the egg and lemon rind, then stir in the flour to make a soft dough.

Roll small pieces of dough into balls about the size of walnuts. Wet your hands under cold running water to prevent the mixture from sticking to them. Place the balls well apart on the baking sheets and flatten them slightly with a fork.

Bake for 20–25 minutes, until the biscuits are spread, risen and brown. Leave the biscuits on the baking sheets for a minute or so, then transfer them to a wire rack to cool.

MAKES 25–30

REFRIGERATOR BISCUITS

The dough for refrigerator biscuits is prepared, shaped and wrapped in foil.
Then it is chilled until firm and slices into biscuits. The uncooked dough can
be stored in the refrigerator for one to two weeks.

fat for greasing
150 g / 5 oz butter
100 g / 4 oz caster sugar
5 ml / 1 tsp vanilla essence
1 small egg, beaten
225 g / 8 oz plain flour

Thoroughly grease two or more baking sheets. Cream the butter with the sugar and vanilla until very pale and soft. Beat in the egg, then stir in the flour to make a soft dough.

Press the mixture together with a spatula, then turn it out on to a sheet of foil. Roughly shape the dough into a roll, then wrap the foil over it. Roll the wrapped dough until it forms a smooth, evenly thick roll measuring about 3.75–5 cm / 1½–2 inches in diameter. Open the foil and pat the ends of the roll neatly into shape, then re-wrap the dough and chill it for about 1 hour or until quite firm.

The dough can be stored until the biscuits are to be cooked. Set the oven at 180°C / 350°F / gas 4. Cut the dough into slices about 5 mm / ¼ inch thick, or slightly less, and place them on the prepared baking sheets. Set the biscuits apart to allow room for spreading.

Bake the biscuits for 12–15 minutes, until golden, then leave them on the sheets for about a minute before transferring them to a wire rack.

MAKES ABOUT 50

VARIATION

• **Pinwheel Biscuits** Divide the dough in half and flavour one portion to taste – add cocoa, coffee essence, orange rind or finely chopped nuts. Cut both types of dough in half. Roll out a portion of plain dough into an oblong measuring about 25 x 35 cm / 12 x 14 inches. Roll out a portion of flavoured dough the same size. Lift the flavoured dough on the rolling pin and place it over the plain dough. Roll up the sheets of dough together like a Swiss roll. Press firmly into shape, wrap and chill. Repeat with the remaining portions of dough. Slice and bake the biscuits as in the main recipe.

SHORTBREAD

Shortbread should be handled as lightly – and as little – as possible; if the dough is worked too much, it will toughen. Wooden moulds, carved with an appropriate motif such as a thistle, are sometimes used for this Scottish speciality, but it is easier to shape the dough by hand.

fat for greasing
100 g / 4 oz plain flour
1.25 ml / ¼ tsp salt
50 g / 2 oz rice flour, ground rice or semolina
50 g / 2 oz caster sugar
100 g / 4 oz butter

Invert a baking sheet, then grease the surface now uppermost. Set the oven at 180°C / 350°F / gas 4.

Mix all the ingredients in a mixing bowl. Rub in the butter until the mixture binds together to a dough. Shape into a large round about 1 cm / ¼ inch thick. Pinch up the edges to decorate. Place on the prepared baking sheet, and prick with a fork. Bake for 40–45 minutes. Cut into wedges while still warm.

MAKES EIGHT WEDGES

VARIATIONS

- **Shortbread Biscuits** Roll out the dough on a lightly-floured surface to a thickness of just under 1 cm / ¼ inch. Cut into rounds with a 5–6 cm / 2–2½ inch cutter. Place on 1–2 greased baking sheets, allowing room for spreading. Prick the surface of each biscuit in several places with a fork. Bake for 15–20 minutes. Leave to stand for a few minutes, then cool on a wire rack.
- **Original Scotch Shortbread** Omit the salt and rice flour, and use 225 g / 8 oz plain flour. Reduce the sugar to 25 g / 1 oz. Add 10 ml / 2 tsp caraway seeds. Top the shortbread round with strips of candied peel.

WHOLE ORANGE SHORTBREAD

Zesty orange rind contrasts well with the wholemeal flour in this recipe, adding a lively note of flavour to complement the wholemeal texture.

fat for greasing
175 g / 6 oz butter
75 g / 3 oz caster sugar
grated rind of 1 orange
225 g / 8 oz wholemeal flour
caster sugar for sprinkling

Base-line and grease a 20 cm / 8 inch round sandwich cake tin. Set the oven at 150°C / 300°F / gas 2.

Cream the butter and sugar together until very soft, pale and fluffy. It is important that the creamed mixture is very light. Beat in the orange rind, then work in the flour to make a soft dough.

Lightly knead the dough together in the bowl, then press it into the prepared tin. Prick the shortbread all over with a fork and mark the edges with the fork. Chill the shortbread for at least 15 minutes, preferably for 30 minutes.

Bake the shortbread for 40–50 minutes, until firm and lightly browned on top. Cut into wedges at once but do not remove from the tin. Sprinkle with caster sugar while hot. Leave the shortbread in the tin until it is firm enough to lift out. This will take about 15 minutes. Carefully remove the first wedge by easing the point of a knife all round it; the remaining wedges are easily lifted out of the tin.

Cool on a wire rack and store in an airtight container once cooled.

MAKES EIGHT WEDGES

DOVER BISCUITS

fat for greasing
200 g / 7 oz plain flour
1.25 ml / ¼ tsp salt
2.5 ml / ½ tsp ground cinnamon
50 g / 2 oz currants
100–150 g / 4–5 oz butter or margarine
100–150 g / 4–5 oz caster sugar
1 egg, separated
flour for rolling out
caster sugar for topping

+ ½ - 1 tbs milk

Thoroughly grease two or three baking sheets. Set the oven at 180°C / 350°F / gas 4. Mix the flour, salt and cinnamon in a bowl, then add the currants and stir to coat thoroughly.

In a mixing bowl, beat the butter or margarine until soft, add the sugar and continue to beat until light and fluffy. Beat in the egg yolk, reserving the white. Fold in the flour mixture, first using a knife and then the fingers.

Knead the biscuit dough lightly on a floured surface, then roll out to a thickness of 5 mm / ¼ inch. Cut into rounds with a 6 cm / 2½ inch cutter. Re-roll and re-cut any trimmings.

Place the biscuits on the prepared baking sheets, pricking the top of each in several places. Bake for 10 minutes, then remove from the oven and add the topping: brush the biscuits with beaten egg white and sprinkle with caster sugar. Return to the oven and bake for a further 5 minutes. Leave to stand for 5 minutes, then cool on a wire rack.

MAKES 26 TO 30

SMILES

Children love these cheerful-looking biscuits and
enjoy adding the smiles to the basic shapes.

fat for greasing
200 g / 7 oz plain flour
1.25 ml / ¼ tsp salt
grated rind of 1 orange
100 g / 4 oz butter or margarine
100 g / 4 oz caster sugar
1 egg yolk
flour for rolling out

TOPPING
12–15 jellied orange and lemon slices

Thoroughly grease two large baking sheets. Set the oven at 180°C / 350°F / gas 4. Mix the flour, salt and orange rind in a bowl.

In a mixing bowl, beat the butter or margarine until soft, add the sugar and continue to beat until light and fluffy. Beat in the egg yolk. Fold in the flour mixture, first using a knife and then the fingers.

Knead the biscuit dough lightly on a floured surface, then roll out to a thickness of 5 mm / ¼ inch. Cut the dough into rounds with a 7.5 cm / 3 inch cutter. Re-roll and re-cut any trimmings.

Place the biscuits on the prepared baking sheets. Using a sharp knife dipped in hot water, trim the orange and lemon slices to emphasize the smile shapes. Press one smile on to each biscuit. Use the jelly slice trimmings to make 'eyes', if liked.

Bake for 12–15 minutes. Leave to stand for 5 minutes, then cool on a wire rack.

MAKES TWELVE TO FIFTEEN

JIM-JAMS

fat for greasing
150 g / 5 oz plain flour
50 g / 2 oz ground almonds
1.25 ml / ¼ tsp salt
100 g / 4 oz butter or margarine
100 g / 4 oz caster sugar
1 egg yolk
flour for rolling
strawberry jam for filling
sifted icing sugar for dredging

Thoroughly grease two or three baking sheets. Set the oven at 180°C / 350°F / gas 4. Mix the flour, ground almonds and salt in a bowl.

In a mixing bowl, beat the butter or margarine until soft, add the sugar and continue to beat until light and fluffy. Beat in the egg yolk. Fold in the flour mixture, first using a knife and then the fingers.

Knead the biscuit dough lightly on a floured surface, then roll out to a thickness of 5 mm / ¼ inch. Cut the dough into rounds with a 6 cm / 2½ inch cutter. Re-roll and re-cut trimmings.

Place the biscuits on the prepared baking sheets, pricking the top of each in several places. Bake for 12–15 minutes, until golden. Leave to stand for 5 minutes, then cool on a wire rack.

When quite cold, sandwich the biscuits together in pairs with strawberry jam and dredge with icing sugar, if liked.

MAKES 26 TO 30

MELTING MOMENTS

fat for greasing
100 g / 4 oz margarine or half margarine
and half blended white vegetable fat
75 g / 3 oz caster sugar
30 ml / 2 tbsp beaten egg
125 g / 4½ oz self-raising flour
pinch of salt
rolled oats for coating
4–5 glacé cherries, quartered

Grease two baking sheets. Set the oven at 180°C / 350°F / gas 4.

In a mixing bowl, cream the margarine or mixed fats and sugar until pale and fluffy. Add the egg with a little flour and beat again. Stir in the remaining flour with the salt, mix well, then shape the mixture into 16–20 balls with the hands.

Place the rolled oats on a sheet of greaseproof paper and toss the balls in them to coat them evenly all over. Space the balls on the prepared baking sheets. Place a small piece of glacé cherry in the centre of each.

Bake for about 20 minutes until pale golden brown. Leave to stand for a few minutes on the baking sheets, then cool on a wire rack.

MAKES SIXTEEN TO TWENTY

VARIATION

- **Custard Treats** Substitute 40 g / 1½ oz of the flour with custard powder for a deliciously creamy biscuits with a rich buttery colour. Omit the rolled oats coating.

DIGESTIVE BISCUITS

fat for greasing
75 g / 3 oz wholemeal flour
25 g / 1 oz plain white flour
25 g / 1 oz fine or medium oatmeal
2.5 ml / ½ tsp baking powder
1.25 ml / ¼ tsp salt
15 ml / 1 tbsp soft light brown sugar
50 g / 2 oz butter or margarine
30 ml / 2 tbsp milk
flour for rolling out

Grease a baking sheet. Set the oven at 180°C / 350°F / gas 4. Mix all the dry ingredients in a mixing bowl, sifting the sugar if it is lumpy. Rub in the butter or margarine until the mixture binds together and mix to a pliable dough with the milk.

Knead the biscuits dough lightly on a floured board and roll out to a thickness of just under 5 mm / ¼ inch. Cut into rounds with a 6 cm / 2½ inch round cutter, place on the prepared baking sheet and prick with a fork. Bake for 15 minutes or until golden brown. Leave to stand for a few minutes, then cool on a wire rack.

MAKES ABOUT TWELVE

GINGER SNAPS

fat for greasing
200 g / 7 oz self-raising flour
pinch of salt
5 ml / 1 tsp ground ginger
100 g / 4 oz soft light brown sugar
75 g / 3 oz margarine
100 g / 4 oz golden syrup
1 egg, beaten

Thoroughly grease several baking sheets. Set the oven at 160°C / 325°F / gas 3. Sift together the flour, salt and ginger. Stir in the sugar.

Melt the margarine with the syrup in a large heavy-bottomed saucepan. When the fat has melted, add the dry ingredients and beaten egg alternately and beat until smooth and thick.

Using 2 teaspoons, place rounds of the mixture on to the prepared baking sheets, allowing plenty of room for spreading. Bake for 15 minutes. Leave to stand for a few minutes, then cool on a wire rack.

MAKES ABOUT 56

CINNAMON BARS

fat for greasing
175 g / 6 oz plain flour
5 ml / 1 tsp ground cinnamon
50 g / 2 oz caster sugar
100 g / 4 oz butter
25 g / 1 oz flaked almonds
15 ml / 1 tbsp granulated sugar

Grease a 30 x 20 cm / 12 x 8 inch Swiss roll tin. Set the oven at 180°C / 350°F / gas 4.

Sift the flour and 2.5 ml / ½ tsp of the cinnamon into a mixing bowl and add the caster sugar. Rub in the butter until the mixture resembles firm breadcrumbs and work into a soft dough. Press the mixture into the prepared tin. Flatten and level the surface, then sprinkle with the flake almonds, granulated sugar and remaining cinnamon.

Bake for 15–20 minutes until golden brown. Cut into bars or fingers while still warm.

MAKES ABOUT TWENTY

PIPED ALMOND RINGS

fat for greasing
175 g / 6 oz butter
100 g / 4 oz caster sugar
1 egg, beaten
225 g / 8 oz self-raising flour
50 g / 2 oz ground almonds
1–2 drops of vanilla essence
about 10 ml / 2 tsp milk

Thoroughly grease two baking sheets. In a mixing bowl, cream the butter and sugar until light and fluffy. Add the beaten egg, beating thoroughly and adding a little of the flour if the mixture begins to curdle. Blend in the remaining flour and ground almonds gradually. Add the vanilla essence and enough milk to give a piping consistency. Leave the mixture to stand for about 20 minutes in a cool place.

Set the oven at 200°C / 400°F / gas 6. Put the biscuit mixture into a piping bag fitted with a medium star nozzle, and pipe small rings on to the prepared baking sheets. Bake for 10 minutes or until golden. Leave to stand for a few minutes, then cool on a wire rack.

MAKES ABOUT 24

FLAPJACKS

fat for greasing
50 g / 2 oz margarine
50 g / 2 oz soft light brown sugar
30 ml / 2 tbsp golden syrup
100 g / 4 oz rolled oats

Grease a 28 x 18 cm / 11 x 7 inch baking tin. Set the oven at 160°C / 325°F / gas 3. Melt the margarine in a large saucepan. Add the sugar and syrup, and warm gently. Do not boil. Remove from the heat and stir in the oats.

Press into the prepared tin, then bake for 25 minutes or until firm. Cut into fingers while still warm and leave in the tin to cool.

MAKES ABOUT TWENTY

VARIATIONS

- **Sultana Flapjacks** Add 50 g / 2 oz sultanas to the basic mixture, stirring them in with the oats.
- **Sesame Flapjacks** Sesame seeds contribute their own, distinctive flavour to this traditional recipe. Press the flapjack mixture into the tin, then sprinkle a layer of sesame seeds over the top and press them down well with the back of a spoon. Do not use roasted sesame seeds.
- **Honey Flapjacks** Use clear honey instead of golden syrup; continue as in the main recipe.

SPONGE FINGERS

*Speed is the secret ingredient of successful sponge fingers.
Do not allow the mixture to stand before baking or it will collapse,
resulting in solid rather than spongy biscuits.*

**fat for greasing
caster sugar for dusting
3 eggs, separated
100 g / 4 oz caster sugar
100 g / 4 oz plain flour
pinch of salt**

Grease 18 sponge finger tins and dust with caster sugar. Set the oven at 160°C / 325°F / gas 3. In a bowl, beat the egg yolks with the sugar until pale and thick. Sift the flour with the salt into a second bowl. Fold half the flour into the egg mixture very lightly.

In a clean, dry bowl, whisk the egg whites until stiff. Fold very lightly into the yolk mixture with the rest of the flour. Half fill the prepared tins and bake for 12 minutes. Leave to cool slightly before removing from the tins and cooling completely on a wire rack.

MAKES EIGHTEEN

MERINGUES

This basic meringue mixture may be used for a wide variety
of dishes, from the individual meringues of the various sizes to shells,
cases and toppings. Provided the cooked meringues are dried out
thoroughly, they will keep for 2 weeks in an airtight tin.

4 egg whites
pinch of salt
200 g / 7 oz caster sugar, plus extra for dusting
1.25 ml / ¼ tsp baking powder (optional)
whipped cream, to fill (optional)

Line a baking sheet with oiled greaseproof paper or with non-stick baking parchment. Set the oven at 110°C / 225°F / gas ¼.

Combine the egg whites and salt in a mixing bowl and whisk until the whites are very stiff and standing in points. They must be completely dry. Gradually add half the caster sugar, 15 ml / 1 tbsp at a time, whisking well after each addition until the meringue is stiff. If the sugar is not thoroughly blended in it will form droplets of syrup which may brown, spoiling the appearance and texture of the meringues, and making them difficult to remove from the paper when cooked.

When half the sugar had been whisked in, sprinkle the rest over the surface of the mixture and, using a metal spoon, fold it in very lightly with the baking powder, if used. Put the meringue mixture into a piping bag fitted with a large nozzle and pipe into rounds on the paper. Alternatively, shape the mixture using two wet tablespoons. Take up a spoonful of the mixture and smooth it with a palette knife, bringing it up into a ridge in the centre. Slide it out with the other spoon on to the prepared baking sheet, with the ridge on top.

Dust the meringues lightly with caster sugar, then dry off in the oven for 3–4 hours, until they are firm and crisp but still white. If the meringues begin to brown, prop the oven door open a little. When they are crisp on the outside, lift the meringues carefully off the sheet, using a palette knife. Turn them on to their sides and return to the oven until the bases are dry. Cool on a wire rack and, if liked, sandwich them together with whipped cream. Filled meringues should be served within 1 hour or they will soften.

MAKES 24 TO 30 MEDIUM MERINGUES

VARIATIONS

- **Meringue Fingers** Pipe the meringue mixture into fingers instead of shaping rounds. Dip one end of each meringue in melted chocolate when cool, then leave to set on waxed paper. Alternatively, sandwich the fingers together with whipped cream and coat the top of each with melted chocolate.
- **Meringue Petits Fours** Make half the quantity of mixture. Pipe very small meringues and dry out as in the main recipe, for about 2–3 hours. Set the meringues on small circles of almond paste, attaching them with warmed apricot jam. Alternatively, sandwich them in pairs with whipped cream.

ALMOND MACAROONS

fat for greasing
2 egg whites
150 g / 5 oz caster sugar
100 g / 4 oz ground almonds
10 ml / 2 tsp ground rice
split almonds or halved glacé cherries

Grease two baking sheets and cover with rice paper. Set the oven at 160°C / 325°F / gas 3.

In a clean dry bowl, whisk the egg whites until frothy but not stiff enough to form peaks. Stir in the sugar, ground almonds, and ground rice. Beat with a wooden spoon until thick and white.

Put small spoonfuls of the mixture 5 cm / 2 inches apart on the prepared baking sheets or pipe them on. Place a split almond or halved glacé cherry on each macaroon and bake for 20 minutes or until pale fawn in colour. Cool slightly on the baking sheets, then finish cooling on wire racks.

MAKES SIXTEEN TO TWENTY

VARIATION

- **Ratafias** Ratafias are used in trifles, to decorate desserts, and as petits fours. Follow the recipe above, but reduce the size of the biscuits so that when cooked they are only 2 cm / ¾ inch in diameter. Omit the split almond or glacé cherry topping.

FLORENTINES

oil for greasing
25 g / 1 oz glacé cherries, chopped
100 g / 4 oz cut mixed peel, finely chopped
50 g / 2 oz flaked almonds
100 g / 4 oz chopped almonds
25 g / 1 oz sultanas
100 g / 4 oz butter or margarine
100 g / 4 oz caster sugar
30 ml / 2 tbsp double cream
100 g / 4 oz plain or courverture chocolate

Line three or four baking sheets with oiled greaseproof paper. Set the oven at 180°C / 350°F / gas 4.

In a bowl, mix the cherries and mixed peel with the flaked and chopped almonds and the sultanas. Melt the butter or margarine in a small saucepan, add the sugar and boil for 1 minute. Remove from the heat and stir in the fruit and nuts. Whip the cream in a separate bowl, then fold it in.

Place small spoonfuls of the mixture on to the prepared baking sheets, leaving room for spreading. Bake for 8–10 minutes. After the biscuits have been cooking for about 5 minutes, neaten the edges by drawing them together with the plain biscuit cutter. Leave the cooked biscuits on the baking sheets to firm up slightly before transferring to a wire rack to cool completely.

To finish, melt the chocolate in a bowl over hot water and use to coat the flat underside of each biscuit. Mark into wavy lines with a fork as the chocolate cools.

MAKES 20 TO 24

BRANDY SNAPS

These traditional treats make a popular addition to a buffet table or may be served as a tempting dessert. Fill them at the last moment with fresh whipped cream or Confectioners' Custard (page 148).

fat for greasing
50 g / 2 oz plain flour
5 ml / 1 tsp ground ginger
50 g / 2 oz margarine
50 g / 2 oz soft dark brown sugar
30 ml / 2 tbsp golden syrup
10 ml / 2 tsp grated lemon rind
5 ml / 1 tsp lemon juice

Grease two or three 25 x 20 cm / 10 x 8 inch baking sheets. Also grease the handles of several wooden spoons, standing them upside down in a jar until required. Set the oven at 180°C / 350°F / gas 4.

Sift the flour and ginger into a bowl. Melt the margarine in a saucepan. Add the sugar and syrup and warm gently, but do not allow to become hot. Remove from the heat and add the sifted ingredients with the lemon rind and juice. Mix well.

Put spoonfuls of the mixture on the prepared baking sheets spacing well apart to allow for spreading. Do not put more than 6 spoonfuls on a baking sheet. Bake for 8–10 minutes.

Remove from the oven and leave to cool for a few seconds until the edges begin to firm. Lift one of the biscuits with a palette knife and roll loosely around the greased handle of one of the wooden spoons. Allow to cool before removing biscuits. Alternatively, make brandy snap cups by moulding the mixture in greased patty tins or over oranges.

MAKES FOURTEEN TO EIGHTEEN

WINE BISCUITS

225 g / 8 oz plain flour
1.25 ml / ¼ tsp salt
1.25 ml / ¼ tsp ground cloves
5 ml / 1 tsp ground cinnamon
2.5 ml / ½ tsp bicarbonate of soda
100 g / 4 oz butter
150 g / 5 oz caster sugar
50 g / 2 oz ground almonds
30 ml / 2 tbsp beaten egg
30 ml / 2 tbsp white wine
fat for greasing
flour for rolling out
halved almonds (optional)

Sift the flour, salt, spices and bicarbonate of soda into a mixing bowl. Rub in the butter until the mixture resembles fine breadcrumbs and add the sugar and ground almonds. In a bowl, mix the egg with the wine. Add to the dry ingredients and mix to a stiff dough. Leave to stand for several hours or overnight.

Grease three or four baking sheets. Set the oven at 220°C / 425°F / gas 7. Roll out the dough on a lightly-floured surface to a thickness of 3 mm / ⅛ inch. Cut into rounds with a 5 cm / 2 inch cutter and put these, well apart, on the prepared baking sheets. Place half an almond on each biscuit, if liked. Bake for 10 minutes. Cool slightly on the baking sheets, then complete cooling on wire racks.

MAKES ABOUT 60

BOURBON BISCUITS

fat for greasing
50 g / 2 oz butter or margarine
50 g / 2 oz caster sugar
15 ml / 1 tbsp golden syrup
100 g / 4 oz plain flour
15 g / ½ oz cocoa
2.5 ml / ½ tsp bicarbonate of soda
flour for rolling out

FILLING
50 g / 2 oz butter or margarine
75 g / 3 oz icing sugar, sifted
15 ml / 1 tbsp cocoa
5 ml / 1 tsp coffee essence or 2.5 ml / ½ tsp instant coffee
dissolved in 5 ml / 1 tsp boiling water and cooled

Line and grease a baking sheet. Set the oven at 160°C / 325°F / gas 3.

In a mixing bowl, cream the butter or margarine with the sugar very thoroughly; beat in the syrup. Sift the flour, cocoa and bicarbonate of soda into a second bowl, mix well, then work into the creamed mixture to make a stiff dough. Knead well, and roll out on a lightly-floured surface into an oblong strip about 23 x 13 cm / 9 x 5 inches and 5 mm / ¼ inch thick. Cut in half to form two rectangles about 6 cm / 2½ inches wide. Place on the prepared baking sheet and bake for 15–20 minutes. Cut into equal-sized fingers while still warm. Cool on wire rack.

Prepare the filling. In a bowl, beat the butter or margarine until soft, then add the sugar, cocoa, and coffee. Beat until smooth. Sandwich the cooled fingers in pairs with the filling.

MAKES FOURTEEN TO SIXTEEN

NUT CLUSTERS

50 g / 2 oz soft margarine
50 g / 2 oz sugar
30 ml / 2 tbsp beaten egg
2.5 ml / ¼ tsp vanilla essence
50 g / 2 oz plain flour
pinch of salt
1.25 ml / ½ tsp bicarbonate of soda
50 g / 2 oz seedless raisins
50 g / 2 oz salted peanuts

Set the oven at 190°C / 375°F / gas 5. In a mixing bowl beat the margarine and sugar until light and fluffy. Beat in the egg and vanilla essence.

Sift the flour, salt and bicarbonate of soda into a second bowl and beat them into the creamed mixture in three portions, mixing well after each addition. Stir in the raisins and nuts. Place small portions on two ungreased baking sheets and bake for 9 minutes. Cool on the baking sheets.

MAKES 20 TO 24

PRINCESS PAIRS

fat for greasing
100 g / 4 oz butter or margarine
25 g / 1 oz caster sugar
pinch of salt
100 g / 4 oz self-raising flour
grated rind of 1 orange

FILLING
Buttercream (page 138), using 25 g / 1 oz butter and the grated rind of an orange

Grease two baking sheets. Set the oven at 180°C / 350°F / gas 4. In a mixing bowl, cream the butter or margarine with the sugar. Work in the salt, flour and half the orange rind. Put the mixture in a piping bag fitted with a large star nozzle, and pipe 9 cm / 3½ inch lengths on to the prepared baking sheets, making 20 biscuits. Bake for 15 minutes. Cool on the baking sheets. When cool, sandwich together in pairs with the butter-cream flavoured with the remaining orange rind.

MAKES TEN

ANZACS

These Australian specialities became popular during World War One, when they were often sent to the Anzacs – soldiers of the Australian and New Zealand Army Corps.

fat for greasing
75 g / 3 oz rolled oats
100 g / 4 oz plain flour
150 g / 5 oz sugar
50 g / 2 oz desiccated coconut
100 g / 4 oz butter
15 ml / 1 tbsp golden syrup
7.5 ml / 1½ tsp bicarbonate of soda

Grease two baking sheets. Set the oven at 160°C / 325°F / gas 3. Mix the rolled oats, flour, sugar and coconut in a bowl. In a saucepan, melt the butter and syrup gently. Meanwhile put 30 ml / 2 tbsp boiling water in a small bowl, add the bicarbonate of soda and stir until dissolved. Add to the melted mixture and stir into the dry ingredients.

Spoon scant tablespoons of the mixture on to the prepared baking sheets, leaving plenty of space between them. Bake for 20 minutes. Cool on the baking sheets.

MAKES ABOUT 36

GERMAN SPICE BISCUITS

fat for greasing
100 g / 4 oz plain flour
50 g / 2 oz caster sugar
1.25 ml / ¼ tsp mixed spice
75 g / 3 oz margarine
flour for rolling out

Grease a baking sheet. Set the oven at 160°C / 325°F / gas 3.

Mix the flour, sugar and spice in a mixing bowl. Rub in the margarine until the mixture binds together and forms a pliable dough.

Roll out on a floured board to a thickness of 5 mm / ¼ inch and cut into rounds with a 6 cm / 2½ inch round cutter. Place on the prepared baking sheet. Bake for about 20 minutes until very pale gold in colour. Leave to stand for a few minutes, then cool on a wire rack.

MAKES ABOUT TWELVE

CHOCOLATE-TIPPED CINNAMON STARS

fat for greasing
350 g / 12 oz plain flour
5 ml / 1 tsp bicarbonate of soda
10 ml / 2 tsp ground cinnamon
2.5 ml / ½ tsp ground ginger
150 g / 5 oz butter
100 g / 4 oz sugar
100 g / 4 oz honey
1 egg yolk
30 ml / 2 tbsp milk
flour for rolling out
150 g / 5 oz plain chocolate, broken into squares, to decorate

Thoroughly grease three or four baking sheets. Set the oven at 180°C / 350°F / gas 4. Mix the flour, bicarbonate of soda and spices in a bowl.

In a mixing bowl, beat the butter until soft, add the sugar and continue to beat until light and fluffy. Beat in the honey and egg yolk, then the milk. Fold in the flour mixture.

Knead the biscuit dough lightly on a floured surface, then roll out to a thickness of 3 mm / ⅛ inch. Cut into stars with a 5 cm / 2 inch star-shaped biscuit cutter. Using a straw, make a small hole in each star. The hole should be on a point, but not too near the edge. Transfer the biscuits to the prepared baking sheets.

Bake for about 8 minutes, until golden brown. Cool for a few minutes on the baking sheets then transfer to wire racks.

Melt the chocolate with 15 ml / 1 tbsp water over low heat. Brush the tips of each star with chocolate, then place on a wire rack until the chocolate has set.

When the chocolate is firm, thread a length of ribbon through each biscuit and hang on the Christmas tree.

MAKES ABOUT 60

CHOCOLATE CHIP COOKIES

America's contribution to the biscuit barrel.

fat for greasing
150 g / 5 oz plain flour
1.25 ml / ¼ tsp salt
2.5 ml / ½ tsp bicarbonate of soda
100 g / 4 oz butter or margarine
50 g / 2 oz caster sugar
50 g / 2 oz soft light brown sugar
1 egg, beaten
2.5 ml / ½ tsp vanilla essence
75 g / 3 oz chocolate chips

Thoroughly grease two or three baking sheets. Set the oven at 180°C / 350°F / gas 4. Mix the flour, salt and bicarbonate of soda in a bowl.

Beat the butter or margarine until soft, add the sugars and continue to beat until light and fluffy. Beat in the egg and vanilla essence. Stir in the flour and chocolate chips.

Using a teaspoon, scoop up a little of the dough. Use a second teaspoon to transfer the dough to one of the prepared baking sheets. Repeat with the remaining dough, making the heaps about 5 cm / 2 inches apart.

Bake the biscuits for 10–12 minutes, until golden. Leave to stand for 5 minutes, then cool on a wire rack.

MAKES 26–30

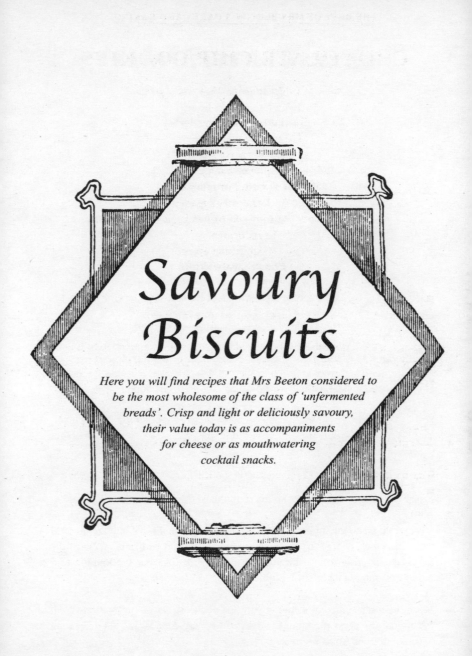

Savoury Biscuits

Here you will find recipes that Mrs Beeton considered to
be the most wholesome of the class of 'unfermented
breads'. Crisp and light or deliciously savoury,
their value today is as accompaniments
for cheese or as mouthwatering
cocktail snacks.

CHEESE BUTTERFLIES

fat for greasing
100 g / 4 oz plain flour
pinch of mustard powder
pinch of salt
pinch of cayenne pepper
75 g / 3 oz butter
75 g / 3 oz grated Parmesan cheese
1 egg yolk
flour for rolling out

TOPPING
100 g / 4 oz cream cheese
few drops of anchovy essence
few drops of red food colouring

Grease two baking sheets. Set the oven at 200°C / 400°F / gas 6.

Sift the flour, mustard, salt and cayenne into a bowl. In a mixing bowl, cream the butter until soft and white, then add the flour mixture with the Parmesan. Stir in the egg yolk and enough cold water to form a stiff dough.

Roll out on a lightly-floured surface to a thickness of about 3 mm / ⅛ inch and cut into rounds about 6 cm / 2½ inches in diameter. Cut half the rounds across the centre to make 'wings'.

With a palette knife, lift both the whole rounds and the 'wings' on to the prepared baking sheets and bake for 10 minutes. Cool on the baking sheets.

Meanwhile make the topping. Put the cream cheese in a bowl and cream until soft with a fork, adding the anchovy essence for flavour and just enough of the red food colouring to tint the mixture a pale pink. Transfer the topping to a piping bag fitted with as shell nozzle.

When the biscuits are quite cold, pipe a line of cheese across the centre of each full round and press the straight edges of two half-rounds into the cheese to make them stand up like wings.

MAKES TWELVE TO EIGHTEEN

VARIATIONS

Use the basic recipe for the biscuits to make a variety of different-flavoured cocktail snacks. This is achieved by varying the flavour of the cream cheese which is piped on to the biscuits.

- **Parmesan and Pine Nut** Add a little grated Parmesan chesses to the cream cheese and omit the anchovy essence and colouring. Sprinkle toasted pine nuts down the middle of the cheese when the 'wings' are in place.
- **Tomato and Olive** Leave out the anchovy essence and colouring, then flavour the cream cheese with a little tomato purée and add a little lemon juice, to taste. Top with a few pieces of black olive when the 'wings' are in place.

CHEESE STRAWS

fat for greasing
100 g / 4 oz plain flour
pinch of mustard powder
pinch of salt
pinch of cayenne pepper
75 g / 3 oz butter
75 g / 3 oz grated Parmesan cheese
1 egg yolk
flour for rolling out

Grease four baking sheets. Set the oven at 200°C / 400°F / gas 6.

Sift the flour, mustard, salt and cayenne into a bowl. In a mixing bowl, cream the butter until soft and white, then add the flour mixture with the cheese. Stir in the egg yolk and enough cold water to form a stiff dough.

Roll out on a lightly-floured surface to a thickness of about 5 mm / ¼ inch and cut into finger, each measuring about 10 x 1 cm / 4 inches x ½ inch. From the pastry trimmings make several rings, each about 4 cm / 1½ inches in diameter.

With a palette knife, transfer both rings and straws to the prepared baking sheets and bake for 8–10 minutes or until lightly browned and crisp. Cool on the baking sheets.

To serve, fit a few straws though each ring and lay the bundles in the centre of a plate with any remaining straws criss-crossed around them.

MAKES 48–60

HOT PEPPER CHEESES

*When freshly cooked, these savouries are inclined to
crumble and break easily. For this reason it is best to allow
them to cool completely, then reheat gently until warm.*

**fat for greasing
200 g / 7 oz plain flour
200 g / 7 oz butter
200 g / 7 oz Lancashire cheese, grated
few drops of hot pepper sauce
1.25 ml / ¼ tsp salt
flour for rolling out**

Grease four baking sheets. Sift the flour into a mixing bowl. Rub in the butter
until the mixture resembles fine breadcrumbs. Add the cheese and seasonings.
Work the mixture thoroughly by hand to make a smooth dough. Use a few
drops of water if necessary, but the dough will be shorter and richer without it.
Chill for 30 minutes.

Meanwhile, set the oven at 180°C / 350°F / gas 4. Roll out the dough on a
floured surface to a thickness of 5 mm / ¼ inch. Cut into rounds or shapes.

With a palette knife, transfer the shapes to the prepared baking sheets and bake
for 10–12 minutes or until lightly browned and crisp. Cool on the baking sheets.

MAKES 40–50

CRISP CRACKERS

These plain crackers are the ideal accompaniment for cheese.
If you use very small cutters to cut the dough, the crackers can
be used as a base for making little canapés – top them with
piped smooth pate or cream cheese, olives and parsley.

fat for greasing
225 g / 8 oz plain flour
2.5 ml / ½ tsp salt
about 125 ml / 4 fl oz milk
1 egg yolk, beaten

Grease two baking sheets. Set the oven at 180°C / 350°F / gas 4. Sift the flour and salt into a bowl, then make a well in the middle and add about half the milk. Add the egg yolk to the milk and gradually work in the flour to make a firm dough, adding more milk as necessary.

Turn the dough out on to a lightly-floured surface and knead it briefly until it is perfectly smooth. Divide the piece of dough in half and wrap one piece in cling film to prevent it from drying out while you roll out the other piece.

Roll out the dough very thinly and use a 7.5 cm / 3 inch round cutter to stamp out crackers. Gather up the trimmings and re-roll them. Place the crackers on the prepared baking sheets and bake them for 12–18 minutes until they are golden. Transfer the crackers to a wire rack to cool.

MAKES ABOUT 24

RUSKS

This is an old Suffolk recipe for simple, dry biscuits which are made from a yeasted bread dough. The original recipe used fresh yeast but this version takes advantage of easy-blend yeast. The sugar may be omitted if preferred.

fat for greasing
225 g / 8 oz strong plain flour
15 g / ½ oz easy-blend dried yeast
25 g / 1 oz sugar
2.5 ml / ½ tsp salt
25 g / 1 oz butter
75 ml / 3 fl oz milk
1 egg, beaten
flour for kneading

Grease a large baking sheet. Set the oven at 220°C / 425°F / gas 7.

Place the flour, yeast, sugar and salt in a mixing bowl. Stir the ingredients together, then make a well in the middle. In a small saucepan, heat the butter and milk together very gently until the butter has melted, then remove the pan from the heat and leave to cool until warm.

Pour the milk mixture into the well in the dry ingredients, add the beaten egg and stir well. Gradually stir in the flour mixture to make a firm dough. Turn the dough out on to a lightly-floured surface and knead thoroughly until smooth and elastic. The dough should be kneaded for about 10 minutes.

Place the dough in a clean, lightly-floured bowl and cover it with a clean cloth. Set the dough to rise in a warm place until it had doubled in bulk. This may take up to 1½ hours.

Lightly knead the dough again, then divide it into six portions. Shape each portion of dough into an oblong roll measuring about 13 cm / 5 inches in length. Place the rolls on the baking sheet and bake them for about 15–20 minutes, or until they are evenly golden.

Remove the rolls from the oven and reduce the temperature to 180°C / 350°F / gas 4. Using a clean tea-towel to protect your hand, split each roll in half lengthways to make a slim rusk. Return them to the baking sheet, cut side uppermost, and cook for a further 30–40 minutes, or until they are crisp and lightly browned on the cut side. The rusks are ready when they are quite dry.

Leave the rusks to cool on a wire rack, then transfer them to an airtight container.

MAKES TWELVE

CARAWAY CRACKERS

Originally, these simple biscuits were sweetened with
50 g / 2 oz caster sugar but the flavour of the caraway seeds makes
such an excellent savoury cracker that the sugar is omitted in this recipe.
However, if you particularly like the flavour of caraway you may like to
try the old recipe and add the sugar to the flour. If you are making the
savoury crackers, try using brown flour instead of white.

fat for greasing
50 g / 2 oz butter
225 g / 8 oz plain flour
30 ml / 2 tbsp caraway seeds
good pinch of salt
1 egg, beaten
milk for glazing

Grease two baking sheets. Set the oven at 180°C / 350°F / gas 4. Place the butter in a small bowl and beat it until it is very soft. Gradually beat in the flour, caraway seeds and salt until the ingredients are thoroughly mixed.

Add the beaten egg and mix well to make a firm dough. Knead the dough briefly on a floured surface, then roll it out thinly and cut out 5 cm / 2 inch circles.

Place the crackers on the baking sheets and brush them with a little milk, then bake them for about 12–15 minutes. Transfer the crackers to a wire rack to cool.

MAKES ABOUT 30

OATCAKES

fat for greasing
50 g / 2 oz bacon fat or dripping
100 g / 4 oz medium oatmeal
1.25 ml / ¼ tsp salt
1.25 ml / ¼ tsp bicarbonate of soda
fine oatmeal for rolling out

Grease two baking sheets. Set the oven at 160°F / 325°F / gas 3.

Melt the bacon fat or dripping in a large saucepan. Remove from the heat and stir in the dry ingredients, then add enough boiling water to make a stiff dough.

When cool enough to handle, knead the dough thoroughly, then roll out on a surface dusted with fine oatmeal, to a thickness of 5 mm / ¼ inch. Cut into wedge-shaped pieces and transfer to the prepared baking sheets. Bake for 20–30 minutes. Cool on a wire rack.

MAKES ABOUT SIXTEEN

Yeasted Breads

*The aroma of freshly-baked bread is unmistakable,
and the results are well worth the effort.
Once you have mastered the basic
techniques and recipes, making
your own bread is fast and
uniquely satisfying.*

BASIC WHITE BREAD

fat for greasing
800 g / 1¾ lb strong white flour
10 ml / 2 tsp salt
25 g / 1 oz lard
25 g / 1 oz fresh yeast or 15 ml / 1 tbsp dried yeast
2.5 ml / ½ tsp sugar
flour for kneading
beaten egg or milk for glazing

Grease two 23 x 13 x 7.5 cm / 9 x 5 x 3 inch loaf tins. Sift the flour and salt into a large bowl. Rub in the lard. Measure 500 ml / 17 fl oz lukewarm water.

Blend the fresh yeast to a thin paste with the sugar and a little of the warm water. Set aside in a warm place until frothy – about 5 minutes. Alternatively, sprinkle dried yeast over all the warm water and set aside. When frothy, stir well.

Add the yeast liquid and remaining water to the flour mixture and mix to a soft dough. Turn on to a floured surface and knead for about 8 minutes or until the dough is smooth, elastic and no longer sticky. Return to the bowl and cover with cling film. Leave in a warm place until the dough has doubled in bulk – this will take 2 hours, or longer.

Knead the dough again until firm. Cut into two equal portions and form each into a loaf shape. Place the dough into the prepared loaf tins and brush the surface with beaten egg or milk. Place the tins in a large, lightly oiled polythene bag. Leave in a warm place for about 45 minutes or until the dough has doubled in bulk. Set the oven at 230°C / 450°F / gas 8.

Bake for 35–40 minutes, until the loaves are crisp and golden brown, and sound hollow when tapped on the bottom.

MAKES TWO 800 G / 1¾ LB LOAVES

SHAPING YEAST DOUGH

Yeast doughs of all types may be shaped in many ways to make attractive breads. The following ideas may be used for making two loaves from the Basic White Bread dough recipe.

Twist Divide the dough in half and roll each piece into a strip. Pinch the two ends of the strips together on a greased baking sheet, then twist the strips together, tucking the ends under neatly and pinching them in place.

Ring Make a long, fairly slim twist, then shape it in a ring on a greased baking sheet.

Plait Divide the dough from one loaf into three equal portions and roll them into long strips. Pinch the ends of the strips together on a greased baking sheet, then plait the strips neatly. Fold the ends under at the end of the plait, pinching them underneath to secure the plait.

Cottage Loaf Shape two-thirds of the dough into a round loaf and place on a greased baking sheet. Shape the remaining dough into a ball. Make an indentation in the middle of the round loaf, then dampen the dough in the middle and place the ball on top. Make a deep indentation with your fingers or a wooden spoon handle down through the ball of dough and the round base. Before baking, score several slits down the side of the base of the loaf.

TOPPINGS FOR BREAD

Before baking, the risen dough may be glazed with beaten egg or milk for a golden crust. Brushing with water makes a crisp crust. Then the dough may be sprinkled with any of the following:
- Poppy seeds – dark or white.
- Sesame seeds – black or white, for flavour as well as texture and appearance.
- Cracked wheat – good on wholemeal loaves.
- Caraway, fennel or cumin seeds – when used generously these all contribute flavour.

FANCY ROLL SHAPES

Divide the risen Basic White Bread dough (page 190)
into 50 g / 2 oz pieces and shape as below:

MAKES 24

- **Small Plaits** Divide each piece of dough into three equal portions; then shape each of these into a long strand. Plait the three strands together, pinching the ends securely.
- **Small Twists** Divided each piece of dough into two equal portions, and shape into strands about 12 cm / 4½ inches in length. Twist the two strands together, pinching the ends securely.
- **'S' Rolls** Shape each piece of dough into a roll about 15 cm / 6 inches in length, and form it into an 'S' shape.
- **Cottage Rolls** Cut two-thirds off each piece of dough and shape into a ball. Shape the remaining third in the same way. Place the small ball on top of the larger one and push a hole through the centre of both with one finger, dusted with flour, to join the two pieces firmly together.

DINNER ROLLS

fat for greasing
800 g / 1¾ lb strong white flour
10 ml / 2 tsp sugar
400 ml / 14 fl oz milk
25 g / 1 oz fresh yeast or 15 ml / 1 tbsp dried yeast
10 ml / 2 tsp salt
50 g / 2 oz butter or margarine
1 egg
flour for kneading
beaten egg for glazing

Grease two baking sheets. Sift about 75 g / 3 oz of the flour and all the sugar into a large bowl. Warm the milk until lukewarm, then blend in the fresh yeast or stir in the dried yeast. Pour the yeast liquid into the flour and sugar and beat well. Leave the bowl in a warm place for 20 minutes.

Sift the remaining flour and the salt into a bowl. Rub in the butter or margarine. Beat the egg into the yeast mixture and stir in the flour mixture. Mix to a soft dough. Turn on to a lightly-floured surface and knead for about 5 minutes or until the dough is smooth and no longer sticky. Return to the bowl and cover with cling film. Leave in a warm place until the dough had doubled in bulk – this will take 2 hours, or longer.

Knead the dough again until firm. Cut into 50 g / 2 oz pieces, then shape each piece into a ball. Place on the prepared baking sheets 5–7.5 cm / 2–3 inches apart. Brush with beaten egg. Cover with sheets of lightly oiled polythene. Leave in a warm place for about 20 minutes or until the rolls have doubled in bulk. Set the oven at 220°C / 425°F / gas 7.

Bake for 12–15 minutes until the rolls are golden brown.

MAKES 24

ENRICHED BREAD

fat for greasing
900 g / 2 lb strong white flour
10 ml / 2 tsp sugar
400 ml / 14 fl oz milk
25 g / 1 oz fresh yeast or 15 ml / 1 tbsp dried yeast
10 ml / 2 tsp salt
100 g / 4 oz butter or margarine
2 eggs
flour for kneading
milk for glazing

Grease two 23 x 13 x 7.5 cm / 9 x 5 x 3 inch loaf tins. Sift about 75 g / 3 oz of the flour and all the sugar into a large bowl. Warm the milk until lukewarm, then blend in the fresh yeast or stir in the dried yeast. Pour the yeast liquid into the flour and sugar and beat well. Leave the bowl in a warm place for 20 minutes.

Sift the remaining flour and the salt into a bowl. Rub in the butter or margarine. Beat the eggs into the yeast mixture and stir in the flour mixture. Mix to a soft dough. Turn on to a lightly-floured surface and knead for about 6 minutes or

continued overleaf...

until the dough is smooth and no longer sticky. Return to the bowl and cover with cling film. Leave in a warm place until the dough has doubled in bulk – this will take 2 hours, or longer.

Knead the dough again until firm. Cut into two equal portions and form each into a loaf shape. Place the dough in the prepared loaf tins. Place the tins in a large, lightly oiled polythene bag. Leave in a warm place for about 30 minutes or until the dough had doubled in bulk. Set the oven at 220°C / 425°F / gas 7. Brush the surface of the dough with milk. Bake for 35–40 minutes until the loaves sound hollow when tapped on the bottom.

MAKES TWO 800 G / 1¾ LB LOAVES

VARIATIONS

- **Bread Plait** Make as for Enriched Bread. Cut the risen dough into two equal portions. Cut one of these into three equal pieces. Roll each piece into a strand 25–30 cm / 10–12 inches long and plait the strands together. Repeat, using the second portion. Place the plaits on a greased baking sheet. Cover, leave to rise and bake the plait as for Enriched Bread.
- **Cheese Bread Plait** Make as for Bread Plait but add 200 g / 7 oz grated Cheddar cheese to the dry ingredients.
- **Caraway Bread** Make as for Enriched Bread but add 10 ml / 2 tsp dried sage, 5 ml / 1 tsp grated nutmeg and 15 ml / 1 tbsp caraway seeds to the dry ingredients.
- **Fruit Bread** Make as for Enriched Bread but add 200 g / 7 oz sultanas, currants or raisins to the dough when kneading for the second time.
- **Nut Bread** Make as for Enriched Bread but add 200 g / 7 oz chopped nuts, such as walnuts or peanuts, to the dough when kneading for the second time.
- **Poppy Seed Bread** Make as for Enriched Bread but sprinkle poppy seeds thickly over the dough before baking.
- **Bridge Rolls** Make as for Enriched Bread but cut the risen dough into 50 g / 2 oz pieces. Roll each piece into a finger shape about 10 cm / 4 inches long. Place on a greased baking sheet so that the rolls almost touch each other. Dust the surface of the rolls with flour. Cover and leave to rise for about 20 minutes or until the rolls have joined together. Bake as for Enriched Bread but reduce the baking time to 12–15 minutes. Makes about 28.

RICE BREAD

This unusual bread is moist with a close, slightly elastic, texture. It is delicious thickly slice when warm or cut into this slices when cold.

100 g / 4 oz long-grain rice (not the easy-cook type)
450 ml / ¾ pint milk
25 g / 1 oz fresh yeast or 15 ml / 1 tbsp dried yeast
2.5 ml / ½ tsp sugar
450 g / 1 lb strong plain flour
10 ml / 2 tsp salt
beaten egg to glaze (optional)

Add the rice to a small saucepan of boiling water. Bring back to the boil, then drain. Put the rice back in the pan and add the milk. Bring to the boil, stirring occasionally, then reduce the heat and partially cover the pan. Simmer for 15 minutes.

Blend the fresh yeast to the thin paste with the sugar and 50 ml / 2 fl oz lukewarm water. Set aside in a warm place until frothy – about 5 minutes. Alternatively, sprinkle dried yeast over the water and set aside until frothy, then stir well.

Mix the flour and salt in a bowl. Make a well in the middle and pour in the rice with the cooking milk. Mix in the flour, using a wooden spoon and a cutting action. When the rice and milk are evenly distributed and have cooled slightly, pour in the yeast liquid and mix to a soft dough. The flour should have cooled the rice sufficiently to avoid killing the yeast but the dough should still feel hot.

Turn out on a well-floured surface and knead until smooth and elastic, sprinkling with a little flour to prevent the dough sticking. Place in a bowl, cover and leave in a warm place until doubled in bulk. Meanwhile, grease a baking sheet.

Turn the dough out, knead briefly and divide it in half. Shape two long oval loaves and place them on the baking sheet. Cover loosely with oiled polythene and leave in a warm place until well risen and spread into slightly flattened loaves. Meanwhile, set the oven at 220°C / 425°F / gas 7. Brush the risen loaves with beaten egg and bake for 35–45 minutes, until well browned and firm. The loaves should sound hollow when tapped on the bottom. Cool on a wire rack.

MAKES TWO LOAVES

INDIAN CORN (MAIZE) FLOUR BREAD

fat for greasing
25 g / 1 oz fresh yeast or 15 ml / 1 tbsp dried yeast
5 ml / 1 tsp sugar
450 g / 1 lb strong white flour
25 g / 1 oz butter
225 g / 8 oz maize flour
7.5 ml / 1½ tsp salt
flour for kneading

Grease two baking sheets. Measure 450 ml / ¾ pint lukewarm water. Blend the fresh yeast with the sugar and a little of the lukewarm water. Set aside until frothy. For dried yeast, sprinkle the yeast over all the water, then leave until frothy.

Sift the flour and salt into a bowl. Rub in the butter, then stir in the maize flour. Make a well in the middle and add the yeast liquid. Pour in the remaining water and stir well. Gradually work in the dry ingredients to a firm dough.

Turn out the dough on a lightly-floured surface and knead thoroughly until smooth and elastic – about 10 minutes. Place the dough in a clean, lightly-floured bowl. Cover with cling film and leave in a warm place until doubled in bulk. This will take about 2 hours.

Knead the dough lightly, then cut it in half and shape each portion into a round loaf. Place on the baking sheets, cover loosely with oiled polythene or cling film and leave in a warm place until doubled in bulk again.

Meanwhile, set the oven at 220°C / 425°F / gas 7. When the bread is risen, use a sharp knife to make three slashes across the top of each loaf. Brush with water and bake for about 45 minutes, until golden brown and crisp. The loaf should sound hollow when tapped on the base. Cool on a wire rack.

MAKES TWO LOAVES

MALTED BROWN BREAD

fat for greasing
800 g / 1¾ lb wholemeal flour
15 ml / 1 tbsp salt
25 g / 1 oz fresh yeast or 15 ml / 1 tbsp dried yeast
2.5 ml / ½ tsp sugar
30 ml / 2 tbsp malt extract
flour for kneading

Grease two 23 x 13 x 7.5 cm / 9 x 5 x 3 inch loaf tins. Mix the flour and salt in a large bowl. Measure 500 ml / 17 fl oz lukewarm water.

Blend the fresh yeast to a thin paste with the sugar and a little of the warm water. Set aside in a warm place until frothy – about 5 minutes. Alternatively, sprinkle the dried yeast over all the warm water and set aside until frothy.

Stir the malt extract into the yeast liquid and remaining water. Add to the flour and mix to a soft dough. Turn on to a lightly-floured surface and knead for about 4 minutes or until the dough is smooth, elastic and no longer sticky. Return to the bowl and over with cling film. Leave in a warm place until the dough has doubled in bulk – this takes 2 hours, or longer.

Knead the dough again until firm. Cut into two equal portions and form each into a loaf shape. Place the dough in the prepared loaf tins. Place the tins in a large, lightly oiled polythene bag. Leave in a warm place for about 45 minutes or until the dough has doubled in bulk. Set the oven at 230°C / 450°F / gas 8.

Bake for 35–45 minutes, until the loaves are golden brown and crisp, and sound hollow when tapped on the bottom.

MAKES TWO 800 G / 1¾ LB LOAVES

SCOTTISH BROWN BREAD

fat for greasing
575 g / 1¼ lb wholemeal flour
200 g / 7 oz fine or medium oatmeal
15 ml / 1 tbsp salt
25 g / 1 oz fresh yeast or 15 ml / 1 tbsp dried yeast
2.5 ml / ½ tsp sugar
5 ml / 1 tsp bicarbonate of soda
flour for kneading

Grease two 23 x 13 x 7.5 cm / 9 x 5 x 3 inch loaf tins. Mix the flour, oatmeal and salt in a large bowl. Measure 500 ml / 17 fl oz lukewarm water.

Blend the fresh yeast to a thin paste with the sugar and a little of the warm water. Set aside in a warm place until frothy – about 5 minutes. Alternatively, sprinkle dried yeast over all the warm water and set aside until frothy, then stir.

Add the bicarbonate of soda to the yeast liquid and remaining water, then stir this into the flour mixture to form a soft dough. Turn on to a ligthly floured surface and knead for about 4 minutes or until the dough is smooth and not longer sticky. Return to the bowl and over with cling film. Leave in a warm place until the dough had double in bulk – this will take 2 hours, or longer.

Knead the dough again until firm. Cut into two equal portions and form each into a loaf shape. Place the dough in the prepared loaf tins. Place the tins in a large, lightly oiled polythene bag. Leave in a warm place for about 45 minutes or until the dough has double in bulk. Set the oven at 230°C / 450°F / gas 8.

Bake for 20 minutes, then reduce the oven temperature to 190°C / 375°F / gas 5. Continue baking for 25–35 minutes, until the loaves are crisp and golden brown, and sound hollow when tapped on the bottom.

MAKES TWO 800 G / 1¼ LB LOAVES

WHEATMEAL BREAD

fat for greasing
400 g / 14 oz wholemeal flour
400 g / 14 oz strong white flour
10 ml / 2 tsp salt
25 g / 1 oz lard
25 g / 1 oz fresh yeast or 15 ml / 1 tbsp dried yeast
2.5 ml / ½ tsp sugar
flour for kneading
salted water

Grease two 23 x 13 x 7.5 cm / 9 x 5 x 3 inch loaf tins. Mix the flours and salt in a large bowl. Rub in the lard. Measure 450 ml / ¾ pint lukewarm water.

Blend the fresh yeast to a thin paste with the sugar and a little of the warm water. Set aside in a warm place until frothy. Alternatively, sprinkle dried yeast over all the warm water and set aside until frothy, then stir well.

Add the yeast liquid and remaining water to the flour mixture and mix to a soft dough. Turn on to a floured surface and knead for about 4 minutes or until the dough is smooth and elastic. Replace in the bowl, over and leave in a warm place until doubled in bulk.

Cut the dough into two equal portions and form each into a loaf shape. Place the dough in the prepared loaf tins, then brush the surface with salted water. Place the tins in a large, lightly oiled polythene bag. Leave the tins in a warm place for about 50 minutes or until the dough has doubled in bulk. Set the oven at 230°C / 450°F / gas 8.

Bake for 30–40 minutes, until the loaves are golden brown and crisp, and sound hollow when tapped lightly on the bottom.

MAKES TWO 800 G / 1¾ LB LOAVES

RYE COBS

fat for greasing
900 g / 2 lb strong white flour
25 g / 1 oz fresh yeast or 15 ml / 1 tbsp dried yeast
2.5 ml / ½ tsp sugar
450 g / 1 lb coarse rye flour
500 ml / 17 fl oz skimmed milk
20 ml / 4 tsp salt
60 ml / 4 tbsp molasses
60 ml / 4 tbsp cooking oil
flour for kneading

Grease a baking sheet or four 15 cm / 6 inch sandwich tins. Sift the white flour into a large bowl. Measure 250 ml / 8 fl oz lukewarm water.

Blend the fresh yeast to a thin paste with the sugar and a little of the warm water. Set aside in a warm place until frothy – about 5 minutes. Alternatively, sprinkle dried yeast over all the warm water and set aside until frothy, then stir well.

Mix the rye flour into the white flour. Add the yeast liquid, remaining water, skimmed milk, salt, molasses and oil, then knead to a soft dough. Cover the bowl with cling film. Leave in a warm place until the dough had doubled in bulk – this will take at least 2 hours, or longer. (Rye bread is slow to rise).

When risen, shape into four loaves. Place on the prepared baking sheet or press into the sandwich tins. Place in a large, lightly oiled polythene bag. Leave to rise for 30–40 minutes. Set the oven at 190°C / 375°F / gas 5.

Sprinkle the dough with warm water. Bake for about 40 minutes, until the loaves sound hollow when tapped on the bottom.

MAKES FOUR LOAVES

GRANARY BREAD

fat for greasing
800 g / 1¾ lb granary flour or meal
10 ml / 2 tsp salt
10 ml / 2 tsp molasses
25 g / 1 oz fresh yeast or 15 ml / 1 tbsp dried yeast
10 ml / 2 tsp corn oil
flour for kneading
15 ml / 1 tbsp cracked wheat

Grease two 23 x 13 x 7.5 cm / 9 x 5 x 3 inch loaf tins. Mix the flour and salt in a large bowl. Measure 500 ml / 17 fl oz lukewarm water. Stir in the molasses.

Blend the fresh yeast to a thin paste with a little of the warm water and molasses. Set aside in a warm place until frothy – about 5 minutes. Alternatively, sprinkle dried yeast over all the warm water and molasses and set aside until frothy, then stir well. Add the yeast liquid, remaining liquid and the oil to the flour and mix to a soft dough. Turn on to a floured surface and knead for about 4 minutes or until the dough is smooth, elastic and no longer sticky. Return to the bowl and cover with cling film. Leave in a warm place, until doubled in bulk – this will take about 2 hours, or longer.

Knead the dough again until firm. Cut into two equal portions and form each into a loaf shape. Place the dough in the prepared loaf tins, brush the surface with salted water and sprinkle with the cracked wheat. Place the tins in a large, lightly oiled polythene bag. Leave in a warm place for about 45 minutes or until the dough has doubled in bulk. Set the oven at 230°C / 450°F / gas 8.

Bake for 30–40 minutes, until the loaves are browned and crisp, and sound hollow when tapped on the bottom.

BAKES TWO 800 G / 1¾ LB LOAVES

SAFFRON BREAD

fat for greasing
400 g / 14 oz strong white flour
5 ml / 1 tsp salt
125 ml / 4 fl oz milk
75 g / 3 oz butter
large pinch of powdered saffron
75 g / 3 oz caster sugar
1 egg
25 g / 1 oz fresh yeast or 15 ml / 1 tbsp dried yeast
50 g / 2 oz ground almonds
flour for kneading
50 g / 2 oz chopped mixed peel
50 g / 2 oz currants
50 g / 2 oz raisins
beaten egg for glazing
10 ml / 2 tsp granulated sugar
4 blanched almonds, roughly chopped

Grease a 23 x 13 x 7.5 cm / 9 x 5 x 3 inch loaf tin. Sift the flour and salt together. Measure 100 ml / 3½ fl oz lukewarm water. Warm the milk and butter together until the butter has melted. Transfer to a bowl, add the saffron and leave to stand for 10 minutes. Beat in the caster sugar, reserving 2.5 ml / ½ tsp if using fresh yeast, and add the egg.

Blend the fresh yeast to a thin paste with the reserved sugar and a little of the warm water. Set aside in a warm place until frothy – about 5 minutes. Alternatively, sprinkle dried yeast over all the warm water and set aside until frothy, then stir well.

Add the yeast liquid and remaining water to the milk and saffron mixture and stir in a third of the flour. Leave in a warm place for 20 minutes.

Work in the rest of the flour and ground almonds to form a very soft dough. Turn on to a well floured surface and knead for about 5 minutes or until the dough is smooth. Return to to the bowl and over with cling film. Leave in a warm place until the dough has doubled in bulk – this will take at least 2 hours, or longer.

Work in the dried fruit and form the dough into a loaf shape. Place the dough in the prepared loaf tin. Brush the top with beaten egg. Sprinkle on the granulated sugar and almonds. Place the tin in a large, lightly oiled polythene bag. Leave in a warm place for about 45 minutes or until the dough has doubled in bulk. Set the oven at 220°C / 424°F / gas 7.

Bake for 10 minutes, then reduce the oven temperature to 190°C / 375°F / gas 5. Continue baking for a further 30 minutes, until golden brown.

MAKES ONE 800 g / 1¾ lb LOAF

VARIATION

- **Kulich** Make as for Saffron Bread. After working the fruit into the dough, divide into two equal pieces. Well-grease two 450–500 g / 1 lb circular empty cans. For example, large fruit or coffee cans may be used. They should be washed and dried before use. Shape they pieces of dough to fit the tins and put the dough in them. Place the tins in a large, lightly oiled polythene bag. Leave in a warm place for about 35 minutes or until the dough has reached the top of the tins. Set the oven at 220°C / 425°F / gas 7. Bake for 35–40 minutes, until golden brown. When cold, ice with Glacé Icing (page 139).

MAKES TWO 400 G / 14 OZ KULICH

BAGELS

These ring buns are poached in water before baking. The result is a close-textured, moist bread with a deep golden-coloured crust which is quite thick but not hard. It is worth making a large batch and freezing them: the bagels may be frozen after poaching but before baking, then they should be baked after thawing. Alternatively, they may be fully cooked before cooling and freezing.

fat for greasing
400 g / 14 oz strong white flour
5 ml / 1 tsp salt
30 ml / 2 tbsp sugar
50 g / 2 oz margarine
15 g / ½ oz fresh yeast or 10 ml / 2 tsp dried yeast
1 egg, separated
flour for kneading
poppy seeds

Grease a baking sheet. Sift the flour into a large bowl. Measure 250 ml / 8 fl oz lukewarm water. Put the salt, sugar (reserving 2.5 ml / ½ tsp if using fresh yeast), the margarine and half the water in a saucepan and warm gently until the fat has melted. Leave until lukewarm.

Blend the fresh yeast to a thin paste with the reserved sugar and the remaining warm water. Set aside in a warm place until frothy – about 5 minutes. Alternatively, sprinkle dried yeast over the warm water and set aside until frothy, then stir well.

Whisk the egg white lightly, then add to the flour with the cooled margarine mixture and the yeast liquid. Mix to a soft dough. Cover the bowl with cling film. Leave in a warm place until the dough has almost doubled in bulk – this will take 2 hours, or longer.

Knead the dough again until firm. Cut into 25 g / 1 oz pieces. Roll each piece into a sausage shape 15–20 cm / 6–8 inches in length; then form this into a ring, pinching the ends securely together. Place the rings on a floured surface and leave to 10 minutes or until they begin to rise.

Heat a saucepan of water deep enough to float the bagels, to just under boiling point. Drop in the bagels, a few at a time. Cook them on one side for 2 minutes, then turn them over and cook on the other side for about 2 minutes or until they are light and have risen slightly. Place on the prepared baking sheet. Set the oven at 190°C / 375°F / gas 5.

Beat the egg yolk, brush it over the top surface of the bagels and sprinkle with poppy seeds. Bake for 20–30 minutes, until golden brown and crisp.

MAKES 28

BRIOCHES

fat for greasing
400 g / 14 oz strong white flour
5 ml / 1 tsp salt
50 g / 2 oz butter
15 g / ½ oz fresh yeast or 10 ml / 2 tsp dried yeast
2.5 ml / ½ tsp sugar
2 eggs
flour for kneading
beaten egg for glazing

Grease 22 x 7.5 cm / 3 inch brioche or deep bun tins. Sift the flour and salt into a large bowl. Rub in the butter. Blend the fresh yeast with the sugar and 40 ml / 8 tsp lukewarm water. Set aside in a warm place until frothy. Alernatively, sprinkle dried yeast over the warm water and set aside until frothy.

Beat the eggs into the yeast liquid and stir into the flour to form a soft dough. Turn on to a floured surface and knead for about 5 minutes or until the dough is smooth and no longer sticky. Return to the bowl and cover with cling film. Leave in a warm place for about 45 minutes or until doubled in bulk.

Knead the dough again until firm. Cut into 22 equal pieces. Cut off one-quarter of each piece used. Form the larger piece into a ball and place in a prepared tin. Firmly press a hole in the centre and place the remaining quarter as a knob in the centre. Place the tins on a baking sheet and cover with a large, lightly oiled polythene bag. Leave in a warm place for about 30 minutes or until the dough is light and puffy. Set the oven at 230°C / 450°F / gas 8. Brush with beaten egg. Bake for 15–20 minutes, until golden brown.

MAKES TWELVE

CROISSANTS

Rich, flaky French croissants make the perfect breakfast,
especially when homemade.

fat for greasing
400 g / 14 oz strong white flour
5 ml / 1 tbsp salt
75 g / 3 oz lard
25 g / 1 oz fresh yeast or 15 ml / 1 tbsp dried yeast
2.5 ml / ½ tsp sugar
1 egg, beaten
flour for kneading
100 g / 4 oz unsalted butter
beaten egg for glazing

Grease the baking sheet. Sift the flour and salt into a large bowl. Rub in 25 g / 1 oz of the lard. Measure 200 ml / 7 fl oz lukewarm water.

Blend the fresh yeast to a thin paste with the sugar and a little of the warm water. Set aside in a warm place until frothy – about 5 minutes. Alternatively, sprinkle the dried yeast over all the warm water and set aside until frothy, then stir well.

Stir the egg, yeast liquid and remaining water into the flour and mix to a soft dough. Turn on to a lightly-floured surface and knead for about 8 minutes or until the dough is smooth and not longer sticky. Return the dough to the bowl and cover with cling film. Leave at room temperature for 15 minutes.

Meanwhile, roughly chop the remaining lard and the butter together until well mixed; then chill. On a lightly-floured surface, roll out the dough carefully into an oblong 50 x 20 cm / 30 x 8 inches. Divide the chilled fat into three. Dot one-third over the top two-thirds of the dough, leaving a small border. Fold the dough into three by bringing the bottom third up and the top third down. Seal the edges by pressing with the rolling pin. Give the dough a quarter turn and repeat the rolling and folding twice, using the other two portions of fat. Place the dough in a large, lightly oiled polythene bag. Leave in a cool place for 15 minutes.

Repeat the rolling and folding three more times. Rest the dough in the polythene bag in a cool place for 15 minutes. Roll out to an oblong 34 x 23 cm / 14 x 9 inches and then cut it into six 13 cm / 5 inch squares. Cut each square into triangles. Brush the surface of the dough with beaten egg and roll each triangle loosely, towards the point, finishing with the tip underneath. Curve into a crescent shape. Place on the prepared baking sheet and brush with beaten egg. Place the baking sheet in the polythene bag again. Leave at room temperature for about 1 hour or until the dough is light and puffy. Set the oven at 220°C / 425°F / gas 7.

Bake for 15–20 minutes, until golden brown and crisp. Cool on a wire rack.

MAKES TWELVE

GRANT LOAF

fat for greasing
800 g / 1¾ lb wholemeal flour
15 ml / 1 oz fresh yeast or 15 ml / 1 tbsp dried yeast
2.5 ml / ½ tsp sugar

Grease three 20 x 10 x 6 cm / 8 x 4 x 2½ inch loaf tins. Mix the flour and salt in a large bowl. Have ready 700 ml / scant 1¼ pints lukewarm water.

Blend the fresh yeast to a thin paste with the sugar and a little of the warm water. Set aside in a warm place until frothy – about 5 minutes. Alternatively, sprinkle dried yeast over all the warm water and set aside until frothy, then stir well.

Pour the yeast liquid and remaining water into the flour and stir until the flour is evenly wetted. The resulting dough should be wet and slippery. Spoon it into the prepared loaf tins. Place the tins in a large, lightly oiled polythene bag. Leave in a warm place until the dough has risen by a third. Set the oven at 190°C / 375°F / gas 5.

Bake for 50–60 minutes, until the loaves are golden brown and crisp, and sound hollow when tapped on the bottom.

MAKES THREE 400 G / 14 OZ LOAVES

PRINCESS ROLLS

fat for greasing
400 g / 14 oz strong white flour
250 ml / 8 fl oz milk
15 g / ½ oz fresh yeast or 10 ml / 2 tsp dried yeast
15 ml / 1 tbsp caster sugar
50 g / 2 oz margarine
5 ml / 1 tsp salt
flour for kneading
about 150 g / 5 oz butter

Grease a baking sheet. Sift the flour into a large bowl. Warm the milk until lukewarm. Blend the fresh yeast to a thin paste with 2.5 ml / ½ tsp of the sugar and half of the warm milk. Set aside in a warm place until frothy. Alternatively, sprinkle dried yeast over the warm milk and set aside until frothy.

Add the margarine, remaining sugar and salt to the remaining milk, and heat until the fat has melted. Leave until lukewarm. Stir with the yeast liquid into the flour and mix to a soft dough. Turn on to a lightly-floured surface and knead until smooth. Return the dough to the bowl and over with cling film. Leave in a warm place until doubled in bulk.

Lightly knead the dough again. Roll out on a floured surface to 8 mm / ⅓ inch thickness. Cut into rounds, using a plain 7.5 cm / 3 inch cutter. Place a small piece of butter on one half of each round. Fold over the other half and pinch the edges firmly together. Place the rolls on the prepared baking sheet. Put the sheet in a large, lightly oiled polythene bag. Leave in a warm place for about 30 minutes or until the rolls have almost doubled in size. Set the oven at 220°C / 425°F / gas 7. Bake for 10–15 minutes, until golden brown.

MAKES EIGHTEEN

SALLY LUNN

Sally Lunn was a cake seller in Bath during the 18th century and her cake, or bun, became very famous.

fat for greasing
400 g / 14 oz strong white flour
5 ml / 1 tsp salt
50 g / 2 oz butter
150 ml / ¼ pint milk
15 g / ½ oz fresh yeast or 10 ml / 2 tsp dried yeast
2.5 ml / ½ tsp sugar
1 egg
15 ml / 1 tbsp caster sugar for glazing

Grease two 15 cm / 6 inch round cake tins. Sift the flour and salt into a large bowl. Rub in the butter. Warm the milk until lukewarm.

Blend the fresh yeast to a thin paste with the sugar and warm milk. Set aside in a warm place until frothy – about 5 minutes. Alternatively, sprinkle dried yeast over the warm milk and set aside until frothy, then stir well.

Beat the egg into the yeast liquid and stir into the flour mixture to form a very soft dough. Beat well. Pour the mixture into the prepared cake tins.

Place the tins in a large, lightly oiled polythene bag. Leave in a warm place until the dough has doubled in bulk – this will take 2 hours, or longer. Set the oven at 220°C / 425°F / gas 7.

Bake for 20–25 minutes, until golden brown. To make the glaze, boil together 15 ml / 1 tbsp water and the sugar until syrupy. Brush the hot glaze over the top of the Sally Lunns.

To serve, split each Sally Lunn crossways, into three rounds and toast each piece on both sides. Butter thickly or fill with clotted cream, re-form the cake, and cut into slices or wedges.

MAKES TWO 15 CM / 6 INCH SALLY LUNNS

CHALLAH

fat for greasing
800 g / 1¾ lb strong white flour
10 ml / 2 tsp sugar
25 g / 1 oz fresh yeast or 15 ml / 1 tbsp dried yeast
10 ml / 2 tsp salt
100 g / 4 oz butter or margarine
2 eggs
flour for kneading
beaten egg for glazing

Grease two baking sheets. Sift about 75 g / 3 oz of the flour and all the sugar into a large bowl. Measure 400 ml / 14 fl oz lukewarm water. Blend the fresh yeast into the water or stir in the dried yeast. Pour the yeast liquid into the flour and sugar and beat well. Leave the bowl in a warm place for 20 minutes.

Sift the remaining flour and the salt into a bowl. Rub in the butter or margarine. Beat the eggs into the yeast mixture and stir in the flour mixture. Mix to a soft dough. Turn on to a lightly-floured surface and knead for about 6 minutes or until the dough is smooth and no longer sticky. Return to the bowl and cover with cling film. Leave in a warm place until the dough has doubled in bulk – this will take up to 2 hours, or longer.

Knead the dough again until firm. Cut into two equal portions. Cut one of these into two equal pieces and roll these into long strands 30–35 cm / 12–14 inches in length. Arrange the two strands in a cross on a flat surface. Take the two opposite ends of the bottom strand and cross them over the top strand in the centre. Repeat this, using the other strand. Cross each strand alternatively, building up the plait vertically, until all the dough is used up. Gather the short ends together and pinch firmly. Lay the challah on its side and place on the prepared baking sheet. Brush with beaten egg. Repeat, using a second portion. Cover with lightly oiled polythene. Leave in a warm place for about 30 minutes or until the dough has doubled in bulk. Set the oven at 220°C / 425°F / gas 7.

Bake for 35–40 minutes, until the loaves are golden brown and sound hollow when tapped on the bottom.

MAKES TWO 800 G / 1¾ LOAVES

Sweet Yeast Doughs

The perfect weekend treat, yeasted tea breads and buns are ideal candidates for batch baking and freezing.

DANISH PASTRIES

200 g / 7 oz plain flour
pinch of salt
25 g / 1 oz lard
15 g / ½ oz fresh yeast or 10 ml / 2 tsp dried yeast
2.5 ml / ½ tsp caster sugar
1 egg, beaten
flour for dusting
125 g / 4½ oz butter, chilled

Sift the flour and salt into a bowl. Rub in the lard.

Blend the fresh yeast to a thin paste with the sugar and 75 ml / 3 fl oz lukewarm water. Set aside in a warm place until frothy – about 5 minutes. Sprinkle dried yeast over the warm water and set aside until frothy, then stir well. Add the beaten egg.

Pour the yeast liquid into the flour mixture and mix to a soft dough. Turn on to a floured surface and knead lightly until smooth. Return the dough to the bowl and cover with cling film. Leave in a cool place for 10 minutes.

Shape the butter into a long rectangle about 1 cm / ½ inch thick. Roll out the dough to about 25 cm / 10 inches square. Place the butter down the centre. Fold the sides of the dough over the middle to overlap about 1 cm / ½ inch only. Roll the dough into a strip 40 x 15 cm / 16 x 6 inches. Fold it evenly into three. Place the dough in a large, lightly oiled polythene bag. Leave for 10 minutes. Roll and fold the dough in the same way twice more, letting it rest for 10 minutes each time. The dough is now ready for making the pastry shapes. Each batch of dough makes 16 pastries. Choose two shapes, using half the dough for each.

Windmills Roll out half the dough to about 40 x 20 cm / 16 x 8 inches. Cut into eight 10 cm / 4 inch squares; place the squares on a baking sheet. Put a little Almond Paste (page 134) in the centre of each square (about 50 g / 2 oz in all). Brush the paste lightly with beaten egg. Make a cut from the corners of each square towards the middle. Fold the corners of each triangular piece towards the centre, then press the points into the almond paste firmly. Brush with beaten egg. Cover the pastries with oiled polythene and leave in a warm place for about 10–15 minutes until puffy. (It is important not to have the temperature too warm or the butter will run out.) Set the oven at 220°C / 425°F / gas 7 and bake the pastries for about 10 minutes. When cool, place a little raspberry jam in the centre of each pastry.

MAKES EIGHT

Fruit Snails Cream together 50 g / 2 oz butter, 50 g / 2 oz caster sugar and 10 ml / 2 tsp ground cinnamon. Roll out half the dough into a 40 x 15 cm / 16 x 6 inch rectangle. Spread with the spiced butter and scatter 25 g / 1 oz sultanas over it. Roll up from the short side to make a fat roll. Cut it into eight slices and place on a baking sheet. Flatten slightly. Prove and bake as above. Decorate with Glacé Icing (page 139) when cold.

MAKES EIGHT

Cockscombs Roll out half the dough and cut it into squares as for windmills. Spread the middle of each square with a little bought chocolate hazelnut spread and top with a thin sausage shape of Almond Paste (page 134). Fold each square in half and pinch the edges together to seal in the filling. Make four or five cuts into the pastries, then place on a baking sheet, curving them slightly to open the slits . Prove and bake as for windmills. Brush with Apricot Glaze (page 134) when cool.

MAKES EIGHT

SWEET ALMOND BREAD

A layer of almond paste is baked into this bread.

fat for greasing
200 g / 7 oz strong white flour
5 ml / 1 tsp sugar
100 ml / 3½ fl oz milk
15 g / ½ oz fresh yeast or 10 ml / 2 tsp dried yeast
2.5 ml / ½ tsp salt
25 g / 1 oz butter or margarine
1 egg

continued overleaf...

flour for kneading
milk for glazing
sifted icing sugar for dredging

ALMOND PASTE
75 g / 3 oz icing sugar, sifted
75 g / 3 oz ground almonds
5 ml / 1 tsp lemon juice
few drops of almond essence
beaten egg white

Grease a baking sheet. Sift about 50 g / 2 oz of the flour and the sugar into a bowl. Warm the milk until lukewarm. Blend in the fresh yeast or sprinkle on the dried yeast. Pour the yeast liquid into the flour and sugar, then beat well. Leave the bowl in a warm place for 20 minutes.

Sift the remaining flour and salt into a bowl. Rub in the butter or margarine. Beat the egg into the yeast mixture and stir in the flour and fat mixture. Mix to a soft dough. Turn on to a lightly-floured surface and knead for about 5 minutes or until the dough is smooth and no longer sticky. Return to the bowl and cover with cling film. Leave in a warm place until the dough has doubled in bulk – this will take about 40 minutes, or longer.

To make the almond paste, mix the icing sugar, ground almonds, lemon juice and almond essence with enough egg white to bind the mixture together.

Roll out the dough on a lightly-floured surface to a 25 cm / 10 inch round.

Break the almond paste in lumps and sprinkle them on to half the dough round. Fold the uncovered half of the dough over to cover the paste. Press the edges of dough firmly together. Brush the surface with milk. Place on the prepared baking sheet and cover with oiled polythene. Leave for about 30 minutes to rise. Set the oven at 220°C / 425°F / gas 7.

Bake for 10 minutes, then lower the oven temperature to 190°C / 375°F / gas 5. Continue baking for 15–25 minutes, until golden brown. When cold, dredge the bread with a little sifted icing sugar.

MAKES ONE 400 G / 14 OZ LOAF

BARA BRITH

fat for greasing
450 g / 1 lb strong plain flour
75 g / 3 oz lard or butter
50 g / 2 oz chopped mixed peel
150 g / 5 oz seedless raisins
50 g / 2 oz currants
75 g / 3 oz soft light brown sugar
5 ml / 1 tsp ground mixed spice
pinch of salt
25 g / 1 oz fresh yeast
5 ml / 1 tsp sugar
250 ml / 8 fl oz lukewarm milk
1 egg, beaten
flour for kneading
honey for glazing

Grease a 20 x 13 x 7.5 cm / 8 x 5 x 3 inch loaf tin. Sift the flour into a bowl and rub in the lard or butter. Stir in the peel, raisins, currants, brown sugar, mixed spice and salt. Blend the fresh yeast to a thin paste with the sugar and milk. Set aside in a warm place until frothy – about 5 minutes.

Make a well in the centre of the dry ingredients and add the yeast mixture and the beaten egg. Mix to a soft dough, then cover the bowl with cling film. Leave in a warm place until the dough has doubled in bulk – this will take about 2 hours, or longer.

Turn out the dough on to a floured board and knead well. Place in the prepared loaf tin, pressing it well into the corners. Place the tin in a large, lightly oiled polythene bag. Leave for a further 30 minutes to rise. Set the oven at 200°C / 400°F / gas 6.

Bake for 15 minutes, then lower the oven temperature to 160°C / 325°F / gas 3. Continue baking for about 1¼ hours. Turn out on to a wire rack and brush the top with clear honey.

MAKES TWELVE SLICES

PLAIN BUNS

These may be varied by adding a few currants,
some chopped candied peel or mixed peel, or caraway seeds.

fat for greasing
25 g / 1 oz fresh yeast or 15 ml / 1 tbsp dried yeast
75 g / 3 oz plus 5 ml / 1 tsp caster sugar
300 ml / ½ pint lukewarm milk
450 g / 1 lb strong plain flour
5 ml / 1 tsp salt
50 g / 2 oz butter, melted

Grease a baking sheet. Blend the fresh yeast with the 5 ml / 1 tsp caster sugar and a little of the lukewarm milk. Set aside until frothy. For dried yeast, sprinkle the yeast over all the milk, then leave until frothy.

Sift the flour and salt into a bowl, then stir in the remaining sugar. Make a well in the middle and pour in the yeast liquid with the remaining milk. Stir in the melted butter and gradually mix in the dry ingredients to a firm dough.

Turn out the dough on a lightly-floured surface and knead thoroughly until smooth and elastic – about 10 minutes. Place the dough in a clean, lightly-floured bowl. Cover with cling film and leave in a warm place until doubled in bulk. This will take 2 hours or longer, depending on the warmth of the room.

Knead the dough lightly, then cut it into 12 equal pieces and quickly knead them into egg shapes. Arrange in neat rows on the baking sheet, cover loosely with oiled polythene or cling film and leave until doubled in bulk.

Meanwhile, set the oven at 220°C / 425°F / gas 7. Brush the risen buns with a little milk and bake for 15–20 minutes, until risen and golden. Cool on a wire rack.

MAKES TWELVE

CORNISH SPLITS

fat for greasing
400 g / 14 oz strong white flour
50 g / 2 oz sugar
125 ml / 4 fl oz milk
15 g / ½ oz fresh yeast or 10 ml / 2 tsp dried yeast
5 ml / 1 tsp salt
50 g / 2 oz butter
flour for kneading

Grease a baking sheet. Sift about 75 g / 3 oz of the flour and 5 ml / 1 tsp of the sugar into a large bowl. Warm the milk and 125 ml / 4 fl oz water until luke-warm. Blend in the fresh yeast or sprinkle on the dried yeast. Pour the yeast liquid into the flour and sugar, then beat well. Leave the bowl in a warm place for 20 minutes.

Sift the rest of the flour and sugar and the salt together in a bowl. Rub in the butter. Stir into the yeast mixture and mix to form a soft dough. Turn on to a lightly-floured surface and knead for about 6 minutes or until the dough is smooth and no longer sticky. Return to the bowl and cover with cling film. Leave in a warm place until the dough has doubled in bulk – this will take 2 hours, or longer.

Knead the dough again until firm. Divide into 50 g / 2 oz pieces and form each into a round bun. Place the buns on the prepared baking sheet. Place the sheet in a large, lightly oiled polythene bag. Leave in a warm place for about 30 minutes or until the buns have doubled in size. Set the oven at 220°C / 425°F / gas 7.

Bake for 15–20 minutes, until golden brown. Serve cold, split the buns and spread with cream and jam.

MAKES FOURTEEN

CHELSEA BUNS

fat for greasing
400 g / 14 oz strong white flour
5 ml / 1 tsp sugar
200 ml / 7 fl oz milk
25 g / 1 oz fresh yeast or 15 ml / 1 tbsp dried yeast
5 ml / 1 tsp salt
50 g / 2 oz butter plus 15 ml / 1 tbsp
1 egg
flour for kneading
150 g / 5 oz currants
50 g / 2 oz chopped mixed peel
100 g / 4 oz soft light brown sugar
honey for glazing

Grease a baking sheet. Sift about 75 g / 3 oz of the flour and the sugar into a large bowl. Warm the milk until lukewarm. Blend in the fresh yeast or sprinkle on the dried yeast. Pour the yeast liquid into the flour and sugar, then beat well. Leave the bowl in a warm place for 20 minutes.

Sift the remaining flour and the salt into a bowl. Rub in the 50 g / 2 oz butter. Beat the egg into the yeast mixture and add the flour and fat mixture. Mix to a soft dough. Turn on to a lightly-floured surface and knead for about 6 minutes or until the dough is smooth and no longer sticky. Return to the bowl and cover with cling film. Leave in a warm place until the dough has doubled in bulk.

On a floured surface, roll out the dough to a 50 cm / 20 inch square. Melt the remaining butter and brush it all over the surface of the dough. Sprinkle with the dried fruit and sugar. Roll up the dough like a Swiss roll. Cut the roll into 16 equal pieces. Place the buns, about 2.5 cm / 1 inch apart, on the prepared baking sheet with the cut side uppermost. Place the baking sheet in a large, lightly oiled polythene bag. Leave in a warm place for about 30 minutes or until the buns have joined together and are light and puffy. Set the oven at 220°C / 425°F / gas 7.

Bake for 15–20 minutes, until golden brown. While still hot, brush with honey.

MAKES SIXTEEN

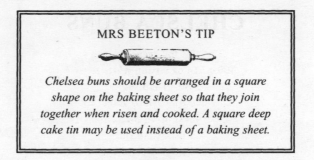

MRS BEETON'S TIP

Chelsea buns should be arranged in a square shape on the baking sheet so that they join together when risen and cooked. A square deep cake tin may be used instead of a baking sheet.

VARIATIONS

- Use this classic recipe as a basis for making rolled buns with different fillings. Try chopped ready-to-eat dried apricots with chopped walnuts and a little honey; chopped dates with orange marmalade and some grated cooking apple; or chocolate chips with chopped hazelnuts and chopped mixed peel.

CHRISTMAS STOLLEN

This is the classic German Christmas bread.

butter for greasing
1 kg / 2¼ lb plain flour
75 g / 3 oz fresh yeast
200 ml / 7 fl oz lukewarm milk
350 g / 12 oz butter
grated rind and juice of 1 lemon
250 g / 9 oz caster sugar
2 egg yolks
5 ml / 1 tsp salt
500 g / 18 oz seedless raisins
225 g / 8 oz sultanas
150 g / 5 oz blanched slivered almonds
100 g / 4 oz chopped mixed peel
flour for dusting
100 g / 4 oz unsalted butter
icing sugar for dusting

continued overleaf...

Butter a baking sheet. Sift the flour into a bowl. Blend the yeast with the warm milk and 50 g / 2 oz of the flour. Set aside until frothy.

Meanwhile, melt the butter. Cool slightly, then blend into the remaining flour with the lemon juice. Add the milk and yeast liquid together with the lemon rind, sugar, egg yolks and salt. Beat well together. Knead the dough until it is very firm and elastic, and leaves the sides of the bowl. Cover with cling film. Leave in a warm place until the dough has doubled in bulk. This will take about 2 hours.

Meanwhile, mix the dried fruit with the nuts and mixed peel. Knead the dough again, pull the sides to the centre, turn it over and cover once more. Leave to rise for a further 30 minutes. When the dough has doubled in bulk again, turn it on to a floured surface and knead in the fruit and nut mixture.

Divide the dough in half and roll each half into a pointed oval shape. Lay each on the prepared baking sheet. Place a rolling pin along the length of each piece of the dough in the centre. Roll half the dough lightly from the centre outwards. Brush the thinner rolled half with a little water and fold the other half over it, leaving a margin of about 5 cm / 2 inches all around which allows the dough to rise. Press well together; the water will bind it. Cover the stollen and leave to rise in a warm place until doubled in bulk again. Set the oven at 190°C / 375°F / gas 5.

Melt 50 g / 2 oz of the unsalted butter and brush it over the stollen. Bake for about 1 hour, until golden. When baked, melt the remaining unsalted butter, brush it over the stollen, then sprinkle with sifted icing sugar. Keep for a day before cutting.

The stollen will remain fresh for many weeks if well wrapped in foil or grease-proof paper and stored in an airtight tin.

MAKES TWO LOAVES, ABOUT 24 SLICES EACH

REVEL BUNS

These take a day to prove.

fat for greasing
large pinch of powdered saffron
125 ml / 4 fl oz milk
20 g / ¾ oz fresh yeast
100 g / 4 oz caster sugar
450 g / 1 lb plain flour
2.5 ml / ½ tsp ground cinnamon
pinch of salt
100 g / 4 oz butter
150 ml / ¼ pint double cream
2 eggs, beaten
100 g / 4 oz currants
beaten egg for glazing

Put the saffron in a heatproof jug. Warm the milk until steaming and pour it over the saffron. Leave to infuse for 30 minutes.

Strain 60 ml / 4 tbsp of the milk and leave until lukewarm. Blend the yeast to a thin paste with 2.5 ml / ½ tsp of the sugar and the strained warm milk. Set aside in a warm place until frothy – about 5 minutes.

Sift the flour with the cinnamon and salt into a bowl. Rub in the butter. Strain the remaining saffron-flavoured milk and cream into the dry ingredients, with the eggs and yeast mixture. Mix thoroughly, then add the currants. Knead well. Cover and prove in the refrigerator overnight.

Next day, grease a baking sheet. Shape the mixture into 12 buns. Place on the prepared baking sheet and leave to rise for 20–30 minutes. Set the oven at 190°C / 375°F / gas 5. Brush the tops with beaten egg and sprinkle with the remaining sugar. Bake for about 15 minutes. Serve warm or cold with butter.

MAKES TWELVE

HOT CROSS BUNS

flour for dusting
400 g / 14 oz strong white flour
5 ml / 1 tsp sugar
125 ml / 4 fl oz milk
25 g / 1 oz fresh yeast or 15 ml / 1 tbsp dried yeast
5 ml / 1 tsp salt
7.5 ml / 1½ tsp ground mixed spice
2.5 ml / ½ tsp ground cinnamon
2.5 ml / ½ tsp grated nutmeg
50 g / 2 oz butter
50 g / 2 oz caster sugar
100 g / 4 oz currants
50 g / 2 oz chopped mixed peel
1 egg
flour for kneading

GLAZE
30 ml / 2 tbsp milk
40 g / 1½ oz caster sugar

Sift about 75 g / 3 oz of the flour and the 5 ml / 1 tsp sugar into a large bowl. Warm the milk and 75 ml / 3 fl oz water until lukewarm. Blend in the fresh yeast or sprinkle on the dried yeast. Pour the yeast liquid into the flour and sugar, then beat well. Leave the bowl in a warm place for 20 minutes.

Sift the rest of the flour, the salt and spices into a bowl. Rub in the butter. Add the caster sugar and dried fruit. Beat the egg into the frothy yeast mixture and add the flour, fat and fruit mixture. Mix to a soft dough. Turn on to a lightly-floured surface and knead for about 5 minutes. Return to the bowl and cover with cling film. Leave in a warm place until the dough has almost doubled in bulk.

Knead the dough again until firm. Cut into 12 equal pieces and shape each into a round bun.

Place on a floured baking sheet. With a sharp knife slash a cross on the top of each bun, or make crosses with pastry trimmings. Cover with oiled polythene. Leave for about 35 minutes, until the dough has doubled in bulk. Set the oven at 220°C / 425°F / gas 7. Bake for 15–20 minutes, until golden. Boil the milk, sugar and 30 ml / 2 tbsp water for 6 minutes. Brush over the hot buns.

MAKES TWELVE

LARDY CAKE

fat for greasing
¼ quantity risen Basic White Bread dough, about 350 g / 12 oz (page 190)
flour for rolling out
125 g / 4½ oz lard
100 g / 4 oz caster sugar
100 g / 4 oz sultanas or currants
5 ml / 1 tsp ground mixed spice
10 ml / 2 tsp caster sugar for glazing

Grease a 20 cm / 8 inch square cake tin. Roll out the dough on a floured surface to a strip 2 cm / ¾ inch thick. Place a third of the lard in small pats over the dough. Sprinkle one-third of the sugar, dried fruit and spice over. Fold the dough into three, bringing the bottom third up and the top third down. Repeat the rolling twice more.

Roll out to fit the tin. Score diamond shapes in the surface of the dough with a sharp knife. Place the tin in a large, lightly oiled polythene bag. Leave in a warm place for about 45 minutes or until risen by half. Set the oven at 200°C / 400°F / gas 6.

Bake for 40 minutes, until golden. To make the glaze, boil the sugar and 15 ml / 1 tbsp water in a saucepan until syrupy, then brush over the warm cake.

MAKES EIGHTEEN TO TWENTY SLICES

BATH BUNS

fat for greasing
400 g / 14 oz strong white flour
5 ml / 1 tsp sugar
125 ml / 4 fl oz milk
25 g / 1 oz fresh yeast or 15 ml / 1 tbsp dried yeast
5 ml / 1 tsp salt
50 g / 2 oz butter
50 g / 2 oz caster sugar
150 g / 5 oz sultanas
50 g / 2 oz chopped mixed peel
2 eggs / beaten egg for glazing
50 g / 2 oz sugar lumps, coarsely crushed

Grease a baking sheet. Sift about 75 g / 3 oz of the flour and the 5 ml / 1 tsp sugar into a large bowl. Warm the milk and 75 ml / 3 fl oz water until luke-warm. Blend in the fresh yeast or sprinkle on the dried yeast. Pour the yeast liquid into the flour and sugar, then beat well. Leave the bowl in a warm place for 20 minutes.

Sift the rest of the flour and the salt into a bowl. Rub in the butter. Add the caster sugar and dried fruit. Beat the eggs into the yeast mixture and add the flour, fat and fruit mixture. Mix to a very soft dough. Use your hand to beat the dough for 3 minutes. Cover the bowl with cling film. Leave in a warm place until the dough has almost doubled in bulk – this will take about 45 minutes, or longer.

Beat the dough again for 1 minute. Place 15 ml / 1 tbsp spoonfuls of the mixture on the baking sheet, leaving plenty of space between them. Place the baking sheet in a large, lightly oiled polythene bag. Leave in a warm place for about 20 minutes or until the buns have almost doubled in size. Set the oven at 220°C / 425°F / gas 7.

Glaze each bun with egg and sugar. Bake for 15–20 minutes, until golden brown.

MAKES TWELVE

Breads Without Yeast

Here are breads that rely on alternative raising
agents, including Irish soda bread.
These are ideal if you want
to make an impact
at short notice.

SOUR DOUGH RYE BREAD

fat for greasing
500 g / 18 oz rye flour
200 g / 7 oz strong white flour
10 ml / 2 tsp salt
15 ml / 1 tbsp sugar
15 ml / 1 tbsp oil

STARTER PASTE
100 g / 4 oz strong white flour
50 g / 2 oz sugar
175 ml / 6 fl oz milk

To make the starter paste, sift the flour and sugar into a bowl. Warm the milk until hand-hot, then stir into the flour. Beat to a smooth paste. Place the starter paste in a screw-topped jar and leave in a warm place for 4 days.

Grease two 23 x 13 x 7.5 cm / 9 x 5 x 3 inch loaf tins. Put the flours, salt and sugar in a large bowl. Add the starter paste, 375 ml / 13 fl oz warm water and the oil, then mix to a slack dough. Beat with a wooden spoon for 3 minutes. Place the dough in the prepared loaf tins. Cover with a large, lightly oiled polythene bag. Leave at room temperature for about 24 hours or until the dough reaches the top of the tins. Set the oven at 230°C / 450°F / gas 8.

Bake for 10 minutes, then lower the oven temperature to 190°C / 375°F / gas 5. Continue to bake for 30–35 minutes, until the loaves are well browned and sound hollow when tapped on the bottom.

MAKES TWO 800 G / 1¾ LB LOAVES

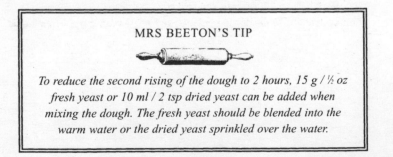

MRS BEETON'S TIP

To reduce the second rising of the dough to 2 hours, 15 g / ½ oz fresh yeast or 10 ml / 2 tsp dried yeast can be added when mixing the dough. The fresh yeast should be blended into the warm water or the dried yeast sprinkled over the water.

BASIC QUICK BREAD

fat for greasing
400 g / 14 oz self-raising flour or a mixture of white and brown self-raising
flours or 400 g / 14 oz plain flour and 20 ml / 4 tsp baking powder
5 ml / 1 tsp salt
50 g / 2 oz margarine or lard
250 ml / 8 fl oz milk or water or a mixture, as preferred
flour for kneading

Grease a baking sheet. Set the oven at 200°C / 400°F / gas 6. Sift the flour,
baking powder (if used) and salt into a large bowl. Rub in the margarine or lard.
Mix in enough liquid to make a soft dough.

Turn the dough on to a floured surface and knead lightly for 1 minute. Shape
the dough into two rounds and place them on the prepared baking sheet. Make
a cross in the top of each with the back of a knife.

Bake for 30–40 minutes. Cool on a wire rack.

MAKES TWO BUN LOAVES

VARIATIONS

- **Wholemeal Quick Bread** Substitute 400 g / 14 oz wholemeal flour for the
  plain flour in the basic recipe. Note that the wholemeal flour will give a
  closer-textured loaf.
- **Nut Bread** Make Wholemeal Quick Bread. Add 75 g / 3 oz chopped nuts and
  50 g / 2 oz sugar to the dry ingredients, and add 1 beaten egg to the liquid.
- **Apricot and Walnut Loaf** Make the Basic Quick Bread, but use butter as
  the fat. Add 100 g / 4 oz dried and soaked chopped apricots and 50 g / 2 oz
  chopped walnuts to the dry ingredients, and add 1 beaten egg to the liquid.

BASIC SOURED MILK QUICK BREAD

fat for greasing
400 g / 14 oz plain flour
5 ml / 1 tsp salt
10 ml / 2 tsp bicarbonate of soda
10 ml / 2 tsp cream of tartar
about 250 ml / 8 fl oz soured milk or buttermilk

Grease a baking sheet. Set the oven at 220°C / 425°F / gas 7. Sift the flour, salt, bicarbonate of soda and cream of tartar into a large bowl. Mix to a light spongy dough with the milk.

Divide the dough into two equal pieces and form each into a round cake. Slash a cross on the top of each loaf with a sharp knife. Place on the prepared baking sheet.

Bake for about 30 minutes, until golden brown. Cool on a wire rack.

MAKES TWO LOAVES

MRS BEETON'S TIP

The keeping quality of this bread will be improved
if 50 g / 2 oz lard is rubbed into the sifted flour.

IRISH SODA BREAD

fat for greasing
575 g / 1¼ lb plain flour
5 ml / 1 tsp bicarbonate of soda
5 ml / 1 tsp salt
5 ml / 1 tsp cream of tartar (if using fresh milk)
300 ml / ½ pint buttermilk or soured milk or fresh milk
flour for dusting

Grease a baking sheet. Set the oven at 190–200°C / 375–400°F / gas 5–6. Mix all the dry ingredients in a bowl, then make a well in the centre. Add enough milk to make a fairly slack dough, pouring it in almost all at once, not spoonful by spoonful. Mix with a wooden spoon, lightly and quickly.

With floured hands, place the mixture on a lightly-floured surface and flatten the dough into a round about 2.5 cm / 1 inch thick. Turn on to the prepared baking sheet. Make a large cross in the surface with a floured knife to make it heat through evenly.

Bake for about 40 minutes. Pierce the centre with a thin skewer to test for readiness; it should come out clean. Wrap the loaf in a clean tea-towel to keep it soft until required.

MAKES ONE 750 G / 1¾ LB LOAF

TEXAS CORNBREAD

This golden bread makes an ideal accompaniment to soups, stews and casseroles.

fat for greasing
125 g / 4½ oz bacon fat or beef dripping
125 g / 4½ oz cornmeal (polenta)
50 g / 2 oz plain flour
5 ml / 1 tsp salt
5 ml / 1 tsp baking powder
2.5 ml / ½ tsp bicarbonate of soda
200 ml / 7 fl oz buttermilk or fresh milk with a squeeze of lemon juice
2 eggs, beaten

Grease a 20 cm / 8 inch cake tin. Set the oven at 230°C / 450°F / gas 8. Melt the bacon fat or dripping, then leave to cool slightly.

Mix the cornmeal, flour, salt, baking powder and bicarbonate of soda in a bowl. Add the buttermilk or soured milk, eggs and melted fat or dripping. Mix well. Turn into the prepared cake tin.

Bake for 30 minutes. The bread should be firm to the touch when done. Serve warm.

MAKES ONE 225 G / 8 OZ CORNBREAD

MIXED GRAIN
SODA BREAD ROLLS

fat for greasing
225 g / 8 oz wholemeal flour
225 g / 8 oz plain flour
5 ml / 1 tsp bicarbonate of soda
5 ml / 1 tsp cream of tartar
5 ml / 1 tsp salt
60 ml / 4 tbsp rolled oats
60 ml / 4 tbsp sunflower seeds
60 ml / 4 tbsp sesame seeds
60 ml / 4 tbsp cracked wheat
300 ml / ½ pint milk plus extra for glazing
flour for kneading

Grease a baking sheet. Set the oven at 200°C / 400°F / gas 6. Mix both types of flour in a bowl. Stir in the bicarbonate of soda, cream of tartar, salt, oats, sunflower seeds, sesame seeds and cracked wheat. Mix in the milk to make a soft dough. Turn the dough out on a lightly-floured surface and knead very briefly into a smooth ball.

Divide the dough into 12 equal portions and quickly knead each portion into a round roll. Place the rolls well apart on the baking sheet. Use a sharp knife to cut a cross in the top of each roll. Brush with a little milk, then bake for about 30 minutes, until well risen, golden brown and cooked through. Cool on a wire rack.

MAKES TWELVE

Muffins, Crumpets & Teabreads

*Ensure your table is laden with delicious
traditional tea-time goods,
for the ultimate in
culinary comfort.*

AMERICAN MUFFINS

Unlike English muffins, American muffins are quick breads.
They are light, savoury or sweet buns made with a slightly more puffed,
richer dough than scones. They are very popular breakfast breads.

butter for greasing
200 g / 7 oz plain flour
15 ml / 1 tbsp baking powder
2.5 ml / ½ tsp salt
50 g / 2 oz granulated sugar
50 g / 2 oz butter
1 egg
200 ml / 7 fl oz milk

Butter twelve 6 cm / 2 ½ inch muffin tins or deep bun tins. Set the oven at 200°C / 400°F / gas 6. Sift the dry ingredients into a bowl.

Melt the butter. Mix with the egg and milk in a separate bowl. Pour the liquid mixture over the dry ingredients. Stir only enough to dampen the flour; the mixture should be lumpy. Spoon into the prepared muffin tins, as lightly as possible, filling them only two-thirds full.

Bake for about 15 minutes, until well risen and browned. The cooked muffins should be cracked across the middle. Cool in the tins for 2–3 minutes, then turn out on to a wire rack to finish cooling.

MAKES TWELVE

VARIATIONS

- **Walnut Muffins** Increase the sugar to 100 g / 4 oz. Add 75 g / 3 oz chopped walnuts before adding the liquids. After filling the muffin tins, sprinkle with a mixture of sugar, cinnamon, and extra finely chopped walnuts.

MRS BEETON'S TIP

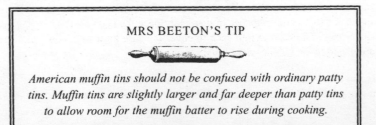

American muffin tins should not be confused with ordinary patty
tins. Muffin tins are slightly larger and far deeper than patty tins
to allow room for the muffin batter to rise during cooking.

Blueberry Muffins Reserve 50 g / 2 oz of the flour. Sprinkle lightly over 225 g / 8 oz firm blueberries. Stir into the mixture last.

- **Jam Muffins** Before baking, top each muffin with 5 ml / 1 tsp sharp-flavoured jam.
- **Raisin Muffins** Add about 50 g / 2 oz seedless raisins before adding the liquids.
- **Orange Apricot Muffins** Add 50 g / 2 oz chopped ready-to-eat dried apricots and 15 ml / 1 tbsp grated orange rind before adding the liquids.
- **Wholemeal Muffins** Substitute 100 g / 4 oz wholemeal flour for 100 g / 4 oz of the plain flour. Do not sift the wholemeal flour, but add it after sifting the plain flour.

CRUMPETS

200 g / 7 oz strong white flour
2.5 ml / ½ tsp salt
2.5 ml / ½ tsp sugar
100 ml / 3½ fl oz milk
10 ml / 2 tsp dried yeast
pinch of bicarbonate of soda
fat for frying

Sift the flour, salt and sugar into a large bowl. Place the milk in a saucepan, add 125 ml / 4 fl oz water and warm gently. The mixture should be just hand-hot. Pour the mixture into a small bowl, sprinkle the dried yeast on top and leave for 10–15 minutes or until frothy.

Add the yeast liquid to the flour and beat to a smooth batter. Cover the bowl with a large lightly oiled polythene bag and leave in a warm place for about 45 minutes or until the batter has doubled in bulk.

Dissolve the bicarbonate of soda in 15 ml / 1 tbsp warm water; beat into the batter. Cover and leave to rise again for 20 minutes.

Heat a griddle or heavy-bottomed frying pan over medium heat, then grease it when hot. Grease metal crumpet rings, poaching rings or large plain biscuit cutters about 7.5 cm / 3 inches in diameter. Place the rings on the hot griddle, pour a spoonful of batter into each to cover the base thinly and cook until the top is set and the bubbles have burst.

Remove the rings and turn the crumpets over. Cook the other side for 2–3 minutes only, until firm but barely coloured. Cool the crumpets on a wire rack. Serve toasted, with butter.

MAKES TEN TO TWELVE

ENGLISH MUFFINS

The correct way to serve muffins is to split each one open around the edges almost to the centre. Toast slowly on both sides so that the heat penetrates to the centre, then pull the muffin halves apart, butter thickly, put together again and serve at once.

400 g / 14 oz strong white flour
5 ml / 1 tsp salt
25 g / 1 oz butter or margarine
225 ml / 7½ fl oz milk
10 ml / 2 tsp dried yeast
1 egg
fat for frying

Sift the flour and salt into a large bowl. Rub in the butter or margarine. Place the milk in a saucepan and warm gently. It should be just hand-hot. Pour the milk into a small bowl, sprinkle the dried yeast on top and leave for 10–15 minutes until frothy. Beat in the egg.

Add the yeast liquid to the flour to make a very soft dough. Beat the dough by hand or with a wooden spoon for about 5 minutes until smooth and shiny. Cover the bowl with a large lightly oiled polythene bag and leave in a warm place for 1–2 hours or until doubled in bulk. Beat again lightly.

Roll out on a well floured surface to a thickness of about 1 cm / ½ inch. Using a plain 7.5 cm / 3 inch cutter, cut the dough into rounds. Place the rounds on a floured baking sheet, cover with polythene and leave to rise for about 45 minutes or until light and puffy.

Heat a griddle or heavy-bottomed frying pan, then grease it. Cook the muffins on both sides for about 8 minutes until golden.

MAKES TWENTY

APPLE LOAF

fat for greasing
200 g / 7 oz plain flour
pinch of salt
5 ml / 1 tsp baking powder
2.5 ml / ½ tsp ground mixed spice
100 g / 4 oz butter or margarine
150 g / 5 oz caster sugar
50 g / 2 oz currants
100 g / 4 oz seedless raisins
200 g / 7 oz cooking apples
5 ml / 1 tsp lemon juice
2 eggs
about 25 ml / 1 fl oz milk
50 g / 2 oz icing sugar, sifted
1 tart red-skinned eating apple

Grease a 23 x 13 x 7.5 cm / 9 x 5 x 3 inch loaf tin. Set the oven at 190°C / 375°F / gas 5. Sift the flour, salt, baking powder and mixed spice into a large bowl. Rub in the butter or margarine. Add the sugar and dried fruit.

Peel and core the cooking apples, slice thinly, then toss in the lemon juice. Add to the dry mixture. Stir in the eggs and enough milk to make a soft dropping consistency. Put the mixture into the prepared loaf tin.

Bake for about 50–60 minutes, until the loaf is golden brown and a skewer pushed into the centre comes out clean. Cool on a wire rack.

Add enough cold water to the icing sugar to make a brushing consistency. Core the eating apple, cut it into thin segments, and arrange these in a decorative pattern on the loaf, Immediately brush the apple with the icing sugar glaze to prevent discoloration. Leave the glaze to set before serving.

MAKES ABOUT TWELVE SLICES

BANANA BREAD

The riper the bananas used for this popular teabread,
the more flavoursome will be the result.

fat for greasing
300 g / 11 oz plain flour
pinch of salt
5 ml / 1 tsp bicarbonate of soda
75 g / 3 oz margarine
100 g / 4 oz granulated sugar
3 eggs, beaten
3 ripe bananas
15 ml / 1 tbsp lemon juice

Grease a 23 x 13 x 75 cm / 9 x 5 x 3 inch loaf tin. Set the oven at 190°C / 375°F / gas 5. Sift the flour, salt and bicarbonate of soda together.

Cream the margarine and sugar in a bowl. Beat in the eggs. Mash the bananas with the lemon juice. Add to the creamed mixture, then work in the dry ingredients. Put the mixture into the prepared loaf tin.

Bake for 50–60 minutes, until golden brown. Cool on a wire rack.

MAKES ABOUT TWELVE SLICES

BANANA AND WALNUT BREAD

fat for greasing
3 ripe bananas
50 g / 2 oz walnuts, chopped
200 g / 7 oz self-raising flour
5 ml / 1 tsp baking powder
1.25 ml / ¼ tsp bicarbonate of soda
125 g / 4½ oz caster sugar
75 g / 3 oz soft margarine
grated rind of ½ lemon
2 eggs
50 g / 2 oz seedless raisins

Grease a 23 x 13 x 7.5 cm / 9 x 5 x 3 inch loaf tin. Set the oven at 180°C / 350°F / gas 4. Mash the bananas.

Mix all the ingredients in a large bowl. Beat for about 3 minutes by hand using a wooden spoon, or for 2 minutes in an electric mixer, until smooth. Put the mixture into the prepared loaf tin.

Bake for 1 hour 10 minutes, or until firm to the touch. Cool on a wire rack.

MAKES ABOUT TWELVE SLICES

MALT BREAD

fat for greasing
400 g / 14 oz self-raising flour
10 ml / 2 tsp bicarbonate of soda
100 g / 4 oz sultanas or seedless raisins
250 ml / 8 fl oz milk
60 ml / 4 tbsp golden syrup
60 ml / 4 tbsp malt extract
2 eggs

Grease a 23 x 13 x 7.5 cm / 9 x 5 x 3 inch loaf tin. Set the oven at 190°C / 375°F / gas 5. Sift the flour and bicarbonate of soda into a large bowl. Add the dried fruit. Warm the milk, syrup and malt extract in a saucepan. Beat in the eggs. Stir the mixture into the flour. Put into the prepared loaf tin.

Bake for 40–50 minutes, until a skewer pushed into the bread comes out clean. Cool on a wire rack.

MAKES TWELVE SLICES

FREEZER TIP

Freeze teabreads and loaf cakes cut into slices.
Separate the slices with freezer film, then re-
shape the loaf and pack it in a polythene bag.
Individual slices may be removed as required.

SWEET DATE BREAD

*Buy blocks of compressed, stoned dates sold specifically for cooking
or look for packets of ready-chopped dates, usually rolled in caster sugar.*

fat for greasing
400 g / 14 oz plain flour
pinch of salt
20 ml / 4 tsp bicarbonate of soda
150 g / 5 oz soft dark brown sugar
125 g / 4½ oz sultanas or seedless raisins
75 g / 3 oz walnuts, chopped
50 g / 2 oz margarine
400 g / 14 oz stoned dates, finely chopped
2 eggs
5 ml / 1 tsp vanilla essence

Grease a 23 x 13 x 7.5 cm / 9 x 5 x 3 inch loaf tin. Set the oven at 190°C / 375°F
/ gas 5. Sift the flour, salt and bicarbonate of soda into a large bowl. Add the
sugar and sultanas or raisins, then the walnuts.

Add the margarine to the dates and pour on 250 ml / 8 fl oz boiling water. Add
the date mixture, eggs and vanilla essence to the dry ingredients and mix thoroughly. Put the mixture into the prepared loaf tin.

Bake for 40–50 minutes, until the loaf is golden brown and a skewer pushed
into the bread comes out clean. Cool on a wire rack.

MAKES ABOUT TWELVE SLICES

HONEY BREAD

fat for greasing
100 g / 4 oz margarine
100 g / 4 oz caster sugar
2 eggs, beaten
90 ml / 6 tbsp liquid honey
250 g / 9 oz self-raising flour or 250 g / 9 oz plain flour
and 15ml / 1 tbsp baking powder
5 ml / 1 tsp salt
about 125 ml / 4 fl oz milk

Grease a 20 x 13 x 7.5 cm / 8 x 5 x 3 inch loaf tin. Set the oven at 180°C / 350°F / gas 4.

Cream the margarine and sugar in a bowl until pale and fluffy. Beat in the eggs and honey. Add the dry ingredients alternately with the milk until a soft dropping consistency is obtained. (Add the milk carefully as the full amount may not be needed.) Put the mixture into the prepared loaf tin.

Bake for 1¼ hours. Cool on a wire rack. When cold, wrap in foil and keep for 24 hours before serving. Serve sliced and buttered.

MAKES ABOUT TWELVE SLICES

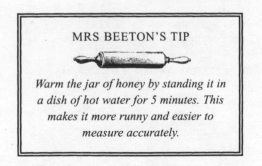

MRS BEETON'S TIP

Warm the jar of honey by standing it in a dish of hot water for 5 minutes. This makes it more runny and easier to measure accurately.

MOGGY

fat for greasing
350 g / 12 oz plain flour
pinch of salt
7.5 ml / 1½ tsp baking powder
75 g / 3 oz margarine
75 g / 3 oz lard
100 g / 4 oz caster sugar
100 g / 4 oz golden syrup
about 50 ml / 2 fl oz milk

Grease a baking sheet. Set the oven at 180°C / 350°F / gas 4. Sift the flour, salt and baking powder in a bowl. Rub in the margarine and lard, then mix in the sugar. Mix the syrup with the dry ingredients, adding enough milk to make the mixture into a stiff dough. Shape into a round or oval flat bun about 2.5 cm / 1 inch thick. Place on the prepared baking sheet.

Bake for 25–35 minutes, until firm and light brown. Serve warm or cold, cut in wedges or slices, and thickly buttered.

MAKES ONE 675 G / 1½ LB BUN

LINCOLNSHIRE PLUM BREAD

Prunes give a delightfully rich taste to this bread.

fat for greasing
100 g / 4 oz prunes
100 g / 4 oz butter
100 g / 4 oz soft light brown sugar
2.5 ml / ½ tsp ground mixed spice
2.5 ml / ½ tsp ground cinnamon
2.5 ml / ½ tsp gravy browning (optional)
2 eggs, lightly beaten
15 ml / 1 tbsp brandy
100 g / 4 oz sultanas
100 g / 4 oz currants
175 g / 6 oz self-raising flour
pinch of salt

Soak the prunes overnight in cold water. Next day, grease and line a 23 x 13 x 75 cm / 9 x 5 x 3 inch loaf tin. Set the oven at 140°C / 275°F / gas 1. Drain the prunes well and pat dry. Remove the stones and chop the prunes finely.

Cream the butter and sugar in a bowl until light and fluffy. Beat in the spices and gravy browning, if used. Mix the eggs with the brandy, then beat into the creamed mixture. Toss the chopped prunes and other dried fruit in a little of the flour. Mix the rest of the flour with the salt. Fold it into the creamed mixture, then fold in all the dried fruit. Turn the mixture into the prepared tin and level the top.

Bake for 3 hours. Cool in the tin. When cold, turn out and store in an airtight tin.

MAKES ABOUT TWELVE SLICES

Scones

A few ideas for some of the easiest and quickest of traditional baked goods. A basic scone recipe is worth mastering, as many delicious variations can then be prepared and baked within half an hour.

PLAIN SCONES

fat for greasing
225 g / 8 oz self-raising flour
2.5 ml / ½ tsp salt
25–50 g / 1–2 oz butter or margarine
125–150 ml / 4–5 fl oz milk
flour for kneading
milk or beaten egg for glazing (optional)

Grease a baking sheet. Set the oven at 220°C / 425°F / gas 7. Sift the flour and salt into a large bowl. Rub in the butter or margarine, then mix to a soft dough with the milk, using a round-bladed knife. Knead very lightly on a floured surface until smooth.

Roll or pat out the dough to about 1 cm / ½ inch thick and cut into rounds, using a 6 cm / 2½ inch cutter. (Alternatively, divide into two equal portions and roll each piece into a round 1–2 cm / ½–¾ inch thick. Mark each round into six wedges.) Re-roll the trimmings and re-cut.

Place the scones on the prepared baking sheet. Brush the tops with milk or beaten egg, if liked. Bake for 10–12 minutes. Cool on a wire rack.

MAKES TWELVE

OTHER RAISING AGENTS

Scones can be made using plain flour with raising agents: for 225 g / 8 oz plain flour, use 5 ml / 1 tsp bicarbonate of soda and 10 ml / 2 tsp cream of tartar. Or use 20 ml / 4 tsp baking powder as the raising agent.

A VARIETY OF SCONE DOUGHS

- **Cheese Scones** Add 75 g / 3 oz grated cheese to the dry ingredients before mixing in the milk. Cut into finger shapes or squares.
- **Savoury Herb Scones** Add 50 g / 2 oz diced cooked ham, 30 ml / 2 tbsp grated Parmesan cheese and 5 ml / 1 tsp dried mixed herbs to the dry ingredients before mixing in the milk.
- **Cheese Whirls** Add 75 g / 3 oz grated cheese to the dry ingredients. Roll out the dough into a rectangle. Sprinkle with another 50 g / 2 oz grated cheese, then roll up the dough like a Swiss roll. Cut into 1 cm / ½ inch slices and lay them flat on greased baking sheets. Brush with milk or egg and bake as in the basic recipe.

continued overleaf...

- **Fruit Scones** Add 50 g / 2 oz caster sugar and 50 g / 2 oz currants, sultanas or other dried fruit to the basic recipe.
- **Griddle Scones** Add 50 g / 2 oz sultanas to the basic recipe. Roll out to 1 cm / ½ inch thick, then cut into 6 cm / 2½ inch rounds. Cook on a moderately hot, lightly-floured griddle or heavy frying pan for 3 minutes or until the scones are golden brown underneath and the edges are dry. Turn over and cook for about another 2 minutes until golden brown on both sides. Cool in a linen tea-towel or similar cloth.
- **Inverary Muffins** Use only 75 ml / 3 fl oz buttermilk or soured milk to make the dough, and add 25 g / 1 oz caster sugar and 1 egg. Roll out 1 cm / ½ inch thick, and cut into 7.5 cm / 3 inch rounds. Cook on a griddle or heavy frying pan in the same way as Griddle Scones but for slightly longer.
- **Nut Scones** Add 50 g / 2 oz chopped nuts to the basic recipe.
- **Syrup or Treacle Scones** Add 20 ml / 4 tsp soft light brown sugar, 2.5 ml / ½ tsp ground cinnamon or ginger, 2.5 ml / ½ tsp mixed spice and 15 ml / 1 tbsp warmed golden syrup or black treacle to the basic recipe. Add the syrup or treacle with the milk.
- **Potato Scones** Use 100 g / 4 oz flour and 100 g / 4 oz sieved cooked mashed potato. Reduce the milk to 65 ml / 2½ fl oz.
- **Rich Scones** Add 25 g / 1 oz sugar to the mixed dry ingredients for the basic recipe. Instead of mixing with milk alone, use 1 beaten egg with enough milk to make 125 ml / 4 fl oz.
- **Wholemeal Scones** Use half wholemeal flour and half plain white flour to make the scone dough.
- **Scones Made with Oil** Use 45 ml / 3 tbsp olive oil or corn oil instead of the fat in the basic recipe. Reduce the milk to 75 ml / 3 fl oz and add 1 egg.

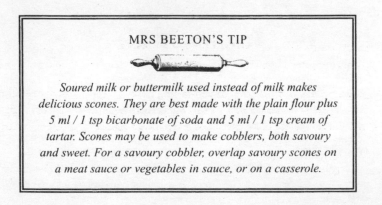

MRS BEETON'S TIP

Soured milk or buttermilk used instead of milk makes delicious scones. They are best made with the plain flour plus 5 ml / 1 tsp bicarbonate of soda and 5 ml / 1 tsp cream of tartar. Scones may be used to make cobblers, both savoury and sweet. For a savoury cobbler, overlap savoury scones on a meat sauce or vegetables in sauce, or on a casserole.

SWEET BROWN SCONES

*These scones are delicious filled with full-fat soft cheese
or butter and spread with honey.*

**fat for greasing
225 g / 8 oz wholemeal or brown flour
2.5 ml / ½ tsp salt
2.5 ml / ½ tsp baking powder
50 g / 2 oz margarine
50 g / 2 oz soft light brown sugar
50 g / 2 oz seedless raisins
1 egg, plus milk to give 125–150 ml / 4–5 fl oz
flour for rolling out**

Grease a baking sheet. Set the oven at 220°C / 425°F / gas 7. Mix the flour, salt and baking powder in a large bowl. Rub in the margarine, then stir in the sugar and dried fruit. Beat the egg and milk together. Reserve a little for brushing the tops of the scones and add the rest to the dry ingredients. Mix to a soft dough. Knead lightly.

Roll out the dough on a floured surface to just over 1 cm / ½ inch thick. Cut into rounds, using a 6 cm / 2½ inch cutter. Re-roll the trimmings and re-cut. Place the scones on the prepared baking sheet. Brush the tops with the reserved egg and milk mixture.

Bake for 10–15 minutes. Serve warm or cold, split and buttered.

MAKES TEN TO TWELVE

VARIATION

- **Bran Scones** Use 175 g / 6 oz self-raising flour, 2.5 ml / ½ tsp salt, 5 ml / 1 tsp baking powder, 25 g / 1 oz soft light brown sugar, 50 g / 2 oz currants or sultanas, instead of the quantities given above. Add 25 g / 1 oz bran when mixing the dry ingredients.

Index